Shared
Storybook
Reading

Shared Storybook Reading

Building Young Children's Language & Emergent Literacy Skills

by

Helen K. Ezell, Ph.D., CCC-SLP
Department of Instruction and Learning
University of Pittsburgh

and

Laura M. Justice, Ph.D., CCC-SLP
Curry School of Education
University of Virginia, Charlottesville

·P·A·U·L·H·
BROOKES
PUBLISHING CO.®

Baltimore • London • Sydney

·P A U L· H·
BROOKES
PUBLISHING CO. ®

Post Office Box 10624
Baltimore, Maryland 21285-0624

www.brookespublishing.com

Typeset by Auburn Associates, Inc., Baltimore, Maryland.
Manufactured in the United States of America by
Versa Press, Inc., East Peoria, Illinois.

Library of Congress Cataloging-in-Publication Data

Ezell, Helen K., 1951–
   Shared storybook reading : building young children's language and emergent
literacy skills / by Helen K. Ezell, Laura M. Justice.
      p.   cm.
   Includes bibliographical references and index.
   ISBN-13:978-1-55766-800-4
   ISBN-10:1-55766-800-0
   1. Reading (Preschool)   2. Children—Books and reading.   3. Reading—
Parent participation. I. Justice, Laura M., 1968–   II. Title
   LB1140.5.R4E99 2005
   372.67'7—dc22   2005023287

British Library Cataloguing in Publication data are available from the British
Library.

Contents

About the Authors

Helen K. Ezell, Ph.D., CCC-SLP, is a speech-language pathologist in the Department of Instruction and Learning at the University of Pittsburgh. She specializes in the study of children's early language development and emergent literacy acquisition. Her research has involved a range of topics, including vocabulary development, print awareness, and reading comprehension. She has published extensively in professional journals and has authored two other books—*Guide to Success in Doctoral Study and Faculty Work* (American Speech-Language-Hearing Association, 2002) and *The Syntax Handbook* (co-authored with Laura Justice, Thinking Publications, 2002). Dr. Ezell served as Director of Communication Development for 8 years at Western Center, a Pennsylvania residential facility for individuals with mental retardation, and as Associate Research Scientist for 5 years with Allegheny-Singer Research Institute before joining the faculty at Ohio University. She currently holds a research position at the University of Pittsburgh with the Pennsylvania Reading First External Evaluation Project.

Laura M. Justice, Ph.D., CCC-SLP, is Assistant Professor of Reading and Communication Disorders at the University of Virginia's Curry School of Education, Charlottesville. She directs the Preschool Language and Literacy Lab at the University of Virginia, which conducts basic and applied research on preschool literacy and language development, language disorders, parent-implemented early childhood language and literacy interventions, and classroom-based language and literacy programs for at-risk preschoolers. Dr. Justice's cross-disciplinary research has received awards from the International Reading Association (2001 Distinguished Finalist, Dissertation of the Year), the Council for Exceptional Children (2003 Early Career Award, Division for Research), and the American Speech-Language-Hearing Association (2004 Editor's Award, *American Journal of Speech-Language Pathology*). She received her doctorate in speech and hearing sciences from Ohio University under the mentorship of Dr. Ezell.

Foreword

Dramatic changes in our understanding of early literacy development have occurred in the past few years. A flurry of studies, consensus reports, and new national early literacy initiatives (e.g., Good Start, Grow Smart) have thrust the field of early literacy into the spotlight. As in Margery Cuyler's witty children's book *That's Good! That's Bad!* (1991), this attention has an upside and a downside. On the upside, because of the recognition of the importance of early literacy experiences to children's later reading success, new resources (such as Early Reading First program funds) have been funneled into the early literacy field. In addition, new research is helping us learn more about what young children are capable of doing and about effective early literacy instruction, what early childhood educators (teachers, administrators, literacy coaches or mentors) need to know and do to ensure that young learners acquire the knowledge and skills important to children's literacy development. On the downside, some preschool teachers worry that whereas once they set individual expectations for children's language and literacy development, allowing children to develop at their own rate, now state-developed pre-kindergarten standards (or foundations or building blocks—states call them by different names) set expectations for the growth of all young children. Such standards now provide an index against which educators are to assess and compare each young child's development (e.g., by the end of the preschool years, all children will . . .). Children must "fit" the expectations. These standards dictate specific content for the preschool language and literacy curriculum and educators' teaching (e.g., vocabulary, oral language comprehension, alphabet knowledge, phonological awareness, print knowledge). Although preschool educators recognize the importance of providing young learners with instruction in these research-supported key language and early literacy skills, some feel pressure to use practices that they know to be developmentally inappropriate (e.g., drill-and-practice worksheets; long group circle times with all children attending to the teacher, who teaches a specific academic skill) to increase their young learners' literacy knowledge. They worry that academic instruction might replace even such traditionally valued activities as sharing quality literature with children.

Therefore, *Shared Storybook Reading: Building Young Children's Language and Emergent Literacy Skills* could not have been published at a better time. Its content takes on special meaning at this time when preschool educators face daunting challenges. How do preschool educators ensure that they provide their preschool children with the core content that young children need in order to be successful readers but do so using developmentally appropriate instructional strategies? With so much to do in so little time (many preschool programs remain half-day programs), how do preschool educators maximize children's learning from each activity?

Helen K. Ezell and Laura M. Justice provide *many* answers to preschool educators' questions. Drs. Ezell and Justice are leading authorities on young children's early language and literacy development. They have contributed to the rich research base on the uses of literature to enhance children's language and literacy development. Their research, supported by that of literally hundreds of others (which they reference extensively), has shown that how teachers, parents, and others read to children is critically important. In *Shared Storybook Reading,* Ezell and Justice use their extensive knowledge of research-based strategies to help early childhood educators to make the most beneficial use of storybook reading. They provide explicit guidance to promote the intentional use of books as a literacy and language learning tool for children. That is, they provide early childhood professionals with specific suggestions on how to introduce and explore a range of key language and early literacy concepts with children. As speech-language pathologists, Ezell and Justice are particularly interested in building readers' knowledge of the five domains of language (semantics, phonology, syntax, morphology, and pragmatics) so that educators can use that knowledge to build children's language (both receptive and expressive language skills) within the context of their storybook reading. Language development is not their sole focus, however. They also provide explicit strategies for teaching the prerequisite or foundation literacy skills (print awareness and phonological awareness) that help children to become successful readers and writers.

Every strategy shared shows how to create storybook reading sessions in which the adult and the child are active participants. *Explicit* does not mean that the adult does all of the talking and the children sit passively attending (or not) to words, words, words. Ezell and Justice also provide specific suggestions and strategies for working with reluctant storybook reading participants. With numerous concrete examples (excerpts from storybook reading sessions), Ezell and Justice help readers look beneath the surface of a storybook reading session to get a close look at the instructional strategies in use. What does it sound like when an adult uses the strategy? What does it sound like when a child is an active participant in a storybook reading session? Certainly, Ezell and Justice do *not* present these examples as scripts to be followed by educators. Rather, their goal is to build preschool educators' knowledge so that they can create their own scripts collaboratively with their young learners.

In short, *Shared Storybook Reading* is the definitive book on implementing storybook reading with young children. It lays the theoretical and research-based foundation for numerous strategies aimed at ensuring quality storybook reading. Whether you are a preschool teacher (or a preschool teacher in training), a literacy mentor or coach, a preschool administrator, a speech-language pathologist working with young children, or an early childhood curriculum specialist, this book provides a comprehensive, practical, userfriendly guide to shared storybook reading. (This is not to suggest that this is a bedtime reading book; you need a Magic Marker to highlight the many points you want to remember and use.) Thanks to Helen K. Ezell and Laura M. Justice for synthesizing what they know so that we can know how to make reading aloud to young children— the activity that has been identified as "the single most important activity for building the knowledge required for eventual success in reading" (Anderson, Hiebert, Scott, & Wilkinson, 1985, p. 23)—even more powerful. *Shared Storybook Reading* will enrich your storybook reading activities, helping you maximize their value to young children.

Carol Vukelich, Ph.D.
Director, Delaware Center for Teacher Education and
Hammonds Professor in Teacher Education
University of Delaware

REFERENCES

Anderson, R.C., Hiebert, E.H., Scott, J.A., & Wilkinson, I.A.G. (1985). *Becoming a nation of readers: The report of the Commission on Reading.* Washington, DC: National Institute of Education.
Cuyler, M. (1991). *That's good! That's bad!* New York: Henry Holt & Co.

Introduction

Reading books with young children is one of the single most important things that adults can do to ensure children's timely development of oral language and emergent literacy skills, both of which are necessary for success in school and, ultimately, in life. The beauty of storybook reading is that young children can learn a multitude of concepts through this one activity. For instance, stories provide information for young children about daily events, people, and animals in an interesting and entertaining way. This builds children's world knowledge and basic vocabulary. Children's books contain illustrations that attract and sustain children's interest and help tell the story, providing important visual support for learning. The written language in books allows children to acquire print awareness and basic knowledge of print conventions. Also, questions and discussions that arise during shared reading between adults and children provide opportunities for children to learn and practice conversational skills and social conventions. Finally, storybooks can be read in a brief period of time, which is perfectly suited for young children's limited attention spans. In short, young children acquire important knowledge every time adults read them a storybook. Table I.1 lists some of the knowledge children may acquire about books, oral language, and written language through regular shared reading.

This book is intended to provide professionals with information and step-by-step guidance for shared reading with young children to promote their language and emergent literacy skills, which in turn builds a strong foundation for future academic learning. Mastery of oral language prepares children for learning about written language. Likewise, children's emergent literacy skills will promote a readiness for formal reading instruction. This foundation is what is meant when educators request that all children enroll for school "ready to learn." It means that valuable learning time in the classroom will not need to be spent on developing necessary prerequisite skills for reading that should have been acquired earlier. In fact, this is the goal of the Early Reading First program funded by the No Child Left Behind Act of 2002 (PL 107-110). In the Early Reading First program, preschool education focuses on four major areas to prepare children for school:

Table I.1.   Examples of skills that are acquired through shared storybook reading

Has knowledge of books
Holds book right side up and knows where the story begins
Identifies the front of a book and points to the title on the cover
Looks at pages from left to right when book is opened
Turns pages one at a time progressing from front to back
Has knowledge of oral language
Shows increased awareness of sounds (phonology)
Develops greater understanding of new words (semantics)
Acquires knowledge of sentence structure (syntax)
Learns correct use of word endings such as plurals (morphology)
Improves conversational skills (pragmatics)
Has knowledge of written language
Knows that text runs from left to right
Knows that print tells the story
Knows that letters make up words
Identifies the first letter of a word
Identifies the space between words

Sources: Adams, 1990; Goodman, 1986; Justice & Ezell, 2000; Mason, 1980; Snow, Burns, & Griffin, 1998.

oral language development, phonological awareness, alphabet knowledge, and print awareness. This book provides strategies for developing children's skills in each of these areas.

This book is organized into 10 chapters. Chapter 1 provides the research and theoretical background explaining how shared reading contributes to children's development. In Chapter 2, the essential elements that create effective shared reading sessions are described so that the reader may understand how effective shared reading sessions should look and sound. Chapters 3 and 5 provide background information on language and emergent literacy skills, respectively. These chapters provide definitions, representative skills, and some important milestones in children's development. They will give the reader an overview for understanding the breadth and complexity of the skills young children need before starting school. Specific strategies to use during shared reading are offered in Chapters 4 and 6. Chapter 4 presents strategies for enhancing children's language skills, in particular those that relate to semantics, phonology, syntax, morphology, and pragmatics. Chapter 6 gives strategies for developing children's emergent literacy knowledge, with a focus on nine print awareness skills and five phonological awareness skills. Chapter 7 describes resistant behaviors that some children exhibit toward books and shared reading. This chapter offers suggestions based on the theory of multiple intelligences for helping reluctant readers. Chapter 8 discusses young children with special needs such as sensory impairments, language impairments, autism, or mental retardation. For those children who lack the necessary prerequisite skills for shared reading (e.g., attending, conversational turn taking) specific strategies are described for developing these skills. Chapter 9 provides guidance for professionals in establishing home reading programs for the children they serve in order to increase their engagement with oral and written language outside of the preschool or child care setting. Chapter 10 discusses some considerations and additional resources for selecting books for shared reading. Appendix A lists some frequently asked questions and answers about shared reading. Appendix B provides general reading strategies. Finally, a glossary is included to provide explanations of important concepts and terms that are used throughout this book.

Professionals are reminded that the numerous activities presented in this book are meant to be accomplished over an extended period of time. There is no advantage to rushing through these suggestions and activities in a few short months. Young children have several years as preschoolers to acquire these important skills, so take each reading session at a leisurely pace and make every effort to create an enjoyable experience for all children.

REFERENCES

Adams, M.J. (1990). *Beginning to read: Thinking and learning about print.* Cambridge, MA: MIT Press.

Goodman, Y.M. (1986). Children coming to know literacy. In W.H. Teale & E. Sulzby (Eds.), *Emergent literacy* (pp. 1–14). Norwood, NJ: Ablex.

Justice, L.M., & Ezell, H.K. (2000). Enhancing children's print and word awareness through home-based parent intervention. *American Journal of Speech-Language Pathology, 9,* 257–269.

Mason, J.M. (1980). When do children begin to read?: An exploration of four-year-old children's letter and word reading competencies. *Reading Research Quarterly, 15,* 203–227.

Snow, C.E., Burns, M.S., & Griffin, P. (Eds.). (1998). *Preventing reading difficulties in young children.* Washington, DC: National Academies Press.

To Craig, for believing in me
–H.K.E.

To Addie, who has patiently allowed me to test
all the strategies described in this book
–L.M.J.

1

Research and Theoretical Background

During their preschool years, children must acquire sufficient knowledge of and facility with language for it to be become a useful tool in their formal education. This means that young children not only need to learn language for personal expression and communication with others but also need it to further their learning in an educational setting. Once formal education begins, children will rely on their reading, writing, speaking, and listening skills, all of which are dependent on an underlying foundation of language competence. Therefore, by helping young children become competent language users, professionals and parents will be building a solid foundation for children's future learning.

This book provides some ideas and strategies for assisting professionals in developing young children's language competence through one particular language-rich experience—that of shared reading. Shared reading has been selected because of its unique quality of presenting both oral and written language simultaneously. This permits children to acquire not only oral language abilities but also early print concepts. Recent important research and policy documents, such as the consensus document *Preventing Reading Difficulties in Young Children* commissioned by the National Research Council (Snow, Burns, & Griffin, 1998) and the position statement *Learning to Read and Write: Developmentally Appropriate Practices for Young Children* prepared jointly by the International Reading Association (IRA) and the National Association for the Education of Young Children (NAEYC) (1998), emphasize the value of providing children generous access to storybooks and engaging them in high-quality interactive reading. These reports stress the role of storybooks in offering valuable experiences with the vocabulary and grammar of oral language, as well as intensive exposure to the sound and print structure of written language that underlies the alphabetic principle.

This book is intended to serve as a guide and resource for all professionals working with young children and their families, including early interventionists, child care providers, early childhood educators, kindergarten teachers, librarians, literacy coaches, speech-language pathologists, special educators, psychologists, social workers, and health care providers. The focus of this book is to help professionals understand the inherent value and versatility of shared reading with young children for building a strong foundation of language and emergent literacy skills. Ultimately, children will apply this foundation to their experiences during the formal reading instruction that occurs in kindergarten and first grade.

DEVELOPING CHILDREN'S LANGUAGE THROUGH SHARED READING

The term *shared reading* is used throughout this book to describe the interaction that occurs between an adult and a child when reading or looking at a book. This interaction may include one adult and one child, or one or more adults and several children. The interaction may occur in any setting (e.g., a child care center, a preschool classroom, an outpatient clinic, children's homes). Several different terms are used by experts to describe this interaction, including *interactive reading, reading aloud, book sharing, book reading, storybook reading, adult–child storybook reading,* and *book-reading interaction.* All of these terms are interchangeable, essentially focused on giving a name to the important interactions that occur between adults and children when they share a storybook. In this book, the terms *book sharing* or *shared reading* are used to emphasize the active involvement and engagement of both the child and the adult in a shared interaction focusing on a book's words, pictures, and story.

This book is based on the premise that shared reading is a unique learning context for young children that involves much more than simply looking at pictures. Although one of the most salient features of storybooks is their illustrations, storybooks also provide children with access to a world of sights, sounds, and words that may be quite different from what they experience in their homes, their communities, and their schools. For example, it is through a storybook that a child may first experience the magic of the animal kingdom (e.g., lions, giraffes, camels, snakes, turtles). One popular book, *Dear Zoo* by Rod Campbell (1982), provides children from the earliest ages with the names of these and other animals, allowing them to experience vocabulary words that are not likely to arise in their everyday environments. A simple and often delightful text for even very young children, *Dear Zoo* exposes children to linguistic concepts that will be important as they develop, including the descriptive adjectives *grumpy, fierce, scary,* and *naughty,* as well as concepts about how to handle objects (e.g., *fragile, heavy*). It is hard to believe that a text containing only 31 different words used in 25 short sentences can help children develop such a range of early yet important concepts.

As another example, Jessica Stockham's *Down by the Station* (2002) allows children to experience a variety of onomatopoeic words describing the sounds of vehicles—the chuff, chuff, chuff of the train; the brrm, brrm, brrm of the bus; the beep, beep, beep of the taxi; and the nee nor, nee nor, nee nor of the fire engine. Clearly, this storybook provides children with early exposure to the sounds of the world around them, all while sitting on the lap of an adult. Professionals can use this book and its systematic attention to words and sounds as a means for heightening children's early sensitivities to the sound structure of oral language and for understanding how words represent diverse aspects of their world, including its sounds.

These examples highlight how storybooks provide children with the words they can use to explore both basic and abstract vocabulary concepts. However, books do much more than teach children new vocabulary. Consider some of the language and early literacy opportunities created during shared reading that are described in Table 1.1. Storybooks increase children's familiarity with the sounds and grammar of their language, expose them to the pragmatic rules that govern the use of language, and provide them with models of how stories and narratives are organized in their culture. At the same time, storybooks teach children fundamental knowledge about how books themselves work and how print is organized, and they provide children with repeated exposure to the alphabet and the way in which letters and sounds map on to one another in an alphabetic language. Not the least important, storybook-reading experiences also provide

Table 1.1. Opportunities for learning language and emergent literacy during book sharing

Adult behavior	Learning oppportunity created
Adult reads narrative text using oral language	Child hears translation of written language
Adult addresses illustrations	Child practices comprehension skills and connects oral events in story to pictures
Adult addresses print	Child associates oral language with written language and learns how print is organized
Adult addresses sounds	Child practices recognition and production of individual phonemes
Adult addresses story content	Child practices comprehension skills and gains contextual understanding of story
Adult converses with child	Child practices language comprehension and expression

children with opportunities to build relationships with the adults in their lives. It is within the context of children's relationships with adults that children's developing competencies about language and literacy may emerge (Pianta, 2000).

With all of the benefits that storybooks offer, it is important to understand that book sharing is not intended to teach children to read. If reading could be taught so easily, nearly all children would be reading by the time they enter school. Instead, book sharing helps children develop a foundation for learning to read. It is not unlike the foundation that children acquire when they listen to music. Listening builds musical skills and knowledge such as becoming aware of pitch and melody, associating sounds with particular instruments (e.g., piano, violin, drum), recognizing that musical notes can be distinguished from one another and can have different meanings, and being able to repeat a tune or sing a song. However, for nearly all children, learning to read music will require explicit instruction. The same is true for learning to read. Consider next some of the research evidence that describes the influence that shared reading has on developing children's foundation skills.

Research on Reading Storybooks with Young Children

Hundreds of studies have appeared in scientific journals during the last several decades on how shared reading contributes to the early language and literacy development of young children. This body of research also has reported on how adults can capitalize on these reading interactions to maximize children's early achievements. Some of the research that provided the impetus for this book has been selected for review in this section and has been organized to consider three major topics:

1. Key findings regarding language and emergent literacy

2. How young children's early shared-reading experiences vary widely

3. Why the quality of shared reading is important

Key Findings Regarding Language and Emergent Literacy

Research has shown that shared reading with young children may affect several aspects of their language and literacy development. With regard to language skills, the dialogic reading technique developed by Grover Whitehurst and his colleagues (Whitehurst et al., 1988) has demonstrated consistent success in increasing children's language skills. Dialogic reading involves gradually shifting the storytelling role from the adult reader to the child through various techniques (e.g., open-ended questions, repetition, modeling). Several studies using the dialogic reading technique during shared reading have shown an increase in children's oral language skills (Arnold, Lonigan, Whitehurst, & Epstein, 1994; Lonigan & Whitehurst, 1998; Valdez-Menchaca & Whitehurst, 1992; Whitehurst, Arnold, et al., 1994; Whitehurst et al., 1988).

A unique aspect of storybooks is how they offer an opportunity to decontextualize language. This means that the events and concepts in storybooks are not restricted to the here and now. Rather, the events may reflect actions, events, and ideas that exist beyond the present—potentially in the past, in the future, or in another world altogether. The events may flow over time ("Once upon a time...") or they may follow a causal chain of events (as in *If You Give a Moose a Muffin* by Laura Numeroff). The events may be placed in the past ("There was an old lady..."), in the future ("When I grow up..."), and even on another planet ("Far away, in another galaxy..."). It is through storybooks that children can experience the eventful forays of a mischievous dog as he discovers chicken coops, ponds, and gardens in *Spot's First Walk* by Eric Hill (1981). These experiences go beyond the incidental language and literacy experiences characteristic of the immediate world of young children; they also prepare them for the decontextualized demands that will pervade elementary schooling.

Unlike decontextualized language, contextualized language concerns the here and now; it is characterized by relatively short and simple grammar, redundant and often nonspecific vocabulary, and a reliance on nonverbal supports (i.e., gestures, eye contact, pointing) to make meaning more specific (Curenton & Justice, 2004; Greenhalgh & Strong, 2001). Although contextualized language is a significant aspect of children's early language achievements, young children also require experience with decontextualized language, or language that goes beyond the immediate context (Westby, 1991). Using decontextualized language means that there are no supports available in the immediate environment to help children get their point across; rather, they must rely on words alone to make meaning. Working with decontextualized language is a challenge for young children because of the cognitive and linguistic demands of the task. It requires children to remember and speak of something that is not immediately in front of them and to use highly precise language to represent their ideas and thoughts so that the listener who may not share this context will understand. When producing decontextualized language, grammar tends to be more complex, vocabulary becomes more specific and precise, and the topic is relatively abstract.

The foundation for being able to succeed in decontextualized discourse is laid in the preschool years, and book sharing offers children an opportunity to experience a world beyond the here and now (Dickinson, de Temple, Hirschler, & Smith, 1992). Experts have suggested that the language contained in storybooks provides children with models for decontextualized discourse (Kaderavek & Sulzby, 2000). Researchers have also suggested that shared reading exposes children to conversations that are more challenging and linguistically complex than occur in other play activities (Girolametto & Weitzman, 2002). Children's early experiences with decontextualized discourse during shared reading help to prepare them for later experiences with cognitive-challenging abstract concepts (van Kleeck, Gillam, Hamilton, & McGrath, 1997). Storybooks expose children to vocabulary that is not commonly used in their everyday conversations with others, and they help children develop a familiarity with the words and grammar that allows them to more precisely discuss concepts within decontextualized discourse (Beck, McKeown, & Kucan, 2002).

We move now to the topic of emergent literacy. Research has shown that when adult readers use verbal and nonverbal references to print during shared reading, children verbalize more about print than when readers do not use such references (Ezell & Justice, 2000). This means that even though preschool children are not yet able to read, they are capable of talking about print when an adult raises the topic. In addition, adults and children discussing print during shared reading affects children's emergent literacy skills. In two studies involving print-referencing strategies, findings showed that in both home (Justice & Ezell, 2000) and preschool settings (Justice & Ezell, 2002), shared reading that focused on print resulted in significant gains in selected emergent literacy skills. For example, in a study involving 30 children in Head Start, gains were evident in children's alphabet knowledge, print recognition, and word awareness (e.g., pointing to words as the adult reads; pointing to the first word on a page) after just 24 small-group reading sessions over 8 weeks (Justice & Ezell, 2002). These findings demonstrate how a simple strategy such as pointing to or commenting about print during shared reading can build some of the skills considered vital for future reading instruction.

Although this review merely highlights a few of the findings involving language and emergent literacy, it suggests the potential impact that skillful shared reading may have. Also, there is reason to believe that certain language and emergent literacy topics may be closely correlated to children's future reading success and perhaps should be given special consideration. In the consensus document by Snow et al. (1998), a summary of numerous research studies was conducted to determine which skills are highly predictive of reading difficulties at the time children enter school. Results of this analysis found the predictors with the strongest correlations to be concepts about print, letter identification, phonological awareness, overall language, and reading readiness (described as pre-reading skills). These results suggest that bolstering children's abilities in these particular areas may have a positive impact on their future reading success at the time of school entry.

How Young Children's Early Shared-Reading Experiences Vary Widely

By the time children enter kindergarten soon after their fifth birthday and begin to experience formal instruction that requires certain language and literacy competencies for success, there is, unfortunately, considerable variation among American school children in their achievement of these competencies. This may be due in part to insufficient exposure to language-rich experiences such as adult–child storybook reading. In early childhood programs, for instance, the extent to which storybooks are a routine part of children's daily educational experiences varies considerably, and this variability influences children's language and literacy achievements in the classroom (Dickinson & Keebler, 1989; Dickinson & Smith, 1994). This is also true in children's homes, where the extent to which parents engage their children in regular storybook-reading experiences may explain some of the variability in children's language and literacy growth during the later preschool years (Bennett, Weigel, & Martin, 2002).

Consider a hypothetical scenario in which in one preschool classroom children experience somewhere around 40 minutes of daily storybook reading and in another classroom children receive only 5 minutes of daily reading. In a month, this difference expands to 800 minutes versus 100 minutes, and over an academic year this equates to a difference of more than 100 hours of book-sharing experience among children in the two classrooms. These numbers illustrate the cumulative effect of shared reading and demonstrate the amount of language exposure that is lost when storybooks are not a high profile component of children's daily routines.

Studies that have attempted to quantify differences among children in the sheer volume of their early book-sharing experiences have had interesting but occasionally distressing findings. Some of the studies have looked at children's homes, whereas other studies have looked into children's classrooms. Studies in both contexts have shown clear variations in the quantity of book-sharing experiences. Purcell-Gates (1996), for instance, looked at the frequency of literacy events in the homes of 4- to 6-year-old low-income children over a 7-day period and found the frequency of literacy events to average about one per hour. Literacy events included any activity in which print was involved (e.g., looking at a book, reading a card, writing a note). Of all of the literacy events observed, storybook reading was not particularly prevalent, accounting for only 5.8% of observed events and occurring on average .09 times per hour for the children observed.

Purcell-Gates's work studied the experiences of 24 children in low-income households specifically. To consider American children more generally, Yarosz and Barnett (2001) studied data for 7,566 toddlers and preschoolers surveyed in 1995 by telephone through the National Household Education Survey. These households were randomly selected from among households in the United States with children, providing a nationally representative sample of American families. The households ranged in ethnic–racial composition (61% white/non-Hispanic, 13.5% African American, 20% Hispanic, and 5.5% other), in educational attainment for the primary caregiver (18% no high school diploma, 30% high school diploma, 29% some college, 23% college degree or beyond), in language spoken (87% spoke English, 13% spoke a language other than English), and in annual household income (47% less than $30,000, 42% between $30,000 and $75,000, 11% more than $75,000). Primary caregivers were questioned as to how often they had read with their toddler or preschooler during the last week, with answer options including not at all (11% of caregivers), once or twice weekly (16%), three or more times weekly (22%), or daily (51%). These data show considerable variation across families in their reading practices, and although the majority of parents reported that they read daily to their children, more than one quarter of caregivers reported reading to their children not at all or only once or twice weekly. Therefore, professionals should not assume that book sharing is a daily event for every child.

It is possible to consider the way in which background characteristics of families interact with the frequency of storybook reading occurring in the home. Many researchers have suggested that socioeconomic status (SES) is a particularly important characteristic that influences the frequency of home reading (e.g., Scarborough & Dobrich, 1994). Others have suggested, however, that it is not SES per se that explains variations in storybook-reading experience across households; rather, such circumstances as limited English proficiency and maternal education (which often co-occur with poverty) are more influential in explaining such variations. Yarosz and Barnett's (2001) research using the National Household Education Survey of 1995 examined these household characteristics and showed—as has been suggested—that SES is less influential on home reading practices than other variables. Specifically, households in which reading experiences were most infrequent were those in which English was not spoken as a primary language, the mother was Hispanic, and maternal education was below 12th grade. In contrast, 66% of English-speaking Hispanic mothers with a college degree reported daily storybook reading with their children.

It is important to note that it is the interaction among these variables—ethnicity, maternal education, and language spoken in the home—that most relates to the quantity of home reading experiences. For instance, considering African American households, 18% of households in which maternal education is less than 12th grade reported never reading to their children, compared with only 4% of African American households characterized by a highly educated mother (bachelor's degree or higher). Thus, when mothers have a college degree and are well educated, it is more likely than not that the children in their households will be read to on a daily basis.

These findings illustrate that language and early literacy experiences of young children in the United States may vary according to several contributing factors such as maternal education, ethnicity, and language spoken in the home. This suggests that such experiences are of even greater importance for some children in child care and preschool settings in order to establish sufficient language and emergent literacy skills for school readiness.

Why the Quality of Shared Reading Is Important   Athough it seems logical to expect that the frequency with which children participate in shared reading during their preschool years will positively influence their language skills, the quality of such interactions may be just as important. Consider the findings of Hart and Risley (1995), who found that the number and variety of words that young children heard in their home environment influenced both the size and variety of words in children's subsequent vocabularies. Thus, both the quality and quantity of word use factored into children's development.

Before discussing quality, consider briefly some research findings regarding quantity. Research that has focused on the amount of shared reading has determined some positive outcomes. For example, Wells (1985) noted that the frequency with which children between 1 and 3 years of age listened to stories was later positively associated with teachers' ratings of these children's oral language when they were 5 years of age. Also, findings contributed to the National Research Council report (Snow et al., 1998) asserting that young children who had fewer experiences with books in the home were at greater risk for reading problems compared with children who had frequent experiences with books. However, there has been some disagreement in the field concerning the extent to which these early shared-reading experiences contribute to children's subsequent skills. A paper published by Scarborough and Dobrich (1994) argued that home storybook-reading experiences may not make as great a contribution to children's language and literacy development as has historically been credited. These researchers studied all of the existing research up to that time on the link between home book sharing and children's later reading performance. They concluded that the quantity of preschool storybook-reading experiences explained only 8% of the variance in children's later literacy achievements. Put simply, when looking at school-age children's reading abilities and considering the wide amount of variation in achievement across children, this research suggested that only 8% of this variation can be attributed to children's early shared reading experiences, leaving 92% of the variability to be explained by other characteristics of the child such as motivation or intelligence.

Current best estimates suggest that the quantity of preschool shared-reading experiences explains about 7%–10% of the variance in children's primary grade reading and language achievements when considering the direct relationship between these variables (Bus, van IJzendoorn, & Pellegrini, 1995; Senechal, LeFebre, Thomas, & Daley, 1998). Although the amount of influence may seem limited, it is important to recognize that this 7%–10% of variability is something that can be influenced by professionals (Lonigan, 1994). In other words, many factors that affect reading and language achievement are well out of professionals' reach (e.g., children's intelligence, temperament, socioeconomic status). However, professionals can have an impact on the amount of shared reading a child experiences through reading programs in child care, preschool, and home settings. Most professionals would agree that maximizing this 10% contribution toward future literacy through regular shared reading is a prudent course of action for all children.

One measure of quality may be the extent to which adults are responsive to children's concerns. The concept of responsiveness is similar to the notion of sensitivity in that an adult reader is sensitive to a child's involvement. A responsive adult gauges a child's interest and comfort with the pace of reading, recognizes words and concepts that are novel to the child, and responds to and builds on his or her communicative attempts. Responsiveness is a valuable way to add quality to shared-reading interactions with young children; consequently, some research addressing this concept will be highlighted.

A high level of responsiveness is characterized by three types of behaviors used by adults: 1) child-oriented behaviors, 2) interaction-promoting behaviors, and 3) language-modeling behaviors (Girola-metto & Weitzman, 2002). Girolametto and Weitzman's research has studied adults' use of these responsive techniques in preschool class-rooms and child care settings. Child-oriented behaviors follow the child's lead, pace, and topic. A responsive adult focuses on the child's object of attention to create periods of joint focus. Two important child-oriented behaviors to use during storybook reading include commenting on the child's object of attention and pausing to allow children to initiate. In a storybook-reading interaction, for instance, when a child says, "Spot pick flower," a responsive adult might respond, "Yes, Spot is picking some flowers. I wonder if they smell good." By contrast, an adult who changes the subject by noting, "Here is a bone on the ground," is not being very responsive to the child's object of attention. In the latter example, the adult has ignored what the child is interested in (i.e., the flower) and has failed to use this topic as a way to build a new language concept.

Interaction-promoting behaviors (Girolametto & Weitzman, 2002) are used by responsive adults to engage children in conversa-tion. A common mistake of adults is to use close-ended questions or yes/no questions to solicit children's involvement. For instance, when an adult asks, "Is this the color red?" the child may respond simply by using a single word response or head nod, which provides minimal practice with language use and adds no new information to the topic. Because of this, close-ended questions are not very useful for engag-ing children in interactions and dialogues; rather, adults need to use different forms and question types to promote children's conversa-tion. One behavior that is useful for promoting interaction is asking *wh-* questions (those beginning with words such as *what, who, where, when, why,* or *which*). In addition, asking open-ended ques-tions, which are questions to which the adult does not have a ready answer, are suggested, as these require children to hypothesize, rea-son, or predict. For instance, during a book-reading interaction, an adult might ask, "Why is the old man picking all the carrots?" or "What do you think the little boy will do next?" An additional tech-nique for maintaining the topic of conversation is to repeat what the child says. This is helpful for maintaining the flow of conversation, for engaging children in dialogue, for ensuring that the adult does not maintain too much control, and for acknowledging children's commu-nicative involvement. For instance, a child might say, "The old lady is pulling on the turnip," to which the adult agrees, "The old lady *is* pulling on the turnip." A simple technique, yes; however, the adult's repetition of what the child says is a responsive and sensitive acknowledgment of the child's contribution to the conversation.

The third adult behavior is language modeling (Girolametto & Weitzman, 2002), which is used by responsive adults to extend children's language and literacy involvement to provide models of more advanced forms and features of oral and written language. Two behaviors most characteristic of language-modeling behaviors are the label and the extension. With labeling, the adult provides the name or label to a concept of which the child does not yet have mastery. For instance, during book reading, the adult might note that "This letter *s* is in your name." This label of the letter *s* creates a model for the child that is beyond his or her independent skills, but the adult uses the content of the storybook to introduce this concept. With labeling, the child is not obligated to respond or participate; rather, the goal is concept exposure. Extension is similar to labeling except that the adult builds on an utterance produced by a child; the adult expands the child's production to include more sophisticated models or concepts. For instance, the child might note that "The cat is holding a sign," which the adult extends to, "Yes, the cat is holding a sign that says 'Danger.'" Of course, there are many ways to extend this utterance (e.g., "The cat is holding a big white sign"). The important point to make is that extensions build on children's current objects of attention and provide valuable language models.

Research focusing on the shared-reading quality has shown that adults have a tendency to be directive by controlling the pace of the task, asking a great many close-ended questions, choosing the topic, and not pausing long enough for children to initiate their own involvement (Girolametto & Weitzman, 2002; Kaderavek & Sulzby, 1998b). However, there is considerable research showing that a more responsive quality of interaction is of greater value in fostering children's development within the book-reading context and promoting their engagement within the interaction itself (Arnold et al., 1994; Bergin, 2001; Kaderavek & Sulzby, 1998b). Studies have shown that teachers' techniques to elicit children's active involvement in book-sharing activities in the preschool classroom—including asking open-ended questions, following children's lead on topics, and giving praise—are powerful tools in building early language and literacy skills (Whitehurst, Epstein, et al., 1994, Whitehurst, Zevenbergen, Crone, Schultz, Velting, & Fischel, 1999). Regarding parents as readers, one recent study that documented the socioemotional quality of parents reading with their preschool children showed quality of book-reading experiences to significantly relate to vocabulary skills at 4 and 7 years of age (Leseman & de Jong, 1998). In fact, the socioemotional quality, defined as an adult's supportive and emotionally positive presence during book reading, was more closely linked to children's language skills during preschool and elementary school than household SES and parents' own literacy practices.

This research has demonstrated that when adults are responsive to children and solicit their active involvement in book sharing, positive developmental gains may be expected. However, having said this, it is important to mention that direct instruction has a place within the reading context. This means that professionals may use shared reading to introduce and explore specific concepts previously unknown to the child (e.g., pinpointing new words, explaining print directionality, associating sounds with particular letters). Engaging children in stimulating conversations that target novel or maturing concepts has a rightful place in shared reading. In fact, integrating explicit teaching opportunities into storybook-reading interactions can be instrumental in fostering children's language and emergent literacy development (Justice & Ezell, 2000, 2002; Penno, Wilkinson, & Moore, 2002). In the end, professionals who balance explicit teaching activities with child-oriented, interaction-promoting, and language-modeling behaviors may be creating the ultimate shared-reading experience for young children.

Theoretical Perspective on the Book-Reading Context

The role that theory plays in working with young children on a day-to-day basis is often considered vague or rather unimportant. However, having a theoretical perspective allows professionals to select which approach may be best suited for helping children grow and develop. Theories give professionals a framework from which to make decisions about children's concerns, to structure adult–child interactions, and to guide intervention.

It is because theory is so important that much of the research in language and emergent literacy is conducted in the first place. Science should, in fact, be used to experimentally confirm or refute theoretical models that represent the nature of the world. Theoretical models of children's development are hypothetical representations of a complex and dynamic event. Scientists conduct research to identify strategies for testing these hypothetical representations to determine how well the models hold up. Those models that hold up over time, despite considerable scrutiny, are then accepted into the mainstream.

It is important for readers to be aware of the theoretical background that supports the language and emergent literacy strategies presented in this book. In essence, it is the theoretical approach that ultimately infuses quality into shared-reading practices. Although many theories are available to describe how children acquire language, such as Piaget's (2001) constructivist theory and Skinner's (1965) behaviorist theory, the present work has been particularly influenced by Vygotsky's (1978) social-interactionist theory.

The social-interactionist theory as it applies to early language and literacy development is grounded in the work of the Russian child psychologist Lev Vygotsky. Vygotsky believed that children's development occurs through socially mediated instruction under the guidance of more knowledgeable and experienced peers. He viewed all knowledge as being socially constructed, whereby children's knowledge moves from a social plane inward to an internal psychological plane. Put another way, a particular concept exists for a child first within the context of an interaction with the knowledgeable person, after which the child internalizes the concept and takes psychological ownership of it. This perspective places a high premium on the value of adult–child interactions to introduce children to concepts. Figure 1.1 shows how a novel concept shared between an adult and a child in shared reading moves from that context to the child having independent ownership of the concept over time.

For learning to occur, it is important for adults to emphasize skills that children have not yet developed rather than to focus on concepts that children already understand. Consider the following excerpt from a shared-reading session to illustrate this point.

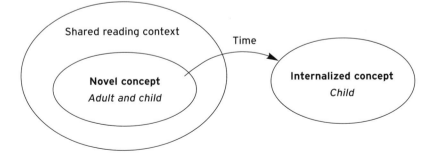

Figure 1.1.   Proposed internalization of novel concept based on Vygotskian theory.

Teacher: This book is called *Red Bear.*

  Child: Red bear.

Teacher: That's right. What color is the bear?

  Child: Red.

Teacher: Right. He's red.

In this excerpt, the child who has previously demonstrated knowledge of colors is asked a question that taps this existing knowledge. Because of this, the adult–child interaction is not instructional. Too often, when adults read books with children, they focus only on concepts that children already understand (e.g., object name, color, size). Although children may find this enjoyable because they readily know the answers, this sort of interaction will not accelerate their learning. Now, consider the following excerpt from a different reading session:

Teacher: This book is called *Red Bear.* Where do you think it says that?

  Child: Right there. (points to picture of bear)

Teacher: Well, that is a picture of a red bear. You are right about that. But we are looking for words. Where are the words *Red Bear*? There are two words.

  Child: Ummm. Here?

Teacher: That says the name of the author, Bodel Rikys. That is a good guess because this time you did find some words. Here, let me show you the words *Red Bear.* (takes child's hand and runs his finger over the title)

In this second excerpt, the teacher is challenging the child in that the instruction precedes the child's development of a concept. The teacher focuses on the concept of book title, which is new to the child, and provides scaffolded assistance using a variety of techniques. These include repeating the question, praising the child, giving an additional clue (by saying "two words"), and providing physical assistance. This is akin to what Vygotsky would call working in the child's zone of proximal development (ZPD), or the zone between what a child can do independently and what he or she can do with maximum adult support. (See the glossary for further discussion of ZPD.) Important to note is that within this zone learning takes place.

To some, this latter interaction may not seem as enjoyable as the earlier interaction in which the child and teacher participate in a series of questions to which the child already knows the correct answer. However, the latter interaction is the one that is most likely to build the child's skills; in particular, it created an opportunity to teach a valuable print concept. This approach also may be used to develop other skills—syntactic, phonological, or vocabulary knowledge, to name just three. Once a concept is understood and internalized by the child, the adult may introduce a new concept into the learning zone, and in this way, the child's knowledge grows and develops one step at a time.

The strategies offered in this book are intended to guide the professional to work within children's ZPD to promote their language and emergent literacy skills. The real advantage of doing this within a shared-reading context is the tremendous flexibility it affords. Stories may be repeated until a child internalizes a concept; new concepts may be introduced with repeated readings of the same story; or new stories may reexamine familiar concepts in new ways. By doing this, shared reading offers endless varieties and opportunities for working within children's ZPD.

Shared reading is not intended for teaching preschoolers to read. Instead, it is a vehicle for children to acquire greater knowledge of and proficiency in oral and written language, which constitutes a foundation for formal reading instruction. Such skills are best learned when professionals focus on quality interactions during shared reading by seeking children's active involvement and by working within children's "learning zones." However, it is equally important to know what topics to address. According to Snow et al. (1998), shared reading that addresses vocabulary development, concepts about print, letter identification, phonological awareness, and overall language skills may promote children's future literacy development. These are precisely the foundation skills to be enhanced through the reading strategies described in this book. To understand more about the characteristics of effective shared reading, continue to Chapter 2, which describes how some of these strategies look and sound when incorporated into shared reading.

2

How Effective Shared Reading Looks and Sounds

In this chapter, an ideal shared-reading session is described. The important elements of shared reading are presented and discussed along with a few illustrative examples. Although shared reading may appear to be a simple activity, in fact, it is not. Several elements must be present for shared reading to be both enjoyable and effective in helping children develop language and emergent literacy abilities. Shared reading is rather like gardening in that the more one pays attention to the presence and timing of the necessary growing elements—sunshine, soil enhancement, watering, fertilizing, weeding, and pruning—the greater the beauty and abundance of one's garden. A mediocre garden is assured when gardeners pay little attention to these elements, but if they are systematic and regular in attending to all elements, a magnificent garden will result. The same is true for shared reading in that care and attention to its important elements may yield impressive results over time with regard to children's language and emergent literacy skills.

The elements that combine to make an effective shared-reading session are not always apparent to the untrained eye. It is easy to overlook an obvious aspect and easier still to underestimate the importance of a simple one. Those who are able to capture the intricacies in a straightforward and pleasing way are the ones who have mastered the art of reading to young children.

AN IDEAL SHARED-READING SESSION

In the ideal shared-reading session, both adult and child are active participants. They sit in a comfortable, quiet location in a way that permits both of them to view the book simultaneously. The atmosphere is relaxed and positive, as demonstrated by the frequent smiles and words of praise being offered by the adult. While the adult reads, discussion involving both the adult and child is interspersed and focused on the characters and events in the story. Speculation as to what future events may occur or how these events relate to the child's everyday experiences may be part of this discussion. Sometimes comments or questions are raised about words, print, and various print concepts. At other times the book's illustrations will be considered. These discussions are initiated by both the child and the adult, and turn-taking opportunities are shared. Observers will hear the adult create story interest by varying the pace and volume of his or her voice and will see the child gazing at the open book or watching the adult's face intently. When the story is concluded, participants may peruse some illustrations again, re-read a favorite part, or discuss new words or the story's events. Both participants are satisfied with sharing the story and look forward to the next reading session. In essence, that is how shared reading should look and sound.

Consider the following excerpt from an ideal reading session that demonstrates some of these features:

Adult: This book is called *Spot Bakes a Cake* by Eric Hill. Hmm. I wonder what kind of cake it will be, chocolate or vanilla.

Child: Chocolate 'cause he's licking a chocolate spoon.

Adult: Well, let's read the story and find out. I'll let you turn the pages, and maybe you can help me read some of the words, okay?

Child: Okay. (opens the book)

Adult: I'll start reading right here. (points to first word) "It's your dad's birthday on Friday, Spot." Spot says, "Let's bake a cake!" (tracks the print while reading)

Child: Is this Spot's mommy? (points to the large dog)

Adult: Yes, *I* think that's his mommy. They look the same except that the mommy is bigger. What do *you* think?

Child: Yeah. That's Spot, and here's his mommy. (points to each one)

Adult: Yes, this page shows Spot and his mommy. (pauses) Spot and his mommy are looking at something that tells when the birthday is. What do you think this is? (points to calendar)

Child: I don't know.

Adult: This is called a calendar. (points to calendar) It helps us keep track of the days.

Child: A calendar? (pauses and looks closely)

Adult: That's right; a calendar tells us the days. What do you see on the calendar?

Child: Mmm. I see a one, a two, a…, a four. (points to numbers as they are named)

Adult: Very good! The one, two, and four are numbers. A calendar is filled with numbers that tell you the date. (quickly tracks the first few lines of numbers with her finger) The calendar has letters, too. Where are some letters?

Child: Up here. (points to the letters at the top of the calendar)

Adult: Yes, you found the letters! Great job! There are seven letters (points to each letter), one for each day of the week. (pauses for the child to look at the page) Ready to turn the page?

Child: Yep. (turns the page)

Adult: Where do I begin reading?

Child: Here. (points to print at top of the page)

Adult: Perfect! It says, "We have to go shopping." (tracks the print while reading and then pauses) Uh-oh, where's Spot?

Child: He's looking in here. (points to Spot)

Adult: Oh, there's Spot looking in the cupboard. Let's see what he found.

Child: (opens flap to see) Hey, a mouse! There's a mouse in there!

Adult: There's a mouse in that cupboard! And the mouse says, "I need some cheese." (uses high-pitched voice, points to the print, and waits for child to look at the picture)

Child: Cheese, the mouse wants cheese. (giggles, looks closely at the mouse, opens and closes the flap several times, and then turns the page)

Adult: Yes, that mouse wants them to shop for cheese.

Adult: "Can you find the chocolate, Spot?" (tracks print with finger while reading) Look, let's read this sign. Give me your finger and we'll read together. (takes child's finger) It says, "Special Today—Chocolate." (assists child in pointing to words while reading) Say, I see a letter in the word *chocolate* that is the same as a letter in your name. Can you find it in this word? (points to *chocolate*)

Child: (looks closely, pauses, and then points to *C*) Here?

Adult: Wow, you found it fast! Very good! What is the name of that letter?

Child: It's an *O*.

Adult: That is a very good try, but this letter (points to the *C*) is *C*. Let's trace it with your finger. (takes child's finger and traces the letter) The word *chocolate* begins with a *C,* and the name *Chad* begins with a *C*.

Child: *C*? Like in my name?

Adult: Yes, exactly. Your name begins with the letter *C*. Now, where were we? (looks back at the sign) Oh, yes, I think there's something under the sign; can you lift the flap?

Child: (lifts flap) Wow, is he ever…he got a lot.

Adult: That's right, Spot has an armful of, of…vanilla, right?

Child: No, *chocolate*!

Adult: Why did Spot get chocolate?

Child: You know, to make chocolate cake.

In the above reading sequence, which lasted only a few minutes, it should be evident that the adult and the child are both active participants. The child is taking conversational turns by asking questions, making comments, and responding to the adult's questions. In addition, he takes opportunities that are offered to point to the print, lift the flaps, and turn the pages. The child appears to be comfortable, involved, and yet challenged to show what he knows and understands. As the adult reads the book, she tracks print; points to letters, words, and pictures; explains new words; pauses for the child to examine the pages; expands some of the child's utterances; and checks for understanding of the story. In doing so, an observer of this session might determine that this child is able to recognize some numbers and can distinguish numbers from letters as seen at the beginning of the session. The child was able to determine what the adult was reading when the adult asked where she should read and the child pointed to the print. The child recognizes the first letter in his name, which appears in another word, but he does not know the letter name. Based on the child's answer to the adult's final question, it appears as though he understands the story up to this point.

Although it may be difficult for each and every reading session to achieve the ideal, it is possible to include many of these features on a regular basis with some forethought. With a little practice, including them may become second nature. The following section describes five important elements that may enhance shared reading with pre-school children.

SHARED READING ELEMENTS

To make the most of shared reading with young children, at least five essential elements should be considered: 1) physical arrangement, 2) social involvement, 3) materials selected, 4) reading style, and 5) conversation. Each of these elements plays a role in creating an enriching, interesting, and fun reading atmosphere in which children can acquire language and emergent literacy skills.

Physical Arrangement

The seating and arrangement of the shared-reading participants is important for ensuring that everyone has sufficient access to the reading material. The adult and child must be seated in a way that both can view the book and handle the pages together. This is vital for the adult who will read and for the child who will follow along. If children are unable to view the illustrations, watch as the adult reads, or touch the pages, they will be unable to join in the activity to the fullest extent possible. Both adult and child should feel that they are active participants in the book-sharing event. Therefore, it is suggested that participants be seated side by side or with the child

seated on the adult's lap so that the book may be shared by both participants simultaneously. Some adjustments to these arrangements
will be necessary when reading to more than one child at a time. If
two children are included, each may sit on either side of the adult.
When three or more children participate, they may be seated in a
small semicircle in front of the adult. During group reading, the adult
must find a way to share the book with the group by either using a
big book, which is designed specifically for group reading, or by turning the book around for the children to see after reading each page.
When reading with a group of children, it may be helpful for the
adult to begin the reading session by showing how the book will be
displayed to reassure the children that they will be able to see it.
This might reduce some children's concern and scrambling for the
best position.

In addition to how the participants are arranged, it is suggested
that adults remember to supply comfortable seating, a quiet environment free from distractions, and sufficient lighting for reading the
print and examining the illustrations. It may be helpful to have a designated reading space prepared so that it is convenient for shared
reading whenever the opportunity arises. Special "book-reading
zones" can be set up fairly easily in almost any setting. For instance,
an 8-week shared-reading program conducted by the authors in a
Head Start center utilized the distraction-free speech therapy room
for book-reading sessions for small groups of three to five children at
a time (Justice & Ezell, 2002). This was made into a special reading
zone by placing a soft carpet on the floor along with four beanbag
chairs that created a semicircle in front of an adult reader; this created a warm, cozy, and private setting where the storybook was the
center of attention.

When reading with children in a preschool classroom or child
care setting, shared reading may also be conducted in a classroom
library, which provides a specialized niche designed for reading
events. Optimally, the classroom library should include well-
organized and accessible bookshelves with a variety of book genres,
soft carpeting, and comfortable and inviting furniture. Although
shared reading can occur in other settings in the child care environment, the well-configured classroom library is an optimal place for
creating the ideal reading sessions described in this chapter. For
more information on establishing a classroom library, see the valuable
guidelines provided in *Helping Young Children Learn Language
and Literacy* (Vukelich, Christie, & Enz, 2002).

Social Involvement

Any time adults and children interact with one another, a social situation is created. Consequently, every time an adult reads a book with a child, an opportunity for social involvement is presented. When these participants engage in positive and rewarding interactions, they are more likely to enjoy the experience and seek additional opportunities in the future. Therefore, it is important that adults make shared reading fun and interesting so that young children can develop a positive regard for books and reading. This may be done in several ways. First, children need to be given multiple opportunities to take conversational turns during shared reading. This is important not only for children to have a chance to practice their language skills but also for building a relationship with the adult. Relationships are based on sharing, and when children are allowed to share their ideas, thoughts, and feelings, a positive relationship will be formed. Second, children's attempts at answering questions or making comments should be praised and acknowledged to build their confidence and ability. This is vital for creating an accepting atmosphere in which children feel comfortable taking risks to acquire new skills. When adults praise and acknowledge children's contributions to shared-reading interactions, children understand that they are valued members in the exchange and that their contributions are welcome. Third, adults need to create opportunities for warmth and affection during shared reading. Often, it is the warmth and closeness that adults may recall about their early reading experiences that make their personal memories so special. Keep in mind that there are many ways for participants to display affection for one another (e.g., through laughter, smiles, winks, pats on the back, and terms of endearment). By remembering that the social context of shared reading is an essential element for its success, adults will establish an emotional climate that promotes children's growth and well-being.

Consider the feelings and social customs expressed in this conversational excerpt following a reading of *Dear Zoo* (Campbell, 1982).

Parent: Well, the camel was too grumpy. Can you remember what animals came next?

Child: Maybe . . . a bear?

Parent: Oh, a bear might be fierce like the lion, or maybe *hungry* (spoken with a growling voice). I hope they wouldn't send a bear, don't you?

Child: Yeah, me too. (leafs through the pages of the book) They send a snake!

Parent: That's right, they sent a scary snake. Hey, what sound do you hear in the words *scary* and *snake* that is the same? Listen: s-s-scary s-s-snake.

Child: Scary snake. (pauses) I hear the s-s-s sound.

Parent: Right! Well done! You listen *very* well.

Child: (resumes looking through the book) And a monkey, too!

Parent: Yes, they sent a monkey also, but the problem with him was that he was naughty. (pause) What does the word *naughty* mean, do you know?

Child: Being bad, like breaking something or taking things.

Parent: Yes, breaking things or taking something that isn't yours would be naughty. If people do that, what else should they do?

Child: Say they're sorry and give it back?

Parent: Exactly, just like when you said you were sorry and gave back the toy to Becky. That was the *right* thing to do. I was proud of you for giving her your apology (smiling and patting the child on the back)!

In the previous excerpt that occurred after shared reading was finished, the parent and child spent some time discussing the story. During this conversation, the parent praised the child for correct sound identification (e.g., the phoneme /s/ heard in the words *scary* and *snake*). Also, the parent used the opportunity to check the child's understanding of the word *naughty* and the appropriate social custom for correcting the behavior the child described. This was then related to a personal experience of the child. By doing this, the parent reinforced that the described behaviors are inappropriate as well as what corrective behavior is expected to occur. In addition, the parent used this opportunity to praise the child for doing the right thing to correct an earlier mistake. These strategies, used by the parent, help make the child an active part of the reading routine, are useful for building story comprehension, and create a social context in which the parent acknowledges and praises the child's engagement in the shared-reading activity.

Materials Selected

Every attempt should be made to select books that are appealing to young children so that they will become engaged in the reading activity immediately. If children do not become interested in a story within the first few pages, their attention may turn elsewhere, which could bring the reading session to a premature end. Naturally, adults must do their part to engage the child with the book from the beginning. This may be accomplished through conversation and reading style, as discussed in the next section. However, aside from what adults may do to make books interesting, the book itself must do its share.

When selecting books to read with young children, it is advised to consider books that have 1) an interesting story, 2) colorful and appealing illustrations, and 3) limited narrative as indicated by having only a few lines of text per page. When examining books for their stories, the reader will find a wealth of children's books from which to choose and many excellent references that offer advice on books to consider for certain age groups. When choosing books for a particular child, it is suggested that his or her personal interests and previous reaction to certain subjects be considered. For instance, if a child especially likes trucks, he or she may enjoy books about trains, steam shovels, or submarines but may be less interested in books about fish, cats, or elephants. Adults may acquire insight into what interests the child if the child is given opportunities to choose books for storytime, too. Common topics to consider are books about animals, adventures, or even everyday events that children may be familiar with (e.g., making friends, getting a haircut, being afraid of the dark). Concept books that describe shapes, opposites, colors, or numbers may be popular with young children, but sometimes these are not presented in a story context and consequently may be less interesting. As for a book's illustrations, avoid abstract or ambiguous drawings that might be confusing to young children. Also consider page size, especially when reading to groups of children. Big books, which are just like regular children's books but on a large scale, are ideal for group reading because they are big enough for children to see illustrations and print easily. Regarding story length, children's attention spans may be the best guide to follow. As children mature and their attention spans develop, longer books that contain more text may be presented, although any book could be read in installments if desired. Because book selection is deemed vital to effective shared reading, Chapter 10 has been dedicated to this topic. There, the reader will find additional information and a list of available resources that recommend books for young children.

As a final note on selecting books for reading with children, the concept of repeated reading—reading a storybook more than once—is noteworthy. This may occur within the same reading session or across multiple reading sessions. With the first reading of a story-book, children will become familiar with the story line, the characters, the words, and the illustrations. As children read books again and again, they gradually take a more active role in telling the story and predicting what will happen. This outcome is a desirable one as it provides children with valuable practice using language and emerging print concepts. Although adults may find repeated reading of the same book to be rather tedious, this technique is an important vehicle for creating ideal reading sessions in which children are actively and positively involved.

Reading Style

The expression that adults use when they read can bring a story alive for children and make it irresistible to them. Reading expression includes a variety of elements that can enhance children's enjoyment of a story. Varying one's pitch and vocal characteristics is one technique that adds interest to the characters in a story (e.g., talking in a high-pitched voice like a mouse or with a roar like a monster when a story line calls for it). Varying one's volume of speech to express emotion or characters' personalities is another. Changing the pace of the reading is a third technique to use for creating suspense or a sense of urgency. Skilled readers also share their emotions about the story when reading, such as a laugh with the child when things are silly or sadness when unhappy events occur. Also, when the text contains a rhyming pattern or verse, a skilled reader is able to capture the rhythmic quality with proper word stress and cadence.

Consider the expressiveness of the speech-language pathologist (SLP) reading *The Legend of the Tooth Fairy* (Ezell, 2005) in the following excerpt:

SLP: "Fairies are happy and fun-loving (spoken joyfully). They often spend their time playing tricks on people (pause) by using magic (spoken in a whisper)."

Child: Magic? Like what kind of magic?

SLP: I don't know exactly what kind, but it sounds interesting, doesn't it? (turns the page) "Sometimes they tease us by hiding things or making objects seem to disappear."

Child: (giggles at the picture) Look at the fairy hiding his shoes behind the door!

SLP: Yes, it will take a long time to find them. I wouldn't think to look behind a door.

Child: He'll be late for school! (turns the page)

SLP: "Other times they put melodies into our heads that follow us around all day." (begins humming a familiar tune)

Child: (turns to the adult, smiles, and begins to hum along)

SLP: (turns the page) "Some fairies like to make us sleepy." (pretends to yawn, closes her eyes, and pretends to fall asleep)

Child: Hey, wake up. Don't let the fairy put you to sleep!

In this brief example, the SLP created a lot of interest for the child by varying her reading expression and volume. She also brought the story alive by producing a tune and pretending to feel sleepy. Such richness of expression is sure to make the story a favorite with any child.

Conversation

Although each book will present its own language for the reading session—meaning its text—this language should be considered merely a foundation on which to build rather than the only words to be spoken. In other words, effective shared-reading sessions promote conversation rather than strict adherence to the book's text. Unfortunately, sometimes adults do not encourage conversation because they learned from their own childhood experiences that the traditional role of the child is simply to listen. By inviting children to make comments, ask questions, and answer questions, however, adults will be able to capture valuable learning opportunities that arise from shared reading. If conversation is not allowed to occur naturally, then these opportunities will go unused. Once adults accept the concept that conversation may be promoted and how this conversation might be guided, shared reading becomes more effective in enhancing language and emergent literacy abilities by giving children an active rather than a passive role in the activity.

By its nature, shared reading promotes opportunities for discussion. It uses speech, print, and illustrations to tell a story. In essence, each book offers a learning opportunity for young children by presenting a story through its words, which are read by an adult, and its illustrations, which provide a visual representation of the story's events. For young children, this is a perfect situation in which to acquire language because of their limited ability to talk about unseen or abstract events. By introducing conversation into the situation, however, it is possible to make this an even richer language experience. Keep in mind that during the preschool years, children are learning about their world through oral language, and the primary means of this is through conversation. Children acquire this technique and practice it everywhere they go. Conversation during shared reading is no different.

There are three naturally occurring reading styles that have been observed when adults read to young children. In their research, Reese and Cox (1999) described these naturally occurring styles as 1) performance oriented, 2) describer, and 3) comprehender. Each style uses conversation with the child in a slightly different way. In the performance-oriented style, conversation occurs before and after the reading of a book, with no or few interruptions to text reading. These conversations may focus on both lower level aspects of the story (e.g., character names, the setting, major events) and higher level aspects of the story (e.g., reasoning, problem solving). The describer reading style contains conversation that is infused throughout the reading of the text. The focus of these conversations is considered low-demand by describing the events of the story and the illustrations. The comprehender reading style also contains conversation during the reading of the text, but its focus tends to be high-demand through reasoning, predicting, and inferring story events. The important point here is that conversation during shared reading is a flexible concept in that it may be conducted in various ways and may involve a range of topics. For adults or children who do not feel comfortable with the interrupting style, important conversation that builds children's language and literacy skills can occur before and after the reading of a storybook.

It should be noted that the topic of conversation may be directed by either the adult or the child; however, striving for balance across both participants is desired. At its best, conversation will complement a reading session but not dominate it. Young children may comment on events or characters depicted in the illustrations, raise questions about words or ideas that are unfamiliar to them, or focus on a related issue that is foremost in their minds. When adults make language a focus of conversation, they may check for children's understanding of word meaning or provide models of correct sound production. When print becomes the focus of conversation, adults may explain how print is read from left to right or how a letter represents a particular sound. These examples by no means exhaust the list of possible topics to be raised during shared reading. Because a primary focus of this book is to expand the conversational element of shared reading for the purpose of developing language and emergent literacy skills, readers will be offered additional information and specific techniques in Chapters 4 and 6. For the present, consider the following brief example showing how conversation between adult and child may be incorporated within shared-reading sessions as the teacher reads *There's an Alligator Under My Bed* by Mercer Mayer (1987):

Teacher: "So I went to the kitchen to get some alligator bait."

Child: What does *bait* mean?

Teacher: Well, bait is something, usually food, that is used to attract an animal. Like when a fisherman uses bait on a hook to catch a fish.

Child: He's gonna use bait to catch the alligator?

Teacher: Maybe so. I don't know—let's read more to find out.

Child: Okay.

In this example, the brief conversation focuses on word meaning. Although adults may often raise this topic to check for children's understanding, in this instance, it was the child who asked about the word *bait,* which was unfamiliar to him. The teacher provided a quick definition and an illustrative example and then continued with the story. The following dialogue is another example of a shared-reading session using the book *Owen* by Kevin Henkes (1993):

Teacher: " 'Fuzzy goes where I go,' said Owen. And Fuzzy did. Upstairs, downstairs, in-between, inside, outside, upside down." (points to each picture as she reads, showing these locations; pauses while child looks at the pictures)

Child: Here he's in-between, right? (points to correct picture)

Teacher: Yes, good job. He's standing on the stairs in between the upstairs and the downstairs. (points to all three pictures)

Child: And here he's upside down. (points to correct picture)

Teacher: That's right! And here are the words *upside down*. (points to the words and pauses while child looks at them) Can you read them with me? Give me your finger, and we'll point to the words as we say them.

Child and teacher: Upside down (in unison and pointing to the words using child's finger).

Teacher: Very good! You helped me read!

This conversation shows how the teacher gave the child time to study the illustrations on the page, ask a question, and make a comment about them. Then she showed the child the words that represent the picture by pointing them out and asking the child to read them with her. This reinforces the idea that concepts shown in pictures may also be found in written words. Consider the following shared-reading example using the book *The Doorbell Rang* by Pat Hutchins (1986):

Parent: " 'No one makes cookies like Grandma,' said Ma as the doorbell rang."

Child: Ding-dong! (turns the page)

Parent: Say, that sounds like our doorbell! Did you hear that?

Child: (smiles proudly) That was *me*!

Parent: It was? Well, it sounded just like our doorbell.

Child: Yeah, I think it sounds like the pananna.

Parent: You mean *piano*. Say it like this: pee-an-no.

Child: Piano.

Parent: Oh, much better. Yes, a piano and a doorbell are both musical, aren't they? I'm impressed that you noticed that!

Child: Can I make the doorbell sound each time?

Parent: Okay, and you can read the part that says that, too. I'll point to the words when we come to the part just like this (points to words): "as the doorbell rang." Shall we try it here?

Child: (nods head in assent)

Parent: " 'No one makes cookies like Grandma,' said Ma . . ."

Child: ". . . as the doorbell rang." (adult and child both point to the words) Ding-dong!

Parent: Great job!

In this reading excerpt the child created a sound effect for the doorbell, which is a creative contribution to the story. This lead the child to make a comparison between a doorbell and a piano. The adult corrected the child's pronunciation of *piano* and praised the child for observing the musical comparison. When the child volunteered to continue the sound effects, the adult readily consented and added a reading responsibility to it. Although the child is not yet able to read, the adult promoted the idea of reading by having the child repeat the words on her pointing cue. This technique helps the child associate written words with spoken words.

In summary, adults can make reading sessions with young children effective by addressing five major elements: 1) physical arrangement, 2) social involvement, 3) materials selection, 4) reading style, and 5) conversation. The overriding purpose of all of these elements is to ensure children's active engagement in the activity. In doing so, the shared-reading experience will not only enhance children's early language and literacy competencies, it also will promote children's engagement in and enjoyment of storybooks.

In the chapters that follow, particular emphasis is given to the conversational aspect of shared reading. Chapter 4 presents adult conversational techniques that concentrate on children's language, and Chapter 6 gives conversational strategies for emergent literacy growth. In using these techniques, readers are reminded that all essential elements of shared reading remain important even though the conversational element is being moved to the forefront in each of these chapters.

3

Understanding the Building Blocks of Language Development

This chapter defines and explains the five domains of language that serve as the building blocks of children's development. The typical path of children's oral language development is described, and expectations for a few of the major milestones in each language domain during the toddler and preschool years are highlighted. Also, a few notable aspects of language are defined and explained for a broader view of children's language development.

WHAT IS ORAL LANGUAGE?

Oral language is the term describing children's understanding and use of language expressed through speech. The term *language* describes children's acquisition of a rule-governed productive system relying on the use of symbols for expression and representation of thoughts and feelings. Although language may be expressed in many ways—through gestures, icons, or printed words—oral language involves the use of speech sounds, which are referred to as phonemes. In producing oral language, children speaking the standard dialect of American English use about 43 phonemes, which may be arranged in various combinations to form thousands of unique words.

Language involves comprehension and production, and both skills are important for mastery. Comprehension involves understanding oral language and is also known as receptive language. Production refers to language use and is referred to as expressive language. Receptive language involves listening and understanding, whereas expressive language involves speaking and writing. As a general rule, most people are able to comprehend more language than they can produce, meaning that receptive language vocabularies are larger than expressive vocabularies. This means that children often understand words they hear in their environment before using them in their everyday speech. Therefore, professionals are cautioned to give children time to process and internalize new words before expecting them to use new words correctly.

Key Areas of Development: Five Language Domains

When considering the five language domains, it may be useful to visualize five connecting links in a circular chain with each link representing a key area of development. These five domains are 1) semantics, 2) phonology, 3) syntax, 4) morphology, and 5) pragmatics. Each link in this language chain is important for language mastery and competence, and all of the domains are interrelated. If one is weak or missing, the others will be affected to some degree. These domains are briefly defined in Table 3.1. It should be noted that although the five language domains may apply to various languages, this chapter will discuss aspects pertinent to the English language only.

What follows is an explanation of each domain along with a description of a few important milestones representing the progression of typical development. This information is taken from works by Gleason (2000), Hoff (2000), and Owens (2000). Readers interested in additional information on each topic in this chapter may consult these and other texts detailing the nature of children's language development.

Semantics   Semantics is the aspect of language involving word meaning. The primary feature of semantics is the child's vocabulary, or individual repertoire of words. Children's early semantic knowledge begins with first acquiring a literal meaning of words; for example,

Table 3.1.   The five domains of language

Semantics: Knowledge of the rules governing word meanings
Phonology: Knowledge of the rules governing the sound system of oral language
Syntax: Knowledge of the rules governing how sentences are arranged internally
Morphology: Knowledge of the rules governing how words are structured internally
Pragmatics: Knowledge of the rules governing how language is used in social situations

understanding that the word *letter* means something that a postal carrier delivers. Gradually, children begin to understand that some words may have more than a single meaning. This aspect of semantics is more advanced and appears when children begin to understand various uses of multiple-meaning words such as *letter* (meaning an alphabet symbol or what a postal carrier delivers) and *tire* (meaning to feel fatigued, or a circular rubber fitting that goes on the wheel of a car) to name just two. Over time, children begin to understand and use figurative language, which is usually acquired after they begin school. Figurative language includes idioms (e.g., bury the hatchet, raining cats and dogs), metaphors (e.g., fists of steel), similes (e.g., fresh as a daisy, as white as snow), and proverbs (e.g., a stitch in time saves nine). This progression demonstrates how children's vocabularies develop complexity and refinement rather than simply grow in number of words.

Vocabulary development is an important aspect of oral language ability that ties into reading achievement. Children who know more words have an easier time understanding what they read. Children who have better vocabularies can read higher level texts than those with underdeveloped vocabularies, which enables them to move their language learning forward. Preschool children who have larger receptive and expressive vocabularies are usually better readers in elementary school than children without such skills. Therefore, it is particularly important to support children's vocabulary development in the preschool years, as these early achievements directly support later accomplishments. Three important milestones in children's semantic development are noted below and are summarized in Table 3.2.

Receptive Vocabulary Knowledge When the First Word Is Spoken   Generally speaking, by the time a first word is spoken, children's receptive vocabularies may contain 10 or more words and

Table 3.2.   Selected milestones in children's semantic development

Receptive vocabulary knowledge when the first word is spoken: Children may understand 10 or more words.

Early expressive vocabulary: Words represent people, objects, or actions seen in their environments. Early words may be accompanied by gestures.

Rapid vocabulary growth: By 18 months of age, children may have approximately 50 words; by 2 years of age, large vocabularies of several hundred words may be expected.

phrases. So even though children may say only a single word, they may understand as many as 10 and sometimes even more. For example, when children can speak only one word such as "mama," they may be able to recognize names of all family members and several familiar objects such as a favorite toy, some clothing items, and preferred food, as well as follow simple instructions such as "Get that ball" or "Wave bye-bye."

Early Expressive Vocabulary   Children's early expressive vocabulary will contain more nouns than verbs, and these words will pertain to a person, an object, or an action that is in their environment. Examples may include "mama," "juice," "doggy," "shoe," "up," and "bye-bye." It is common to see children accompany their early words with gestures such as raising their arms when speaking "up" or waving a hand when saying "bye-bye." Also, these early words may appear in general terms first, with specificity developing later. For example, children may say "flower" for all flowers and anything that resembles a flower (e.g., a blossom on a flowering tree or bush) before they acquire more specific words such as "tulip," "pansy," or "rose."

Rapid Vocabulary Growth   At first, new words are added somewhat slowly to the initial vocabulary that starts with the first word, with about 10 words added per month. However, at about 18 months of age, the situation changes quite suddenly, and children enter what is often called a word spurt or word explosion. At 18 months (give or take a few months), typically developing children usually have approximately 50 words in their expressive vocabularies, although the number of words understood is actually much higher, ranging from 200 to more than 300 words. When this magic number of 50 words is reached, the word spurt begins; from here on, until first grade or so, children may acquire one or more new words per day, averaging an increase in vocabulary of greater than 30 words each month. By 2 years of age, children have up to 500 words in their expressive vocabularies, and by 3 years, as many as 1,000 words. When children enter first grade, they typically have about 10,000 words in their spoken repertoire.

How do children acquire so many new words so rapidly? A number of studies have shown that children are often able to add a new word to their receptive vocabulary through only one or two exposures to the word. Those who have spent time with young children are well aware of how true this is, as when adults let an off-color word slip and a child begins using it immediately! Interestingly, to acquire a new word, this word does not even have to be addressed to the child. One study found that preschoolers were just as likely to add new words to their vocabulary when these words were overheard in a conversation as when the new words were directly addressed to them (Akhtar, Jipson, & Callanan, 2001). We call this phenomenon *incidental learning*. Incidental learning means that children acquire new skills or new knowledge through their everyday experiences rather than through direct instruction or deliberate teaching. Most words in children's vocabularies are acquired this way—through exposure to new words in their environment during the normal course of events (e.g., in a grocery store, at the dinner table, during book reading). Considerably fewer words are acquired by children through direct instruction by parents or teachers.

Phonology   Phonology refers to children's understanding and use of speech sounds or phonemes. In American English, there are about 43 phonemes, including both vowels and consonants. (Interested readers may wish to consult the glossary, which provides a complete list of English consonants.) By about 5 years of age, children use nearly all of these sounds correctly. Phonology also includes knowing which sounds can go together and which sounds cannot, which is referred to as phonotactics. Phonotactics also governs where in words and syllables sounds can appear. For example, in English, the phonemes /n/ and /ʤ/ are rarely found together at the beginning of a word; however, they appear together in the middle of words such as *banjo, engine,* and *dungeon,* or at the end of words such as *sponge* and *lunge.* In contrast, the phonemes /s/ and /t/ regularly appear together in the beginning of words as in *story, stay,* and *stop*; in the middle as in *master* and *faster*; or at the end as in *best, lost,* and *wrist.* Obviously, children are not taught these rules about phonology; rather, they acquire them through their experiences with oral language. Noted next and summarized in Table 3.3 are four important milestones in children's phonological development.

Recognizing Sounds in the Native Language   Every language has its own set of phonemes that are used to create the words of the language. American English uses a set of about 43 phonemes; other languages use fewer phonemes and some use more. The job of young

Table 3.3.   Selected milestones in children's phonological development

Recognizing sounds in the native language: Begins in infancy and is mastered by 1 year of age

Developing oral control to produce sounds: Begins during infancy with babbling and gradually improves with age; mastery occurs around 7 years of age

Using sounds to produce the first word: First words usually appear around 1 year of age. Early words often contain phonemes such as /p/, /b/, /n/, /m/, or /w/.

Producing a variety of sounds: By 3 years of age, most children have mastered /g/, /f/, /d/, and /j/. By 3½ years of age, many can produce /s/ and /v/. By 4 years of age, most children can articulate /t/, /r/, /l/, /z/, /ʃ/, and /tʃ/.

children is to learn the sounds that are specific to the language used in their environment. Much of the groundwork for the development of the phonological system is laid in very early infancy. Young children are equipped to learn the phonological system of any language— Chinese, English, French, German, Italian, Spanish, Swahili, or others. However, at birth, the language selection is made for newborns as their brains begin to "soak up" the speech sounds they hear being used by others. By 1 year of age, young children have acquired receptive repertoires of the sounds unique to their native language.

Developing Oral Control to Produce Sounds   In contrast to children's rapid recognition of speech sounds in their native language, their ability to produce the range of speech sounds occurs much more gradually, sometimes taking the entire first 7 years of life. This has much to do with the fact that production of speech sounds requires sophisticated muscular command of the oral structures (i.e., lips, jaw, tongue, and palate). Developing muscular agility for speech takes time because infants' control of these oral structures is quite immature. This is one reason why feeding infants and toddlers can be so messy. Infants and even toddlers have to learn muscular control and coordination for both eating and talking.

Infants begin practicing sound production through various forms of babbling. Once the first word is spoken, usually around 12 months of age, children continue to develop and refine their movements for producing speech sounds. Many sounds may be produced as an approximation of the standard form well before correct articulation is achieved. An example of this is when young children say "fum" for the word *thumb,* and "lellow" for the word *yellow.* Although these may be considered errors by adults, such productions are quite systematic and show children's developing competencies toward mastery of the phonology of their language.

Using Sounds to Produce the First Word Being able to speak the first word is a major milestone for all children. The first 12 months of life are critical for setting the stage for achieving this milestone. The first word is usually spoken around 1 year of age. When children say their first word, it typically contains one of the following phonemes: /p/, /b/, /n/, /m/, or /w/ (e.g., "papa," "baba," "mama"). These sounds are the easiest for young children to produce and therefore are often mastered first. Most children have mastered these five sounds by about 2 years of age, and many children's first words contain these phonemes. It is probably no coincidence that the words used to describe children's most important early caregivers, *mama* and *papa*, contain these sounds. And this is not just an English phenomenon—across many cultures and languages, the words for *mother* and *father* are composed of these early sounds.

Producing a Variety of Sounds The phonemes that are mastered next are typically /g/, /f/, /d/, and /j/ (as in y̲am), usually around 3 years of age. The phonemes /s/ and /v/ are acquired around $3\frac{1}{2}$ to 4 years of age. The more difficult phonemes, which include /t/, /r/, /l/, /z/, /ʃ/ (as in s̲h̲oe) and /tʃ/ (as in c̲h̲in), are mastered by children by about 4 to $4\frac{1}{2}$ years of age. Some phonemes, such as /dʒ/ (as in J̲ack), /θ/ (as in t̲h̲in), and /ð/ (as in t̲h̲at), can take even longer for some children.

Syntax Syntax is the grammar of language, or the set of rules governing how sentences are structured. Although speakers often do not realize that their sentences are arranged according to a set of rules, they are in fact strictly governed by a variety of rules that are intuitively understood and adhered to every time a sentence is produced. For example, one simple rule stipulates that all sentences must contain both a subject and a predicate. The subject is basically the "doer" in a sentence, whereas the predicate (which includes the verb) is what is done to the subject or by the subject. This rule allows *Jane swims* to be considered a sentence, whereas *Jane* is not. Another rule requires that articles go in front of nouns and not vice versa. There are three articles in English: *a, an,* and *the.* Per this rule, *The cat* is an acceptable way to start a sentence, whereas *Cat the* is in violation. There are dozens of rules that are not discussed here, but suffice it to say that children acquire these rules rapidly during the first few years of life by listening to adult speech. Three important milestones in children's syntactical development are noted next and summarized in Table 3.4.

When Syntax Begins   Children acquire the rules of grammar very early in their language development. The development of syntax is usually viewed as beginning around 18 months of age, when children start to combine two words. Prior to 18 months, children speak primarily in single-word utterances. At 18 months, however, when children have about 50 words in their expressive vocabularies, they begin to combine words to produce their first "sentences." These sentences contain the same words that were previously spoken in isolation so that "mommy" and "up" may now be produced as "mommy up" (meaning the child wants to be picked up by mommy). Typical utterances may include "mommy no," "daddy bye-bye," or "shoe off." At first, these early sentences do not appear to abide by any particular grammatical rule or order—children may be just as likely to say "mommy up" as they are to say "up mommy." However, it is not much longer before a grammatical rule system begins to emerge and word order starts to stabilize.

Expansion of Two-Word Utterances   By 2 years of age, children's utterances average more than two words in length, and three-word utterances are emerging (e.g., "mommy up car," "no daddy go," "big baby shoe"). Around this time, children begin using questions. Children's early questions are usually marked with an upward or rising intonation at the end without any reordering of words. When this occurs, it is referred to as an intonational question. "Daddy go car?" is an example of this question type. Only later do children learn to reorder words to form their questions as in "Is Daddy going in the car?" or "Where is Daddy going?"

Table 3.4.   Selected milestones in children's syntactic development

When syntax begins: When children reach 18 months of age and have approximately 50 words in their expressive vocabularies, they begin combining words to create two-word utterances.

Expansion of two-word utterances: Around 2 years of age, children begin using three words together ("doggy ball run"). Emergence of intonational questions may be seen.

Emergence of other syntactical forms: By 5 and 6 years of age, typically developing children exhibit a variety of syntactic forms and parts of speech such as adjectives, conjunctions, adverbs, and prepositions.

Emergence of Other Syntactical Forms   From these early three-word sentences, grammatical development emerges quite rapidly over the next 3 years, resulting in a nearly complete system of grammar by the time children reach 5 or 6 years of age. By this time, children may use elaborated noun phrases ("the big black bear in the woods"), complex verb structures ("might be talking"), complex sentence structures (e.g., "The kid in my class whose name I forget was mean to me today, and it made me feel bad"), and all of the traditional parts of speech, including adjectives (e.g., *dirty, large, delicious*), adverbs (e.g., *here, tomorrow, slowly*), conjunctions (e.g., *then, but, so*), and prepositions (e.g., *over, behind, under*).

Morphology   Morphology is the domain of language governing the structure of words. Words can be manipulated in several ways to meet a variety of purposes. The word *break,* for instance, can be manipulated to make *broke, broken, breakable,* and *unbreakable.* Morphology is the set of rules that govern how this word manipulation occurs. It allows plural forms to be added to nouns (e.g., *cat/cats, mouse/mice*) and possession to be demonstrated (e.g., *girl's*), and it is used with verbs to show time of action (e.g., *sing, sang, sung*). Also, it includes the use of prefixes and suffixes, such as *un-* and *-able* as seen in *unbreakable.*

A morpheme is the smallest unit of language that carries meaning. Consider the word *preschools.* This word contains three morphemes: the word *school* (referring to a place children go to learn), *pre-* (referring to something that happens before something else), and *-s* (referring to multiple entities). Some morphemes can stand alone (e.g., *school, dog, book*) and are known as free morphemes. Other morphemes have meaning but cannot stand alone. These are known as bound morphemes. Examples of bound morphemes are prefixes such as *bi-, re-, inter-,* and *un-,* and suffixes such as *-ing, -s,* and *-ed.* Some words consist of only a single free morpheme (e.g., *ant, alligator*), whereas other words are made up of several morphemes. For example, *anthill* (two free morphemes) and *cups* (one free morpheme and one bound morpheme) both contain two morphemes. The words *reopened* and *anthills* each contain three. Three important milestones in children's morphological development are noted next and are summarized in Table 3.5.

Table 3.5.   Selected milestones in children's morphological development

The first morphological form to be used: Children's first 50 words tend to include words that consist of only one morpheme (e.g., *ball, baby, juice*).

Other early morphological forms: Plurals, possessives, and the present progressive *-ing* form appear around 2 and 2½ years of age.

Emergence of additional morphological forms: Other forms acquired during the pre-school years include the past tense (*-ed*), present tense (*-s*), and the contracted forms of the auxiliary verb be (e.g., *she's coming, I'm going, they're calling*).

The First Morphological Form to Be Used   Children's first 50 words tend to consist of only one morpheme (e.g., *ball, baby, juice*). Exceptions are occasional compound words (e.g., *birthday, grandpa*) and diminutive forms in which the long *e* sound (spelled as either *-ie* or *-y*) is added to a word (e.g., *blankie, tummy, kitty, doggy, sissy, daddy*). Typically, the first real morphological form to occur in children's speech is adding *-ing* to verbs as in *washing, eating, sleeping,* or *going.* This is referred to as the present progressive verb form, which indicates ongoing action. Used first in two- and three-word utterances, it is common to see the *-ing* form when children are about 2 years of age.

Other Early Morphological Forms   Not long after the *-ing* form is first used, children start to use plurals (e.g., *puppies, cookies, rocks*) and possessives (e.g., *daddy's, baby's, kitty's*). This occurs around 2½ years of age. The use of present progressive verb forms, plurals, and possessives by 2-year-old children reflects emerging skills in morphology. These forms give children greater specificity and precision in their oral language.

Emergence of Additional Morphological Forms   Other significant milestones in the development of morphology during the preschool period include use of the past tense (*-ed* in verbs, as in *walked*) and the present tense (*-s* in verb forms, as in *eats*), both of which emerge at about 3 years of age. The contracted forms of the auxiliary verb *be* (e.g., I *am,* you *are,* he *is*), as in *she's coming, I'm going,* and *they're calling,* emerge at about 3½ years of age. By 5 years of age, many of children's words consist of multiple morphemes.

Pragmatics   Pragmatics is the domain that governs the social use of language. When communicating with others, speakers and listeners follow a variety of tacit rules. These rules regulate conversational turn taking; appropriate eye contact; the relevance and truthfulness of a message; the amount of information being provided; the volume, emphasis, and pitch used when speaking; the physical distance maintained between the speaker and listener; and so forth. These rules all fall within the pragmatics domain. Having appropriate pragmatic skills is essential for developing one aspect of children's social skills, and children with good social skills usually have an easier time making friends and getting along well with others. Also, children who have well-developed pragmatic skills will initiate conversations with their teachers in the classroom more often and participate in more conversations with adults than children with poor or underdeveloped pragmatics. Children with poor pragmatics may be unskilled at initiating conversations with friends and adults and become frustrated at their inability to express their feelings and wishes.

Pragmatic skills are necessary in all social interactions. One such interaction is a conversation between two individuals. For conversation to flow and be productive for both parties, each person must take conversational turns that are an appropriate length. If this rule is violated, the result is a one-sided conversation in which one person dominates the conversation and does not give the other a chance to speak. Likewise, it may be just as disconcerting to be in a conversation in which the partner fails to take conversational turns when they are offered. Appropriate turn taking is an important element of all conversations, and when turn-taking rules are violated, the result may be a less-than-satisfying social interaction between the two individuals and may affect the opportunity and frequency of future interactions. The ideal situation is one in which each partner allows the other an opportunity for conversational turns and is sufficiently responsive when these opportunities are offered. Four important milestones in children's pragmatic development are noted next and are summarized in Table 3.6.

Early Rituals Set the Stage Children's awareness of the pragmatic protocols of oral language gradually increases over the preschool years. The foundation for pragmatic development is often viewed as occurring in the parent–child rituals of early infancy (e.g., eating, bathing, dressing, playing). When feeding infants, early turn taking may be initiated through a child's cries, which are answered by

Table 3.6.   Selected milestones in children's pragmatic development

Early rituals set the stage: Feeding, bathing, and book reading are early rituals that
  help create an early foundation for future turn taking.

Establishing joint reference: By age 12 months, children may be successful in
  achieving joint reference using a variety of means (e.g., gestures, sounds, words).

Development of communicative functions: Children begin deliberate communication
  around 8 months of age, using eye contact, gestures, and vocalization to achieve
  three primary functions: to comment, to request, and to reject. Around 12
  months of age, words are used to meet these functions.

Development of social register: Children as young as 3 years of age may be able to
  vary their social register when speaking with children who are younger than
  they are.

a parent's verbal response and the introduction of food. When infants
are full, they often fuss or refuse further food, to which parents
usually respond by removing the food and changing the activity.
Another early ritual that promotes turn taking is storybook reading in
which the parent may read and the infant may pat the book, smile, or
babble in response. The infant's sound or action is viewed as a
conversational turn by the parent, and he or she answers back or
interprets what the child is doing. Within these early rituals, children
become increasingly accustomed to the patterns of interaction and
communication that occur with others.

   Establishing Joint Reference   Early interactions such as those
occurring with feeding, bathing, and book reading are not only
important for acquiring an awareness of turn taking but also for developing joint reference. Joint reference occurs when two individuals
share a common focus on a particular action or object (e.g., an article
of food, a toy, a clothing item, a book). With infants, joint reference
first occurs with their mother, father, or older siblings. This sharing of
attention is essential to the development of oral language skills. Joint
attention allows the infant to practice emerging communication skills
such as new words and gestures and for the partner to model more
advanced linguistic concepts that relate to the child's focus of
attention. The development of joint reference during the first year of
life follows a fairly predictable pattern. From birth through 6 months,
parents or caregivers control the initiation and maintenance of joint
reference. For instance, a parent may hold a rattle in front of her
infant and say, "Look. It's a rattle," as she shakes it to produce the
sound. As infants approach 6 months of age, they become
increasingly responsive to their parents' requests, and joint reference
readily occurs. From 6 to 12 months, infants may participate in vocal

turn taking (making sounds) in a game such as Pat-a-cake. A particularly important development occurs at about 7 months of age, when infants begin to instigate periods of joint reference by drawing their parent's attention to objects or actions through pointing or showing behaviors. For instance, a child might point to a cat in the room or hold a rattle up to show someone. By 12 months of age, infants may be consistently successful in achieving joint reference for actions and objects of interest using a variety of means (e.g., gestures, sounds, words). The dialogue between the parent and child that occurs during periods of joint reference is critical to the development of oral language skills.

Development of Communicative Functions   Communicative function refers to the reasons a person communicates, or the intention behind the communication. In other words, every time children speak a sentence, there is a reason behind it, and this is its function or intention. When infants first begin to deliberately communicate, which typically occurs at about 8 months of age, there are three primary functions: to comment, to request, and to reject. At this young age, infants use eye contact, gestures, and vocalizations rather than words for these functions. When the first word emerges, at about 1 year, words are then used to fulfill these functions. A single word such as *dog* can be used for any one of these three functions. The child might say "dog" to comment on a dog being present, to request a favorite stuffed animal, or to question if a particular animal is a dog. Whether by word or by gesture, it is very important that children by about 1 year of age be able to use these three functions in their communication with others. Children with a restricted range of communicative functions will experience problems in expressing themselves fully and having their concerns addressed. In the next several years of life, the number of communicative functions increases to include greeting, protesting, answering, and practicing. Having a full range of communication functions allows children to serve as competent conversational partners.

Development of Social Register   One area that is interesting to observe with respect to pragmatics is children's use of social register. Register refers to the way language style is varied to be appropriate according to specific listeners and situations. For example, adults who speak to someone of authority such as a police officer or a judge use a polite and respectful tone of voice and appropriate vocabulary.

However, when speaking to infants, adults change their tone of voice, sentence length, and vocabulary by raising their voice to a high pitch, speaking in shorter sentences, and using simple and repetitive vocabulary. This type of register is affectionately known as baby talk. Children as young as 3 years old have been observed to vary their social register when speaking with children who are younger than they are. For instance, a 3-year-old playing with a newborn may vary the pitch, sentence structure, and vocabulary used when talking to the infant. Likewise, this same 3-year-old may also be observed changing social register when taking on the role of teacher or police officer during dramatic play with peers.

If Language Fails to Develop Normally

Children may vary in the speed with which they acquire language, so the milestones provided in this chapter should be viewed as guidelines rather than definitive markers. For instance, some children begin speaking words at 10 months of age, whereas others do not begin until 14 months of age. It should be noted, however, that when children have significant problems or delays in one or more of the language domains, such as not speaking until 18 months of age, a language problem may be present. Thus, when children produce fewer sounds than expected for their age, fail to develop an expressive vocabulary beyond a few single words, or display deficits in their pragmatic development, adults should take action. If a delay in development is suspected by parents, physicians, or early childhood specialists, a referral to a speech-language pathologist (SLP) for diagnosis and treatment is recommended. These referrals should be timely, as there will be no advantage to waiting. On the contrary, by waiting for the problem to correct itself, children are likely to lose valuable learning time and will fall further behind, which may have a negative impact on their future learning. The next topics will provide further explanation as to why early intervention is so essential.

THREE IMPORTANT CONCEPTS RELATED TO CHILDREN'S LANGUAGE DEVELOPMENT

There are three concepts related to language development that provide a more comprehensive view of this phenomenon beyond an explanation of language domains and a listing of common milestones.

These three concepts are 1) the critical period, 2) the universal premise, and 3) the particulate principle. Understanding these concepts will assist the reader in appreciating the enormous task that language acquisition is for young children and in learning about some of the more intriguing aspects of this development.

The Critical Period

The years from infancy through preschool are vital to the development of oral language. When it comes to oral language, nothing is more important than the first 5 or 6 years of life, when language development is faster than it will ever be again. Many experts refer to these years as the *critical period*. Some experts believe the critical period to last from birth through puberty, whereas others believe the critical period to be much shorter—from birth to about 5 or 6 years of age. Regardless of perspective, nearly all scholars agree that the first 5 years of life are the most important for oral language development. Never again will the child have the opportunity for such rapid language development.

When children come into the world, their brains are especially dedicated to the task of acquiring language. But not too many years later, children's brains need to turn to other tasks, and the brain is no longer well suited for, or so dedicated to, the task of language development. At about 6 years of age, the child has more or less mastered the language system, and at this point, the rapid pace of language development really starts to slow down. Adolescents and adults attempting to learn a new language tend to have a very difficult time and often will never achieve full mastery of the new language. Adults may easily forget how difficult the task of learning language can be.

Recognizing the language growth that must occur between birth and 6 years of age will help adults understand and appreciate the enormous task that each child faces. Furthermore, the skills learned during this time period will serve as the foundation on which all later language and literacy abilities will build. This is one reason why it is important to seek intervention as early as possible when children show signs of delay.

The Universal Premise

The universal premise refers to the fact that children all across the world, in various cultures and communities, from Australia to Zaire, acquire language in much the same way and along much the same timeline. Children enter the world ready to learn any language; it matters not whether the language is Arabic, Chinese, English, or French. Once children begin to be exposed to their native language (or languages), they will begin a course of language acquisition in that specific language, and this course looks remarkably similar across languages. Children of all languages begin to vocalize at about 2 months of age, start to babble at about 4 months of age, and say their first word at about 1 year of age. Even children acquiring sign language as their first language follow essentially the same sequence and timeline of these major milestones. This is the universal premise.

The Particulate Principle

One interesting aspect of language is its potential for creativity and abundance, which is demonstrated through the particulate principle. This principle applies to situations in which a very small set of elements can be used to create an infinite number of possibilities. Consider the speech sound system of English, which contains only about 43 phonemes. This is actually quite a small number of sounds for children to learn, and, indeed, they have usually mastered them all around the time that formal schooling begins. With this small repertoire of sounds, children have an amazing tool for producing an infinite number of words. They learn that different words are created by reordering sounds (from *pat* to *tap*), by deleting sounds (from *cup* to *up*), and by adding sounds (from *at* to *splat*). By putting just two sounds together, they have short words such as *my,* and by putting more sounds together they have longer words such as *gigantic,* which has eight phonemes. Given the particulate principle, children need only learn a small set of elements (about 43 English phonemes), after which they are able to speak all of the words in the English language.

The particulate principle applies to the grammar system of language as well. For example, one syntactic rule mentioned earlier in this chapter requires that all sentences contain at least two parts: a subject and a predicate. Once children learn this rule, they are able to create an endless number of new sentences. They need not be taught all of the possible sentences in the world; rather, they simply need to know the grammatical rules. Children usually figure out these rules on their own, using the sentences they hear from adults around them as the key to unlocking the code. Once they internalize the rules, they can create any number of original sentences. The entire grammar of language is rule governed; children need only acquire a fairly small set of rules governing the grammar of their language, and they are then able to produce an endless variety of novel sentences and, likewise, to understand a multitude of sentences they have never heard before.

The concept of the particulate principle is important to understand for two reasons. First, it illustrates that the challenge of learning language lies in mastering its underlying principles and rules. Children need not be taught everything about language. Rather, they will benefit more from learning the various rules that govern its sound system and its grammar. Such rules and principles are acquired as children experience language in the world around them; children acquire the rules and gradually come to understand all of the various applications of the rules. Second, knowing that children need to acquire rules to become good language learners, the importance of providing an environment that contains frequent verbal interactions of the highest quality cannot be overstated. It is through children's experiences of hearing and producing language with others that these language rules are understood. By providing children with excellent language models depicting diverse applications of form, function, and use, children will be better able to acquire a high degree of language competence.

These three concepts (the critical period, the universal premise, and the particulate principle) all support the notion that young children require a daily language environment that is supportive, stimulating, and rich in experience in order to develop normally. This means that adults need to provide language to young children during all daily activities such as feeding, bathing, dressing, playing, transporting, and preparing for naptime and bedtime—in short, whenever adults and children interact. One activity that is particularly suited for language acquisition opportunities is shared book reading. This activity combines several elements that make it a natural context for children's language acquisition: a brief entertaining story, colorful illustrations, and written text read by an adult. In the next chapter, strategies for enhancing children's language skills through shared reading are presented.

4

Using Shared Reading to Develop Children's Language Skills

As noted in the previous chapter, there are five interconnected domains that together compose children's language: semantics, phonology, syntax, morphology, and pragmatics. Each of these may be addressed during shared reading using strategies proposed in this chapter to promote and further children's language development.

RECEPTIVE AND EXPRESSIVE LANGUAGE

Professionals may choose to emphasize either receptive or expressive language when conducting shared reading with young children. Receptive language involves the comprehension of oral language, as seen when children show understanding of "Give me the sock" or "Show me two fingers." Such requests typically elicit a nonverbal response (e.g., handing over the sock, holding up two fingers). In contrast, expressive skills require children to formulate a verbal response as seen when they are asked, "What is your name?" or "Where do you live?" As a general rule, expressive language tasks are more challenging than receptive language tasks because they require children to formulate a verbal response. Therefore, when professionals want to present less demanding tasks that involve nonverbal responding, the receptive mode should be chosen; but when a conversational response is desired, the expressive mode should be used. Of course, it is possible to emphasize both modes during shared reading rather than target exclusive use of one or the other. The professional may determine which approach to use based on a child's current language abilities and areas of need. The ultimate goal will be to work within a child's learning zone as discussed in Chapter 1.

Building Receptive Language

Building receptive language during shared reading involves asking children to point, touch, or show rather than requiring them to use expressive language. Although all language skills may be taught receptively, semantics (vocabulary) is probably one of the easiest to teach in this way. This would involve asking children to "point to the picture of _____" to demonstrate that the meaning of a particular word is understood. For children who have small vocabularies or use no speech at all, expanding receptive vocabulary might be a good starting point for language growth. Also, for children who are reluctant to participate in book-sharing conversations, nonverbal responding may serve as an introductory step to active participation.

Professionals may also facilitate receptive language growth by modeling and expanding children's utterances. These techniques have been shown by various researchers, such as Whitehurst et al. (1988) and Girolametto and Weitzman (2002), to be effective in building children's receptive language. Modeling involves presenting and using a new word for the child to hear (e.g., "Look at this." [pointing to a bicycle] "It's called a bicycle. We ride bicycles by pedaling with our feet."). Expansions occur when the professional builds on something the child just said. If a child says, "Hot," an expansion could be, "Yes, the oven is hot" or "Right, the fire looks very hot." Although young children may not demonstrate immediate use of new words or more syntactically complex utterances, over time these forms may emerge through repeated models and expansions.

Building Expressive Language

Building expressive language occurs by engaging children in conversational exchanges that extend their current expressive abilities. One way to engage children in conversational exchanges is the use of *wh*-questions. An example of such a question might be, "What is happening in this picture?" Any time children answer using speech, the expressive mode of language is being tapped. Emphasis on expressive language will elicit the verbal turn taking desired for book-sharing conversations, which is a primary focus of this book. Also, expressive language use by children, when produced in meaningful, conversational contexts, helps children to reinforce their understanding of new words and concepts.

SHARED-READING STRATEGIES FOR DEVELOPING CHILDREN'S LANGUAGE SKILLS

The following sections describe suggested language development strategies that may be incorporated into conversations during shared reading. The reader will notice that all of these strategies are designed to promote children's expressive language; however, adaptations may be made to several of these strategies to promote comprehension without requiring production. For example, asking a child to "point to the picture showing him" or "point to the picture showing her" would be targeting comprehension of pronouns that denote gender.

One strategy for each language domain is provided. It should be noted that these examples do not exhaust the variety of ways to focus on these skills; instead, they offer the reader some tips for getting such conversations started. On another point, the reader will note that each strategy is to be employed three times during a single shared-reading session. This recommendation has been made with the child's enjoyment of the story in mind, as it has been the experience of these authors that continual interruptions reduce children's enjoyment of the story being read. However, there is nothing sacred in this rule of three, and if the reader finds that more frequent interruptions do not cause frustration or compromise children's shared-reading enjoyment, the strategy may be used more often.

Throughout the strategies described in this chapter and in future chapters, professionals will find recommendations to provide praise and feedback to children during shared reading. It is the opinion of the authors that all children acquiring new skills depend on this praise and feedback for gaining mastery. Little is to be gained when children are confused on this matter and think that any and all responses are equally correct. Therefore, it is suggested that professionals praise children's positive performance, task engagement, and persistence. When children make errors, corrections may be made through "think aloud" strategies or modeling to help children come up with the right answer. Of primary importance is that corrections and "think aloud" strategies be offered using an accepting and understanding tone so that children feel comfortable and supported by the adult. As noted by Schuele (2004), this adult feedback will help shape children's performance to increasingly higher levels.

One final point concerning how sounds are presented in the reading samples in this and other chapters is noteworthy. Although the technical term for a sound is *phoneme,* adults rarely use this term when speaking with preschoolers. Therefore, when adult/child dialogue is presented, target sounds appear in quotation marks and will be described in a way that adults and children typically speak (e.g., "The first sound in the word *pony* is 'puh' ").

Conversational Target: Semantics

Professionals' initiating conversations that focus on semantics during shared reading will have a positive impact on children's vocabulary knowledge. Sometimes these conversations occur spontaneously when children ask what a particular word means or when they demonstrate a misunderstanding of word knowledge by their words or actions. However, it is possible to create opportunities for these conversations, too. The procedures that follow will describe one way the topic of semantics may be addressed.

Selecting a Vocabulary Target and a Storybook   In theory, it is possible to use the vocabulary found in any storybook to build language skills, but taking an organized or methodical approach will allow the professional to have greater control and precision in the task. Therefore, it is suggested that some thought be given to which vocabulary words to target and which books may offer conversational opportunities about these words. When selecting a storybook for potential vocabulary targets, preview it ahead of time to determine what concepts or words might be new or challenging for the child or classroom of children. Select up to three words to include in conversation during shared reading of that book. These can be nouns, adjectives, adverbs, or verbs. Make note of how often the words are used, how they are represented in print, and whether they are depicted in the book's illustrations. In doing so, it will be possible to know in what ways the word may be emphasized. For example, if a word appears several times throughout the storybook, it may be discussed when it is first illustrated and then reviewed again later. It is recommended that these words be written down somewhere, perhaps on a slip of paper to use as a bookmark, to serve as a reminder of the ones selected. For additional information about book selection, the reader is referred to Chapter 10, which describes selection considerations in greater detail.

Conducting the Shared-Reading Session   Begin the shared-reading activity by reading the title of the storybook and then having a conversation speculating on what the story may involve. As the reading progresses, interrupt the story for a brief conversation about the selected words as planned. This conversation could include a comment, a question, or a request about the target words that is intended to elicit a verbal response from the child. For example, if the professional selects *The Very Hungry Caterpillar* (Carle, 1987) and a target word is *cocoon*, ask the child if he or she knows what a cocoon is or if he or she has ever seen a cocoon. An explanation of the word *cocoon* might be required, or perhaps the child will relate an experience with a caterpillar or other insect. This conversation may be only momentary before returning to the story, but it will have served its function by calling the word to the child's attention and explaining its meaning to facilitate comprehension. Consider the following example using a storybook created by the preschool children about their recent visit to the local post office:

Teacher:	"We saw lots of signs in the post office." (pauses) Look right here (points to the word *fragile* in the photograph). The sign on this box says *fragile.* Can you point to the word *fragile* for us, Molly?
Molly:	Here? (points correctly)
Teacher:	That's right, this word is *fragile.* (points to the word again) Does anyone know what the word *fragile* means?
Jeremy:	That means it breaks.
Suzanne:	No, it means, "Be careful!"
Alex:	Don't touch it.
Teacher:	Very good! All of you have the right idea. It means to be very careful with the package because it can be damaged in some way. If it was a piece of glass, it might break. If it was an animal, it could be hurt if you bump it or drop it.
Jeremy:	Yeah, it could get a broken leg.

Alex: Or a broken foot.

Teacher: Absolutely! The box must be lifted very gently so nothing
           is hurt or broken. Well done! Now let's keep reading to see
           what comes next.

When children participate actively in the discussion, be sure to
provide praise to reinforce the concept that their contributions are
valued. Repeat this procedure with the other selected target words as
shared reading continues. Do not overwhelm the children with repeated interruptions that may interfere with their enjoyment of the
story. This is the reason that no more than three target words are recommended for discussion. When the storybook is finished, praise the
children for listening and talking about the story. A brief synopsis of
this procedure is provided in Table 4.1.

If repeated readings of the same storybook are conducted, children may initiate conversations about these new words again. This
will provide opportunities for the professional to introduce additional
information about these words or concepts and for the child to practice using the words in conversation. If a different storybook is presented that also contains these new words, the professional may initiate a conversation about these words to see whether the child
remembers and understands them in a new situation.

As an alternative, professionals may discuss new vocabulary
words before shared reading begins by presenting the words orally, in
print, and/or through illustration. This conversation could include a
brief definition of the word and the use of it in a sentence. Then the
professional might ask the child to listen for the word as the story is
being read. This gives the child an opportunity to initiate a conversation about the word when he or she hears it in the story.

Table 4.1.   Conversational target: semantics

Select a storybook that contains three words that may be new or challenging for
the child. Consider how these words are presented in the text and in the illustrations to plan for conversational opportunities.

During the reading, interrupt the story on three occasions (once for each target
word) for a brief conversation. Conversations may involve asking the child if he
or she has heard the word before or knows its meaning. The professional may
also point to an illustration depicting the meaning or may show the child the
printed word in the book that represents the spoken word.

Keep conversations limited and brief so as not to reduce the child's enjoyment of
the story. Praise the child's correct responses and conversational attempts.

Conversational Target: Phonology

Conversations about phonology will focus on developing children's speech production as well as their awareness of speech sounds. Awareness of sounds is also critical for emergent literacy development, specifically phonological awareness. Conversations about phonology embedded in shared reading can help children learn correct pronunciation of consonant sounds that are mastered during their preschool years, such as the first sounds found in the words *bed, pen, hand, time, dog, kind, foot, yellow, go, no, me,* and *we.* Developing consonants such as /s/, /r/, /θ/, /ʒ/, and /ð/ may be emphasized when children are older, but they are not recommended targets when children are young preschoolers. The reader may have noticed that vowel sounds have been omitted in this discussion. This is because of the numerous variations that occur in vowel production as a result of the location of the vowel within words and the influence of regional dialectal differences. For these reasons, it was decided that awareness of vowel sounds might best be introduced during formal reading instruction when children enter school.

Integrating attention to phonology is suitable for children who are verbal and can be easily understood. It could be especially helpful to children who exhibit occasional mispronunciations in their speech. It may not be appropriate when children have many mispronunciations or can be understood by only select people. The presence of multiple mispronunciations and limited intelligibility may signal a significant language delay. When limited intelligibility is an issue for children, they should be referred to an SLP for a thorough evaluation. If children are diagnosed with a language disorder, their SLP will be able to provide appropriate goals and individualized guidance for promoting language development during shared-reading activities.

Selecting a Target Sound and a Storybook   Begin by selecting a target consonant sound for the child or a group of children and locating a storybook that includes words containing this sound. Ideally, the storybook selected will have at least three different words that begin with the target sound and will depict these words in the illustrations. It is easier for children to hear and distinguish sounds at the beginning of words, so avoid making the task too difficult by choosing words in which the sound appears in the middle or at the end of words. Likewise, avoid words that use the target consonant in a consonant cluster in which it is placed adjacent to another consonant such as /bl/, /br/, /kl/, /pr/, or /dr/. Hearing and producing the sounds in consonant clusters is more challenging because the two consonants blend together, which slightly alters their production. The target consonant will be clearer for the child and easier to produce if it is followed by a vowel. As an example, if the target consonant sound is /f/, the words *foggy* or *fable* would be preferred over *freedom* or *fly*. One final consideration is the meaning of the words containing the target sound to be discussed. When children are asked to focus on a word, it is always possible for them to ask about its meaning, which introduces the opportunity to extend the conversation into the semantics realm. Therefore, it will be important to be prepared to address such questions in case they arise.

A few suggested books for emphasizing particular sounds are included in the list below. One excellent resource for finding other books that feature specific sounds is *Books Are for Talking Too!* (Gebers, 1990), which is listed in Chapter 10.

For the consonant /b/: *The Blue Balloon* (Inkpen, 1990)

For the consonant /p/: *Hop on Pop* (Seuss, 1963)

For the consonant /t/: *Where's Tim's Ted?* (Whybrow, 2000)

For the consonant /d/: *If You Give a Mouse a Cookie* (Numeroff, 1985)

For the consonant /k/: *The Doorbell Rang* (Hutchins, 1986)

For the consonant /g/: *Good Night, Gorilla* (Rathmann, 1994)

For the consonant /f/: *Owen* (Henkes, 1993)

For the consonant /m/: *Five Little Monkeys Jumping on the Bed* (Christelow, 1989)

For the consonant /n/: *Nuts to You!* (Ehlert, 1993)

For the consonant /w/: *Spot Goes to a Party* (Hill, 1992)

Conducting the Shared-Reading Session   Preview the chosen book in advance to determine where to introduce conversation about the target sound and how it is produced. If desired, the child or children could be told in advance that the story will be interrupted a couple of times to practice saying some words; however, this step is optional. Begin reading the storybook and introduce conversation about the target sound when coming to the first selected word in the story. This may be introduced through saying the word and pointing to a relevant illustration. Point out the sound that begins the word and say the sound in isolation (i.e., say only the individual sound), asking the child to watch carefully to see what to do. Produce the sound two or three times while the child watches and listens. Then ask the child to try saying the sound. Provide as much assistance as needed—pointing out where the tongue should be placed, how the lips move, if voice is used, or how air comes out of the mouth. Praise the child's attempts and tell him or her when the sound is produced correctly. Ask the child to say the sound in the first target word once he or she is able to produce the sound correctly in isolation. After the child produces or attempts the sound or word once or twice, resume the story, saying something like "Good work! Let's see what happens next in the story, and maybe we'll try that sound again." Repeat this procedure a second and third time as the remaining two target words are encountered. Have the child try the target words only if he or she can correctly produce the sound in isolation; otherwise, focus only on the individual sound. The reason for this is that saying the sound within a word is more difficult than saying the sound in isolation, so if the child has problems saying the sound alone, avoid making the task even harder by expecting correct production within words. Also, do not interrupt the storybook more than three times to practice the sound even if the target words appear more frequently because this may disrupt the flow of the story too much. The following excerpt from a shared-reading session of *Owen* (Henkes, 1993) provides an example of this strategy:

Parent: "Haven't you heard of the blanket fairy? Owen's parents hadn't. Mrs. Tweezers filled them in." (pause) I hear that "fuh" sound again. Do you hear it, too? It's in the word *fairy*. Listen to the word: fuh-fuh-fairy.

Logan: Vuh-vuh-vuh.

Parent: That was a good try, but not exactly right. This time say it like a whisper—softer and with more air like this: fuh-fuh.

Logan: Fuh-fuh.

Parent: Well done—you've got it! Try it again.

Logan: Fuh-fuh.

Parent: Perfect! Now, try the "fuh" sound in the word *fairy*. Start with the sound "fuh-fuh-fairy."

Logan: Fuh-fuh-very.

Parent: That was a nice try, but it's not quite right. Try it again with a whisper and with more air.

Logan: Fuh-fuh-fairy.

Parent: Wow! You did it! That was great! Do it again, and say, "fairy."

Logan: Fairy.

Parent: That's correct. Good work! Let's keep reading, and we'll practice again later, okay?

Logan: Okay.

Some children need only a little practice before they master saying the sound alone as in the example above, whereas others may need to practice for several days or even weeks. Offer continued practice with new words by introducing them through different storybooks, using the same procedure. However, if the child is unable to master it quickly and is showing some signs of frustration, try another sound or focus on a different language strategy and return to this sound at a later time. Do not continue to frustrate children with a difficult sound that might be mastered more easily when they are a few months older. Table 4.2 provides a brief synopsis of this procedure for quick reference.

Table 4.2.   Conversational target: phonology

Select one consonant sound to emphasize. This should be a consonant that most young children master at an early age. Some examples are the initial sounds in the words bed, pen, hand, time, foot, dog, kind, yellow, go, me, no, and we.

Select a storybook that has three different words that contain the target consonant sound in the beginning position. Do not select words that contain the sound in the middle or end of words. Also, avoid words that contain the sound in a consonant cluster. Whenever possible, try to select words that are depicted in illustrations.

As the story is read, initiate a conversation with the child about the sound when the first selected word is encountered. Model the correct production and ask the child to watch closely. Encourage the child to try making the sound a couple of times. Praise all attempts (e.g., "That was a good try") and reinforce correct productions (e.g., "You did it right that time," "That was perfect!"). Ask the child to try the sound in the first target word only if he or she is able to produce the sound correctly in isolation.

Repeat this procedure on two more occasions with the remaining target words. Praise the child again at the end of the session for trying some new sounds and/or words.

For continued practice, introduce new words containing this sound in different storybooks using the same procedure.

Conversational Target: Syntax

When focusing on syntax, many different types of structures may be targeted. Basic sentences are formed with a subject and a predicate (e.g., *Bear swims*) and may expand from there to include noun phrases (e.g., *The baby bear*), verb phrases (e.g., *swims fast*), and prepositional phrases (e.g., *in the cold water*). By paying attention to a child's typical sentence patterns, likely syntactic structures to be targeted may be determined. Consider a few examples. If a child does not use a variety of adjectives to modify nouns, noun phrases might be targeted; likewise, verb phrase expansion could be selected if a child rarely uses adverbs. Also, if a child is known to omit words (e.g., saying, "He going" for "He is going") or to use words incorrectly (e.g., saying, "Her do it" for "She does it"), these structures could be addressed. When a child speaks in two- or three-word utterances, simply expanding the utterance length by one word could be a goal. However, vocabulary expansion should not be confused with syntactic development. When the goal is to increase a child's vocabulary, the adult helps the child understand the meaning of a word but may not require the child to use the new word immediately in sentences. When the professional focuses on syntactic development, immediate (or eventual) incorporation of the word within a child's utterance is the main objective. Given the numerous ways that syntactic knowledge may be addressed, this language skill may be an appropriate target for almost all young children.

Selecting a Syntactic Target and a Storybook   As noted previously, a child's typical sentence structure may serve as a guide in selecting a syntactic target. If the child uses only one-word utterances (e.g., "doggie"), then expanding his or her utterances to include verbs would be appropriate (e.g., "Doggie is sleeping," "Doggie is eating," or "Doggie is running"). After children can produce sentences with a subject and a predicate, it is typical for them to add a direct object (e.g., "Doggie is chasing a *cat*" or "Doggie is eating a *bone*"). Expansion of noun phrases (e.g., "*The big doggie* is eating") and verb phrases (e.g., "The doggie is *jumping high*") may be a next logical step. Encouraging the use of prepositional phrases (e.g., "The doggie is running *around the tree*") might be considered as well. Indirect objects (e.g., "The dog is giving the slipper to *Daddy*"), object relative clauses (e.g., "The dog belongs to the girl *who lives on the corner*"), and passive sentences (e.g., "The dog is carried by the boy") should be reserved for older children because these syntactic constructions are more advanced. It is important to remember that when children are developing syntax, they often omit key grammatical markers; for example, they may say, "The doggie is chasing cat," leaving out the article *the* preceding the direct object in "The doggie is chasing *the cat*." Such omissions are normal and are not cause for alarm. Simply provide models of the more adult-like form (e.g., *the cat*) and emphasize the word to be added. With repeated modeling, it is likely that the child will begin using the missing word.

Although professionals may select practically any storybook for developing specific syntactic forms, two suggestions are offered. First, it is recommended that a storybook be reviewed with the particular target in mind so that opportunities for using the structure may be found in advance. It may be helpful to make a note as to where these conversations should occur to serve as a reminder during the shared-reading session. As described in the previous strategies, it is recommended that three conversational opportunities be identified. Keeping the number of opportunities to three provides some practice for the child without disrupting the story to a great degree. A second consideration is to select a familiar storybook so that the child has some prior knowledge of the words used in the story. The reason for this suggestion is that it may be easier for the child to use familiar words within new syntactic structures than unfamiliar ones.

Conducting the Shared-Reading Session　As the storybook is being read, begin a brief conversation with the child to model correct use of the target syntactic structure. This may be initiated with a question that leads into the desired topic such as asking about a character in the story (e.g., "What is the girl doing now?") or an illustration (e.g., "Tell me what you see on this page"). After the child responds, provide an expansion that adds further information and uses the target structure. For instance, if the child says, "Mouse," an expansion could be "The mouse *is sleeping*" or "The mouse *is washing*," depending on events in the story. With these examples, the portions in italics may be spoken with emphasis in order to call them to the child's attention. This is referred to as focused stimulation. The child is not required to repeat what is modeled, but if he or she attempts to repeat it, provide praise. If the child says nothing further, simply resume reading the storybook and repeat the same procedure at the predetermined times.

The goal is to provide expansions using the target structure on three occasions during shared reading so as not to disrupt the flow of the story too often. Praise all attempts and praise again at the end of the session for talking about the story. As the child becomes more proficient in using the target syntactic structure, he or she will be able to do so in response to the model or independently. Table 4.3 provides a brief summary of this strategy for quick reference.

As an example, consider the following excerpt from a shared-reading session targeting a prepositional phrase (e.g., *on the stairs*) from *There's an Alligator Under My Bed* by Mercer Mayer (1987):

Teacher: What is the boy doing in this picture?

Nathan: He got the food.

Teacher: That's right, the boy got some food for the alligator. Where is he putting it?

Nathan: Right here. (points to the food)

Teacher: Yes, the food is right here *on the stairs.* (points to the food on the stairs)

Nathan: Food is on stairs.

Teacher: Very good! The boy is putting the food *on the stairs.*

Nathan: I see a carrot. (points to the carrot)

Table 4.3. Conversational target: syntax

Select a target syntactic structure that the child does not exhibit in his or her speech on a regular basis such as including a direct object (e.g., "The girl is buying *a present*").

Choose a book that the child has read before or one that contains familiar vocabulary words. Locate three places in the story where the target syntactic structure may be modeled. Favorable locations in the story may be found through specific events or illustrations.

Interrupt the story for a brief conversation on three occasions that were determined in the previous step. Ask the child a question about the story or a picture that might be followed with a model of the targeted syntactic structure. For instance, if the professional asks a question (e.g., "What is the man doing in this picture?") and the child answers (e.g., "He is washing"), the professional could respond with an expansion that includes the target structure (e.g., "Yes, he is washing *the car*").

Provide praise whenever the child repeats the model. Upon completion of shared reading, praise the child again for listening and speaking well.

Teacher: Yes, the carrot is *on the stairs,* too.

Nathan: Carrot is on stairs?

Teacher: Yes, the carrot *is* on the stairs. Very good! Now let's see
            what he does next.

Conversational Target: Morphology

As explained in Chapter 3, morphology involves the use of word endings that provide additional meaning to the nouns or verbs to which
they are attached. In typical language development, children acquire
some word endings at a relatively early age. Two examples are the
present progressive *-ing,* which is added to verbs (e.g., *talking,*
sleeping, thinking) and the plural *-s,* which is added to nouns (e.g.,
cats, books, movies). Other forms may be acquired a little later; for
example, the superlative form *-est* (e.g., *biggest, fastest*), the regular
past tense form *-ed,* which is added to verbs to indicate past action
(e.g., *walked, opened, pushed*), and irregular past tense forms in
verbs (e.g., *ate, slept, threw, sat*).

Morphology involves a more refined language skill. Consequently,
this strategy is suitable for children who exhibit large expressive
vocabularies, who can speak intelligibly, and who use sentences containing at least three to four words. Morphology would be considered
a lower priority for children who have minimal vocabularies, unintelli-
gible speech, or utterances containing only one or two words.

Selecting a Morphological Target and a Storybook   Observe
the child's typical language and choose a target morphological form
that he or she uses infrequently or not at all. Some target forms to
consider include the present progressive verb tense *-ing,* (e.g.,
dancing, reading, skipping), the possessive *-'s* (e.g., *Tommy's*
shoe, the boy's bike, the girl's notebook), the plural *-s* (e.g.,
elephants, crayons, shoes), regular past tense *-ed* (e.g., *shaved,*
stirred, skated), or the comparative form *-er* (e.g., *wider, smaller,*
taller).

When considering a storybook for shared reading, be sure that
several actions are pictured in the book if a verb ending is selected
(e.g., *-ing -ed*). If the plural *-s* form is selected, try to find a book,
such as a counting book, that contains more of one item in which plurals may be used easily. Targeting the comparative form *-er* will be

easier if the book uses several adjectives. Be sure the book contains at least three occasions in which the targeted form might be used so that there are enough instances for practice.

Conducting the Shared-Reading Session　　The same general procedure of interrupting the story for a brief conversation on three occasions will be followed. Begin the conversation with a question whose answer would normally involve the use of the targeted morphological form. For example, if the target is the present progressive form *-ing,* a question that might be posed is, "What is the boy doing here?" An expected response from the child could be, "He is running" or "The boy is running." However, if the child responds by saying, "He run," the professional would provide the correct model by saying, "He is running." As another example, if the target is the possessive *-'s* form, the adult might ask, "Whose ball is this?" expecting a response such as "Spot's ball." If the child responds by saying, "It Spot ball," the professional would model the correct form by saying, "It is Spot's ball." After the model is given, pause for the child to respond. If the child uses the form after the model, praise should be provided. If no response is given, simply continue with the story. Providing and emphasizing these models of specific morphological forms can be useful for advancing children's language development.

Some children may need to hear the model on several occasions before beginning to respond using the targeted form, especially when they have never used the target form previously. Praise all correct responses that the child provides. If the child responds incorrectly after hearing the model, provide further assistance (e.g., emphasize the final part of the word as the model is provided again). However, do not belabor the point too long because the child will be eager to

Table 4.4.　　Conversational target: morphology

Select a target form that the child uses infrequently or not at all. Review the storybook in advance to determine three occasions where the form could be used.

Interrupt the story on three occasions to pose a question or request that might elicit the child's use of the target form. For example, if the target is the plural *-s*, the professional might say, "This picture has lots of *balloons*. I count one, two, three...." The professional would pause at that point for the child to say the word *balloons*. If the child does not respond, the professional could model the correct plural form again.

Provide praise whenever the child repeats the model. Give assistance if the child responds incorrectly. Upon completion of shared reading, praise the child again for listening and speaking well.

return to the story. Repeat the procedure on two more occasions. At the end of the reading session, provide praise for listening well, paying attention, or learning some new words. Table 4.4 provides a review of this procedure for quick reference.

In the following shared-reading excerpt, the regular past tense -*ed* form is emphasized using *Spot Bakes a Cake* (Hill, 1994):

Parent: What did Spot and his mommy do?

Kelly: He bake a cake.

Parent: That's right, Spot bak<u>ed</u> a cake.

Kelly: He baked a cake.

Parent: Very good! Yes, he bak<u>ed</u> a birthday cake.

Kelly: He baked it in here? (opens the oven door to reveal the cake inside)

Parent: That's right—he bak<u>ed</u> the cake in the oven just the way we do.

Kelly: Yep! (turns the page)

Conversational Target: Pragmatics

As described in Chapter 3, pragmatics governs the social use of language. This involves not only which words an individual chooses when speaking but how the message is delivered. Using appropriate pragmatic skills means speaking with the proper tone and volume at a comfortable distance from the listener. It includes using an appropriate amount of eye contact when speaking. It involves social graces such as introducing oneself and using phrases such as "please," "thank you," "you're welcome," and "excuse me." It recognizes that some listeners may be less able to understand and makes appropriate adjustments for this fact. Also, it regulates conversational turn taking, topic maintenance, and suitable topics of conversation, given the situation.

Children's pragmatic skills are developed over time, from early childhood into adulthood. These skills will be acquired through life experiences and will be shaped by the child's culture. All adults in children's lives play a valuable role in developing early pragmatic skills by monitoring children's language use and explaining acceptable forms of expression in a variety of contexts. Although this assistance may occur in casual daily interactions, shared reading provides an additional opportunity for monitoring and practicing appropriate pragmatic skills with young children.

Selecting a Pragmatic Target and a Storybook   A few pragmatic skills that may be easily incorporated into conversations during shared reading include establishing eye contact, maintaining a conversational topic, and regulating speaking volume. Naturally, the need to address such skills would depend on the child's typical conversational behavior. For instance, if the child establishes eye contact easily, this target would not be chosen. However, if the child appears to avoid eye contact, it could be a reasonable target. The same is true for maintaining a conversational topic and using an appropriate speaking volume (neither too loud nor too soft) as well.

If other pragmatic skills are an issue, they might be addressed by selecting a storybook that deals with the relevant topic through a social situation in the story. Examples could include learning to ask questions, introducing a friend, extending a personal invitation, accepting a compliment, or using polite language. Some children's books address these and other types of social situations that may provide opportunities for the professional and child to discuss expected or appropriate behavior. For instance, if a story deals with a character's lack of polite language (e.g., saying "please" and "thank you"), the professional and child could discuss the character's resulting problems. In this conversation the professional could explain why these words are important to say and point out how people in the story react when the character forgets to say them. This conversation may help the child to view the situation from a different perspective and to be more sensitive toward others' feelings in the future.

Practically any storybook could be used for shared-reading sessions to emphasize eye contact, topic maintenance, or speaking volume. If other pragmatic skills are to be targeted through the story's theme or content, it will be important to read the storybook ahead of time to know how the pragmatic skill is addressed in the story and to plan how the target skill might be discussed. An ideal situation might be to find a storybook whose topic deals with one of the target behaviors to be practiced with the child (e.g., a story about talking too loud). This would allow the child a chance to relate to the character in the story and practice a new speaking voice at the same time.

Table 4.5.   Conversational target: pragmatics

Select an appropriate pragmatic target based on the child's typical conversational behavior.

Choose a book that would interest the child and stimulate conversation.

On three occasions, interrupt the shared reading to have a conversation about the story

- To increase eye contact, look at the child and pause. If the child does not establish eye contact, say the child's name and pause again. If the child is still unresponsive, ask, "Will you look at me, please?" Praise the child when he or she achieves momentary eye contact and proceed with a brief conversation.

- To improve topic maintenance, pose a question to the child regarding the story. If the child answers off topic, continue posing the question two or three times until receiving a relevant response. Praise all relevant answers.

- To improve speaking volume, provide a gentle request such as "Could you speak a little softer?" but do not interrupt the child's conversational turn to do so. Praise the child's appropriate volume adjustment. The verbal prompt may be shortened (e.g., "Softer, please") or replaced with a visual prompt (e.g., placing index finger to closed lips) and given only when needed.

Conducting the Shared-Reading Session   As in all previous strategies presented, shared reading will be interrupted on three predetermined occasions to emphasize and/or practice the targeted skill. Strategies for the three pragmatic skills mentioned earlier—eye contact, topic maintenance, and speaking volume—are described next and summarized in Table 4.5.

If the child needs reminders to use appropriate eye contact, it will be important that the professional attempt to establish eye contact with the child on three occasions in order to hold a brief conversation. When the professional reaches the first conversational point, he or she should look at the child and pause for a few seconds for the child to establish eye contact independently. If the child does not do so, the professional should say the child's name to get his or her attention. If after a few seconds the child still has not established eye contact, the professional may provide a prompt to do so by saying, "Will you look at me, please?" An appropriate response from the child would be to look at the professional for a brief moment. When the child establishes eye contact, even for an instant, the professional should provide praise and then begin a brief conversation. The child is not expected to sustain eye contact for a long period of time, as the primary focus will be to look at the storybook. Therefore, do not expect the child to sustain eye contact through the entire conversation. The goal is to establish appropriate momentary eye contact when a child fails to do so as it is appropriate to conversation. The professional will need to use some judgment to determine what is reasonable and natural, but generally speaking, eye contact that is a few seconds in duration would be an acceptable length of time given the nature of the activity. The following example demonstrates this strategy through an excerpt from a shared-reading session from *Spot Goes to the Beach* (Hill, 1985):

Teacher: Spot wants to buy something. Can you lift the flap to see what Spot's doing?

Brian: I remember . . . he wants a sailor hat! (lifts the flap)

Teacher: Yes, that's right! He wants to buy one of these sailor hats. (pauses and attempts to establish eye contact with the child and waits several seconds)

Brian: (continues looking at book)

Teacher: Brian.

Brian: (continues looking at book)

Teacher: Brian, can you look at me? I want to ask you something.

Brian: (looks up briefly and establishes eye contact with the teacher)

Teacher: (smiles when eye contact is established) Thank you! I like it when you look at me. Now I was wondering, which one of these would you want if *you* were at the beach?

Topic maintenance is an ideal target if a child changes the subject whenever taking a conversational turn rather than contributes to the topic that has just been introduced. When interrupting the story for a conversation, introduce a topic that is related to the story's character or action by posing a question such as "Who is that in the circus tent?" If the child responds by changing the subject (e.g., "I like chocolate candy"), ask the question again (e.g., "Who do you think this is?"). If the child still does not respond on topic, ask a third time by saying, "Can you answer my question, please? Who does Spot see in the circus tent?" Although it is not desirable to ask each question two or three times, it may be necessary to do so in the beginning so that the child understands that he or she is expected to answer the question or contribute a comment, even if the answer is "I don't know." Praise all relevant responses the child attempts by saying something like "That's a good answer!" Over time, the child may realize that the professional will keep asking until he or she provides a relevant comment. Plan to use this strategy on three occasions during shared reading so that the story is not disrupted too often. In the following example of a shared-reading session of *The Paper Bag Princess* (Munsch, 1980), the parent uses this strategy successfully to elicit a response from her child that is appropriate to the topic:

Parent: That dragon can sure make a lot of fire come out of his mouth! How do you think he does that?

Michael: Can we go to the zoo?

Parent: Yes, sometime we'll go. But how do you think he makes all that fire? (points to the dragon)

Michael: (no response)

Parent: You still have not answered my question. How do you think the dragon makes all that fire?

Michael: It comes from his belly where it's real hot, and every time he breathes, the fire and smoke come out.

Parent: Wow, that was a terrific answer! I always wondered how they did that.

A target of regulating volume would be appropriate if a child consistently speaks using a volume that is either too soft or too loud. Often, all that is required is a reminder or two for the child to adjust his or her speaking volume to an appropriate level. Therefore, when interrupting the shared reading to have a brief conversation about an event or character in the story and the child speaks too softly, provide a gentle request to speak louder such as, "Could you please speak a little louder so I can hear you better?" Avoid interrupting what the child is saying to make this request. Instead, wait until he or she has finished a conversational turn and then request it. Likewise, if the child speaks too loudly, a possible request might be similar: "Could you please use a quieter voice?" When the child complies with the request, provide praise such as, "That is much better! Thank you for speaking softer (or louder)." After making a few such requests, the reminder may be shortened to "Softer, please" or "A little louder, please." At some point, it may be possible to replace verbal prompts with visual prompts. For example, to request a softer voice, the professional could raise an index finger up to closed lips; for a louder voice, the prompt could be cupping an ear with his or her hand. Once the child begins using an appropriate volume level, verbal and visual prompts may be eliminated except as occasional reminders. This strategy may be seen in the following shared-reading excerpt of *Spot Sleeps Over* (Hill, 1990):

Teacher: This book is called *Spot Sleeps Over.* What do you think Spot is carrying here? (points to the front cover of the book)

Brandon: He's got a flashlight! (speaks in loud voice)

Teacher: Yes, it *is* a flashlight. But I need to ask you something before we read any more. Can you speak more softly? I want you to use your "inside" voice when we read, okay?

Brandon: Okay. (speaks in loud voice)

Teacher: Brandon, that's still too loud. Try to make it even quieter.

Brandon: Okay. (speaks with lower volume)

Teacher: That's very good—I like that much better.

The strategies in this chapter have focused on enhancing young children's language skills through shared reading. Suggestions for addressing targets in the five domains of language (i.e., semantics, phonology, syntax, morphology, and pragmatics) have been described. The reader is cautioned against thinking that these examples represent an exhaustive list of developing skills, as there are many others that have not been addressed in this text. Instead, the proposed activities are provided as a starting point for understanding how conversations during shared reading can offer opportunities for children's language growth. It should also be mentioned that for simplicity's sake, these examples have been separated into five specific areas; however, it is possible to have shared-reading conversations that involve more than one language domain at a time.

5

Understanding Important Foundation Skills for Emergent Literacy

This chapter defines the term *emergent literacy* and describes its two major domains: print awareness and phonological awareness. Explanations of the various elements within these domains are provided.

Emergent literacy describes the concepts, skills, and knowledge that young children have about reading and writing prior to beginning their formal literacy instruction in elementary school (Whitehurst & Lonigan, 1998). In this book, the terms *early literacy* and *emergent literacy* are used interchangeably and refer to the same types of skills. In the 1970s, Marie Clay (1979) recognized the importance of these early skills and their impact on subsequent reading achievement. Clay created an assessment, *Concepts About Print,* as part of *The Early Detection of Reading Difficulties, Third Edition,* which is still used in schools today.

Even though children usually do not start to read and write in a conventional sense until first grade, many prerequisite or foundation skills are acquired in the years leading up to the time of formal reading instruction. For instance, the drawings and scribbles of young children may be viewed as showing emergent literacy behavior, as are knowing how to turn the pages of a storybook, becoming aware of print, and recognizing some alphabet letters. These kinds of early behaviors provide the foundation on which reading and writing skills will build. Even children as young as 2 years of age display many early reading and writing behaviors (Lonigan, Burgess, Anthony, & Barker, 1998). Therefore, it is important to support young children's development of emergent literacy skills because these early accomplishments will help them to become better readers and writers.

EMERGENT LITERACY DOMAINS

The considerable knowledge of reading and writing learned in the toddler and preschool years may be classified into two broad domains: print awareness and phonological awareness (Justice & Ezell, 2001). Print awareness, also referred to as written language awareness and print knowledge, describes children's early understanding of the forms and functions of written language including knowledge of the alphabet. Phonological awareness, in contrast, refers to children's knowledge of the sound structure of oral language. As noted by Adams (1990), awareness of sounds and awareness of print are both needed for reading to occur, for no amount of phonological awareness will benefit children without an understanding of print and individual letters. Therefore, the reader is reminded that developing children's competency in one area should not supersede the other, as both are important foundation skills for children's reading. These terms are described in greater detail in the following sections.

Print Awareness

Print awareness describes children's early discoveries about the orthography of language. Developing an interest in print usually represents children's earliest print achievement (Justice & Ezell, 2004). Print interest is when children view print as an object worthy of their attention. Once children achieve an interest in print, various aspects of print concepts begin to develop. Children acquire knowledge of print functions (that print carries meaning), print conventions (how print is organized), print forms (the names and characteristics of different print units such as alphabet letters), and print part-to-whole relationships (the way in which various print units are combined to create names, words, and sentences). As noted by Adams (1990), these achievements help young children develop a familiarity with and sensitivity to the orthography of their written language, which prepares them for higher level applications of this knowledge when reading instruction begins.

Print awareness may be approached from two different perspectives that are both equally important. The first is from the perspective of a reader, meaning that children begin to understand that print carries meaning and is something that a person reads. This awareness may begin even before children know letters of the alphabet. They understand that the print means something, and they often pretend or attempt to read what they see. For example, a child might point to an exit sign in a store and say, "That sign says 'Go outside,' " point to the word *Crest* on a toothpaste box and say, "This says toothpaste," or point to a dollar bill and say, "This says money." Whether the print is read correctly or not, this kind of behavior is more than just pretend play; it is a valid indicator that emergent literacy is developing and that the child realizes the functionality of print as a communication device (Justice & Ezell, 2004). Looking at signs and logos and thinking about what the print may say is an important behavior that emerges during the preschool years. Some scholars have suggested that this represents the first stage of reading development (Gillam & Johnston, 1985; Goodman, 1986). Such a perspective suggests that reading does not start on the first day of school; rather, reading starts when children learn the function of print or when they notice that print is different from other patterns, as these are the early precursors to reading. By 3 years of age, these types of behaviors are quite common and represent the early stages of emergent literacy.

The second perspective of print awareness is from that of a writer. This means that children begin to understand that they can produce writing to express themselves (Ferreiro & Teberosky, 1982) and that written language is a way to communicate with others. The perspectives of print awareness as a reader and writer often develop simultaneously, so when young children attempt to read, they may also attempt to write. For example, starting at about 3 years of age, children often begin to "sign" their names on pictures they have drawn (Welsch, Sullivan, & Justice, 2003). For a 3-year-old child, a signature might be just a scribble or a line. By 4 years of age, a signature might consist of some odd geometric figures appearing with a random letter or two. Although young children's signatures do not look anything like the conventional writing of a first grader, their abilities at presenting their names and other words in print prior to entering school are strongly correlated with other aspects of emergent literacy, such as alphabet knowledge and phonological awareness (Welsch et al., 2003). These early writing behaviors are considered part of a typical developmental sequence. This sequence of name-writing development begins at about 2 or 3 years of age and continues to develop when the child enters school (see Table 5.1).

Table 5.1.   Common progression of name writing in typically developing children

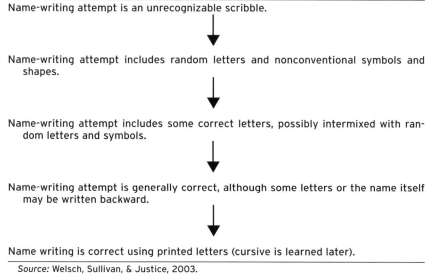

Name-writing attempt is an unrecognizable scribble.

Name-writing attempt includes random letters and nonconventional symbols and shapes.

Name-writing attempt includes some correct letters, possibly intermixed with random letters and symbols.

Name-writing attempt is generally correct, although some letters or the name itself may be written backward.

Name writing is correct using printed letters (cursive is learned later).

Source: Welsch, Sullivan, & Justice, 2003.

When examining this writing sequence, notice how one stage leads to or blends into another stage. This suggests that children's writing skills progress in incremental steps rather than move from a completely unrecognizable signature to a perfectly correct one. This shows how emergent literacy gradually develops over time as a function of experience and cognitive changes. In a sense, the ability to provide a signature starts with these early markings just as the ability to produce words begins with saying the first sounds.

Print Awareness Skills   Print awareness consists of several skills involving both reading and writing as seen in Table 5.2. Obviously, some of these skills are more difficult than others. For example, simple book-reading conventions, such as front-to-back directionality, are generally mastered prior to children's understanding of how words and letters relate to one another (Justice & Ezell, 2001). Likewise, in each skill listed, gradations in development occur, as described previously with children's name-writing representations in which children first write their names using a scribble, followed by increasingly meaningful and legible approximations. Similarly, knowledge of the alphabet letters may occur first through recognizing obvious letter differences (e.g., differentiating the letters *A* and *B*) but perhaps not easily seeing smaller differences (e.g., differentiating

Table 5.2.   Examples of print awareness skills

Awareness of print in the everyday environment (e.g., street signs, product labels, logos)

Ability to handle books correctly (e.g., hold book right side up, turn pages one at a time)

Knowledge of print directionality (e.g., left page to right page, top to bottom, left to right on a line)

Knowledge of major book elements (e.g., cover, title, author)

Knowledge of alphabet letters

Use of literate vocabulary words such as *word, letter, read, page, sentence,* and *write*

Ability to represent own name using pencil and paper, making scribbles, lines, and unconventional shapes

Understanding of the relationship between written language units, including letters, words, and sentences (e.g., that letters make up words, that words are separated by spaces)

the letters C and O). Only later will children be able to identify and produce all of the letters of the alphabet, which is an important skill for profiting from beginning reading instruction (Badian, 2001).

Although developmental norms for the various print awareness skills are still being determined, the information presented in Table 5.3 will provide some idea as to the difficulty level of some of these skills. In a study conducted by the authors (Justice & Ezell, 2001) involving 38 preschoolers from low-income families, 4-year-old children were asked to complete a number of tasks during a storybook activity. In the

Table 5.3.   Sample performance of 4-year-olds on selected print awareness tasks

Print awareness concept	Percentage of children scoring correctly
Child can indicate the title of the book	82
Child can indicate the front (cover) of the book	76
Child can identify one letter	74
Child can differentiate print from pictures	68
Child can indicate the directionality of reading (left page to right page)	66
Child can tell the first letter in own name upon request	45
Child can indicate the directionality of print (left to right on a line)	37
Child can indicate the first line of print to be read	18
Child can differentiate uppercase from lowercase letters	13
Child can point to the short word in the title of a book	8
Child can point to words as the adult reads them	5
Child can point to the last line of print on a page	3

Note: Based on a sample of 38 preschool children from low-income households (Justice & Ezell, 2001).

left column, the print awareness task presented to each child is listed. The corresponding score on the right shows the percentage of children who were able to successfully complete the task. Readers are cautioned that the sample size in this study was both small and specific to low-income families, suggesting that these percentages may change in the event that larger and more diverse groups of children are sampled. However, this information helps to illustrate the varying levels of difficulty of print skills for some preschool children.

Print Awareness Stages   Print awareness accomplishments have been organized into a series of five stages to represent how children develop these skills over the early and later preschool years. Children gradually progress through these stages as they interact on their own with written language and are provided guidance by adults. These stages, which appear below, were developed by early literacy theorist Yetta Goodman (1986). When reviewing these stages, notice that both reading and writing skills are included.

Stage 1: Children begin to respond to and interact with print that is naturally occurring in the environment. They may attempt to "read" print occurring as signs, labels, and logos. Print of this type has many clues that help to decipher it. For example, the word *Pringles* on a canister of potato chips shows pictures of potato chips that help the child read it. Children usually enter this stage at 2 or 3 years of age.

Stage 2: Children begin to interact with written language in connected (nonenvironmental) print, such as print found in storybooks or appearing on lists. Key attainments of this period include acquiring book-handling skills (e.g., orientation, directionality) and developing a vocabulary oriented toward print, including words such as *read, page,* and *story.*

Stage 3: Children begin to experiment with the functions and forms of writing and begin the progression through the stages of writing described previously.

Stage 4: Children become more able to use their oral language skills to talk about written language activities and concepts. Children increasingly use print as a means of communicating, and, in doing so, they begin to use more conventional written symbols in their writing.

Stage 5: Children demonstrate a sophisticated awareness of written language that allows them to explain and reflect on aspects of written language form and function. For example, children may talk about the similarities of two words ("This word starts with an *S* just like my name") or how letters and words relate to one another ("D-O-G spells *dog*!"). Children at this stage are usually about 6 years old and are poised for formal reading instruction.

Phonological Awareness

The other domain of emergent literacy development is phonological awareness. Phonological awareness describes children's sensitivity to the sound structure of oral language (Lonigan, Burgess, et al., 1998). It includes awareness of not only the individual phonemes that make up the English language but also several other larger sound units, including syllables and words. Generally, phonological awareness is thought to include rhyming, alliteration, word awareness, syllable awareness, and phoneme awareness, which are briefly defined in Table 5.4.

Phonological awareness is an essential skill for learning to read (Torgesen, Wagner, & Rashotte, 1994). When children begin reading, they need to be able to decode words. Decoding requires an ability to look at words and "unlock" their meaning and pronunciation by applying the alphabetic code. In order to apply the alphabetic code, children must determine the relationship between sounds and letters, which is known as phoneme–grapheme correspondence. In decoding, children retrieve the sounds represented by the letters and then blend these sounds to create the words. However, before children are able to use phoneme–grapheme correspondence, they must have awareness and knowledge of sounds. Specifically, this awareness or sensitivity constitutes phonological awareness. Without phonological awareness, children will have an extraordinarily difficult

Table 5.4.   Phonological awareness skills

Rhyme awareness: Ability to produce and comprehend rhyme patterns across words

Alliteration awareness: Ability to produce and comprehend shared phonemes across words and syllables, particularly when the common sound appears in the initial position

Word awareness: Awareness of the boundaries between words in spoken sentences or phrases

Syllable awareness: Awareness of the boundaries between syllables in spoken words

Phoneme awareness: Awareness of individual sounds within words time with decoding. Children who come to reading instruction with underdeveloped phonological awareness have great challenges keeping up with early reading instruction (Torgesen et al., 1994).

As an illustration, consider the word *flode.* Even though an individual may never have seen this word before (because it is not a real word), it is possible to read it as though it were a real word. This is achieved through decoding for children who are beginning readers. (More advanced readers attend less to individual letters and sounds and more to familiar orthographic "chunks" such as the *fl* and the *ode.*) When children read, they need to decode the words they come across, and particularly challenging are those words they have never seen before. Nearly all words that beginning readers come across will be new. Therefore, decoding skills are critical. As readers gain experience and become more sensitized to orthographic patterns, they will be able to decode with greater speed and accuracy (Ehri, 1995). However, to get to this level of automaticity, children need extensive reading practice. As long as children struggle with decoding, reading will be a frustrating experience.

How does decoding occur for beginning readers who have yet to achieve automaticity? Simply put, children use their knowledge of individual alphabet letters as well as their knowledge of phonology to represent the relationships between letters and sounds. In the word *flode,* a reader must look at each letter, identify it, and search his or her memory (in a matter of milliseconds) to make the connection between the letters and their corresponding sounds. Doing this, the reader determines that the letter *f* goes with the /f/ phoneme, the letter *l* goes with the /l/ phoneme, the letter *o* makes a long "o" sound because of the silent *e* at the end (a rule stored away from early reading instruction), and the letter *d* goes with the /d/ phoneme. Therefore, in order to apply phoneme–grapheme correspondence for accurate decoding, it is essential that children acquire two major building blocks: 1) knowledge of sounds (phonological awareness) and 2) knowledge of letters (print awareness). Those children who have these building blocks will have an easier time mastering the phoneme–grapheme correspondence necessary for word decoding.

Rhyme Awareness   Rhyme awareness is an ability to produce and recognize rhyming patterns across words. Although recognizing that words rhyme is a form of phonological awareness, it is not generally understood how important rhyming is. Whereas rhyming skills do not correlate strongly with later reading success (Chaney,

1994), children's awareness of rhyme shows that they are beginning to notice the phonological structure of words. That is, when children produce a rhyme, they are playing with the sound structure of a word rather than focusing on its meaning. This is a major step for young children who tend to focus on word meaning rather than word structure.

The making of a rhyme involves taking a word and analyzing its broad phonological structure into two parts, the onset and the rime. For example, the onset in the word *cat* is *c-* and the rime portion is *-at*. The next step is to add a different onset to the rime to create a new word that matches the first in phonological properties; for example, *cat, sat, bat,* and *hat* all have different onsets but share the same rime——*at*. Children begin to hear rhymes when their parents read poems and rhyming books, and around 3 or 4 years of age children may start producing rhymes in their play and other literacy activities. Children who experience rhymes early in life may begin to produce rhymes earlier. This skill sets the stage for being able to identify sounds within words, to recognize similar sounds across words, and to understand how to move sounds from one word to another. By developing mastery of these skills, children progress one step closer to acquiring phoneme–grapheme correspondence.

Alliteration Awareness   Alliteration is another early developing phonological awareness skill. Alliteration simply means that two words or syllables share a common sound, usually the initial sound as in "lucky lady," "galloping gophers," or "wigwam." Children begin to be aware of alliterative patterns as early as 3 years of age (Chaney, 1994). For instance, a child might note that there is something similar between her name and another child's name ("My name Lucy and your name Laura are the same!"). Lucy is commenting on the similarity in the initial sounds appearing in these names, which demonstrates an awareness of alliteration. What Lucy has done is actually quite remarkable: She has focused solely on the phonological structure of the words *Lucy* and *Laura* and recognized the similarity of the two. As with rhyming awareness, alliteration awareness promotes the development of phoneme–grapheme correspondence in that it helps children develop an early familiarity with how language is organized phonologically.

Word Awareness   Word awareness refers to recognizing spoken words as discrete phonological units; for example, the sentence "My cat is white" consists of four separate words. This skill allows children to know where one word stops and another begins so that word boundaries are recognized. When producing oral language, individuals provide a variety of phonological units, including words, syllables, onsets, rimes, and phonemes. Relative to the other phonological units, words are the largest segment and are usually recognized by children earlier than smaller units. Being sensitive to the larger units of phonology is considered shallow (or more concrete) phonological sensitivity, whereas the later developing sensitivity to smaller units of phonology is called deep (or more abstract) phonological sensitivity (Stanovich, 2000). Children's phonological awareness typically moves from shallow levels during the preschool years to deep awareness in kindergarten and the first grade when reading instruction begins.

Consider the following sentence: "Tommy is walking." Native English speakers will be able to identify three distinct words *Tommy*, *is*, and *walking*. Even the *-ing* at the end of *walk* does not change the number of words an experienced native speaker will recognize. However, native speakers of other languages may find it difficult to hear three distinct words until they achieve a certain level of mastery with English. This is the challenge that children face in learning word boundaries—determining where one word stops and another begins. An explicit level of word awareness, as identified through specific tasks, may be seen in 3- and 4-year-olds. By the age of 5, these skills are usually well established. Still, even 6-year-olds may misunderstand spoken words sometimes when word boundaries cannot be distinguished. One example is a 6-year-old who asked his mother why there was a "witch's stand" (i.e., "for which it stands") in the United States Pledge of Allegiance. An ability to recognize word boundaries improves children's comprehension of oral language, which, in turn, may help them identify and map the sounds onto written words when reading instruction begins.

Syllable Awareness   Syllable awareness is an ability to identify syllable boundaries of spoken words. An example would be recognizing that the word *elbow* has two syllables or parts (i.e., *el-bow*), *butterfly* has three parts (i.e., *but-ter-fly*), and *helicopter* has four parts (i.e., *hel-i-cop-ter*). In the sentence "Tommy is walking," the three words contain a total of five syllables (*Tom-my-is-walk-ing*). Recognizing that words are made up of syllables occurs at about the same time children realize that speech can be broken into words, usually around

4 years of age (Lonigan, Burgess, et al., 1998). Syllable awareness helps children recognize word parts, which will complement their phoneme–grapheme correspondence skills when learning to read.

   Phoneme Awareness   Some time after these word- and syllable-awareness skills become established, children are able to do some basic phoneme-level analyses when asked to focus on a sound in a specific position of a word. Children who are 4 or 5 years old may be able to answer a question such as "What is the first sound in the word *pat?*" or "Tell me the last sound you hear in the word *dog."* Phoneme-awareness tasks require greater refinement and will be more difficult for young children than recognizing single words. Also, children will have greater challenges with these tasks when words are longer or when they contain consonant clusters as in the word *stripe,* which is a single-syllable word that begins with a consonant cluster containing three consonants (i.e., /s/, /t/, and /r/; Treiman, 1985). Multisyllabic words, or those that contain consonant clusters, pose a more difficult challenge and are not typically accomplished until a year or two later.

   Attending to all of the sounds in a word represents an even greater challenge for children. Returning to the example "Tommy is walking," many children might be able to recognize that the word *is* contains two sounds (one vowel and one consonant, which are denoted as VC), but they would have more difficulty telling how many sounds are in the word *Tommy* (four sounds: CVCV). It is important to note that there may not be a one-to-one correspondence between the number of sounds that a word has and the number of letters in the word. For example, the word *is* has two sounds that directly correspond with two letters, but the word *Tommy* has four sounds and five letters. In summary, 4-year-old children would have a very difficult time knowing that the word *cat* is made up of three sounds even though they may be able to identify the first or last sound in this word. It is not until about 6 or 7 years of age that children are able to identify the complete phoneme structure of simple words. It should be noted that this skill is further bolstered during early reading instruction when children focus a great deal of attention on thinking about how sounds and letters go together to decode words.

CONCLUSION

In Chapter 6, several strategies are presented that describe how shared reading may promote children's emergent literacy concepts.

These strategies may be used in combination with the language strategies described in the previous chapter if desired. However, the reader is cautioned that for children to understand the concepts discussed in this chapter, a certain amount of metalinguistic knowledge is required. This means that children must be able to recognize language as an object of attention and discussion. For phonological sensitivity to develop, children must be able to listen to the sounds that a word contains rather than try to grasp word meaning. Likewise, for print awareness to emerge, children must be aware of print and begin to understand that print has meaning. Without these essential skills, children will not be prepared to confront these concepts. This means that children with severely limited language such as those with significant language delay may benefit more from the language strategies in Chapter 4 before those in Chapter 6 are attempted.

6

Using Shared Reading to Develop Children's Emergent Literacy Skills

In this chapter, strategies for promoting children's emergent literacy skills are presented. In particular, techniques for developing nine print awareness skills and four phonological awareness skills are described.

INTRODUCING CHILDREN TO EMERGENT LITERACY

As explained in Chapter 5, emergent literacy refers to the concepts, skills, and knowledge that children acquire about books and print prior to formal reading instruction. During their preschool years, children obtain this knowledge primarily through exposure to storybooks and other printed material. For many children, these early experiences provide numerous opportunities for observational learning, which refers to learning that occurs when children watch the behavior of others (e.g., parents, siblings, peers, babysitters). Children learn all sorts of behaviors through observational learning. For example, a child may watch how the parent holds a book and how pages are turned when reading. Later, when the child handles a book, he or she will hold the book and turn the pages in the same way that the parent did. Children become aware of various functions of print in the same way, by watching an adult read a recipe, a shopping list, a map, a road marker, a building sign, a subtitle, a web address, or a number from the telephone book, to name but a few examples. Thus, it is important to provide a rich supply of these early opportunities so that children will learn to recognize print and be familiar with its purpose and potential value.

Although children are often skilled observational learners for some behaviors, they may not be for all behaviors; in other words, the skill may be uneven or at times inconsistent. For instance, a child may be able to distinguish differences between some sounds but not others. Observational skills may also vary according to the level of difficulty of a task as seen when a child easily notices the difference between print and pictures (an easy task) but may have more difficulty identifying specific letters (a more challenging task). Consequently, at times children may need explicit instruction to notice some of the finer distinctions among sounds and print such as the ones described in this chapter.

Before embarking on teaching some of the emergent literacy skills described in this chapter, the reader is reminded of Vygotsky's zone of proximal development (ZPD) in which teaching is guided by what children know and what they may be able to learn with assistance. As described in Chapter 1, the professional will provide whatever assistance a child needs to accomplish a new task. Over time and with practice, the child may require less and less assistance until he or she is capable of complete independence, which suggests that the new concept has been successfully internalized. When that occurs, the professional selects a new concept to introduce. It is the professional's job to ensure that decisions involving the pace of learning, amount of assistance, and need for practice be guided by what occurs within a child's learning zone.

Emergent literacy skills may be enhanced by focusing on the written form or the spoken form of the language. As mentioned in Chapter 5, both forms are important because when children begin to decode words, they will be required to blend both skills to associate sounds with their written form (i.e., phoneme–grapheme correspondence). This chapter lists strategies for written language first; however, the reader may begin with phonological awareness if desired.

Print Awareness

Because children usually gaze at the illustrations in a storybook as they listen to a story, they may not pay much attention to the print. Although preschool children would not be expected to read the print, it is important that they become aware of it in order to acquire various print concepts. Such concepts include knowledge of print directionality and spacing and knowledge that words are made up of letters. Children will learn that sometimes letters are written larger, as capitals (called uppercase lettering), and other times they are written smaller (called lowercase lettering). These are a few of the print concepts that young children may learn before they begin to read. In Chapter 1, Snow et al. (1998) found that young children's concepts about print were strongly correlated with their future reading success at the time of school entry. Based on that finding, this chapter will present several print concepts that are important for children to acquire or, at the very least, be introduced to prior to formal reading instruction.

Listed in Table 6.1 are nine common print concepts that may be acquired during children's preschool years. Although this is not an exhaustive list of print concepts, those included may be easily incorporated into shared-reading conversations. It should be noted that these concepts take time to develop and require children to have an understanding of literacy terms such as *print, word, read, write,* and *letter.* Therefore, professionals need to be selective when choosing a skill to be presented and pace shared-reading conversations according to children's abilities.

Specific Strategies for Print Awareness   The following strategies provide suggestions for brief conversations during shared reading that will assist children in becoming aware of and learning about print. Strategies are provided for each of the nine skills listed in Table 6.1. Also, each strategy may be viewed for quick reference in a summary table that lists the main points. To illustrate these procedures, excerpts from shared-reading examples are provided except where a strategy tends to repeat one that was described

Table 6.1.   Common print concepts

Child differentiates print from pictures.
Child understands print directionality.
Child identifies the top and bottom of a page.
Child knows that print tells a story.
Child identifies some letters (e.g., first letter) in his or her name.
Child knows some letters of the alphabet.
Child understands that words are made up of letters even though he or she may not know the individual letters yet.
Child identifies the space between two words.
Child points to words individually as they are read by an adult.

Source: Justice & Ezell, 2001.

previously. When implementing these strategies, it is best to use storybooks that contain prominent print features such as large print and few words per page. This will help children see and attend to the print more easily.

Differentiates Print from Pictures   There are two ways to help children understand the differences between print and pictures. The first way is to track the print in the storybook as reading takes place. Tracking involves running a finger under the line of print in a smooth continuous motion from left to right. This nonverbal cue shows children what is being read and may help them learn to associate the printed word with the spoken word. A second way to show the difference between print and pictures during shared reading is by explicitly stating the differences. This may be done by pointing to an illustration and saying, "Here is a picture that shows what is happening in the story," followed by pointing to the print and saying, "These are the words that tell the story." Doing this two or three times during one or two reading sessions may be all that is necessary for children to acquire this skill.

After emphasizing this concept in a few reading sessions, determine whether the child understands it by saying, "Show me the words that tell the story." If the child points to the print instead of an illustration (be sure the picture contains no letters or numbers), then an understanding of this concept is evident. If the child points to the illustration or fails to respond, it may be necessary to repeat these two strategies in a few more reading sessions until the child comprehends the concept correctly. Refer to Table 6.2 for a brief review of this strategy.

In the following shared-reading excerpt from *Little Bear* (Namm, 1990), explicit explanation can be seen.

Table 6.2.   Differentiates print from pictures: brief review

Track the print while reading the storybook by running a finger beneath the words in a fluid left-to-right motion.

Point to an illustration and explain, "This picture shows what is happening."

Point to the print and explain, "These are the words that tell the story."

After several sessions, determine whether the child can differentiate print from pictures by saying, "Show me the words that tell the story."

Praise a correct response and provide assistance if the child is unsure or responds incorrectly.

Parent:	What do you see in this picture? (after reading the page to Nikki)
Nikki:	Mommy bear. Baby bear. (points to each)
Parent:	Yes, the mommy bear and baby bear are shopping.
Nikki:	'Cause he's hungry? (turns the page)
Parent:	That's right, bears are *always* hungry. That is why they are shopping.
Nikki:	Uh-huh.
Parent:	Nikki, this picture shows what the bears are doing in the story. (points to the illustration) Right here (points to the print) are the words that tell us the story.
Nikki:	Like saying, "Little bear" (puts finger on the line of print)
Parent:	I can't believe you just did that! That was very good. That's just what *I* do to read the story. Before we know it, you'll be reading the story to *me*!

Understands Print Directionality   Reading print involves three basic directions: 1) reading the left page before the right page, 2) reading left to right on a line, and 3) reading from the top of the page to the bottom. It is suggested that only one direction be emphasized at a time to avoid confusing a child who is just learning this concept. Also, it is recommended that the suggested order be followed so that the broader concept (e.g., reading the left page before the right page) is approached first. For each of these directional concepts, it is recommended that the professional track the print while reading to make the direction more salient for the child.

When emphasizing the left page to right page direction, provide a brief comment or two during shared reading that explains how the book is being read. For example, the professional might say, "I read this page first (pointing to the left page), and then I read this one next (pointing to the right page)." Be sure that print occurs on both pages before providing this comment as some storybooks have print on only one open page. After one to three reading sessions, see if the child can tell you on which page to start by asking, "Show me where to read first, this page (pointing to the left page) or that page (pointing to the right page)?" If the child correctly points to the left page, provide praise. If the child seems confused or points to the incorrect page, provide assistance and further explanation. Repeat this strategy in successive reading sessions until the child is able to answer correctly. Table 6.3 provides a brief review of this procedure for quick reference, and the following reading excerpt from *The Day the Goose Got Loose* (Lindbergh, 1990) illustrates this strategy:

Teacher:	"Her dress got messed and her hair un-styled. The day the goose got loose."
Ethan:	Here's his football . . . and his helmet is up here. He's a football player.
Teacher:	Yes, he is a football player. What team does he play for? Can you read his jersey if we turn the book this way? (turns book upside down and points to the word on the jersey)
Ethan:	What does it say?
Teacher:	It says "Rams"! Isn't that funny—a ram butted the Rams football player! (teacher and Ethan laugh; Ethan turns the page) Ethan, do you remember which page I read first—this one (points to the left page) or that one (points to the right page)?
Ethan:	Here. (points to a line of print in the middle of the right page)
Teacher:	That was a good try, but it is not where I *start*. I *start* reading right here on this page first (points to first line on left page) and then, after I read these words, I go to this page. (points to the right page) Can you show me now?
Ethan:	Oh, yeah, I know. Here first (points to the left page) and then over here (points to the right page).
Teacher:	Very good! You got it right.

Table 6.3.   Identifies directionality of left page to right page: brief review

Say, "I read this page first (pointing to the left page), and I read this one next." (pointing to the right page)

After one to three reading sessions, say, "Show me where I should read first—this page (pointing to the left) or that page." (pointing to the right)

Praise the child's correct response, and provide assistance if the child seems unsure or responds incorrectly.

To emphasize reading left to right on a line, provide a brief explanation during shared reading (e.g., "I start reading here [points to the first word on a line] and go this way" [moves a finger in a left-to-right motion beneath the words]). Make this comment once or twice during several reading sessions. After about a week, see if the child is able to demonstrate an understanding of this concept by saying, "Show me which way to read." (point to the first word on a line of print) When providing a response, the child need not place a finger exactly under the print; just an indication of a left-to-right movement is all that is required for a correct answer. Provide praise when a correct left-to-right movement is indicated. If the child moves a finger right to left or up or down, or points to the next page, provide an explanation so that the child understands the correct direction. Repeat this strategy in successive reading sessions until the child is able to respond correctly. See Table 6.4 for a brief review. A continuation of *The Day the Goose Got Loose* (Lindbergh, 1990) shows this strategy:

Teacher:　Look class. I want you to watch my finger. It will show you how I read the words. "When the goose got loose the cows were tense. The goose provoked a bull named Spense." (tracks the words while reading the text)

Elliot:　You went this way. (makes a left-to-right motion with his hand)

Patty:　It goes to the bend. (meaning where the two pages are joined together)

Teacher:　That's right. You watched very closely that time! I read this word first (points to the word *when*) and then I go this way. (moves finger in a left-to-right motion beneath the words) I always read in the same direction—from left to right. (moves finger from left to right beneath the print) Good job!

Table 6.4.　Identifies directionality of left to right on a line: brief review

During shared reading, provide a brief explanation about the direction of reading by saying, "I start reading here (pointing to the first word on a line) and go this way." (moving a finger in a left-to-right motion beneath the words)

After about a week, check to see if the child understands this concept by saying, "Show me which way I read." (pointing to the first word on a line of print)

Praise the child's correct response and provide assistance if the child seems unsure or responds incorrectly.

For the third directional concept, reading from the top of a page to the bottom, the same explanation strategy is suggested. One way to explain this could be by saying, for example: "I start reading up here (tracks finger beneath the top line on the page) and then I go to the next line (tracks left to right beneath the second line), and read each line until I come to the bottom of the page (moves finger down the page to the bottom line). This means that I read from the top of the page to the bottom." This comment can be offered once or twice during each shared-reading session for about a week. After providing this explanation on several occasions, check to see if the child understands this directional concept. Begin by reading and tracking the first line of print on a page and then stop at the end of the line and ask, "Which way do I read now?" If the child moves a finger down the same page or points out the second line of print, then he or she likely understands this concept. Be sure to praise a correct answer. However, if the child points to the first line (which had just been read) or the next page, the child may need further explanation to understand this concept. Repeat this strategy, as seen in Table 6.5, during shared reading until the child is able to respond correctly. One final example from *The Day the Goose Got Loose* (Lindbergh, 1990) is provided next:

Teacher: On this page (points to the left page), the story is just at the top. But on this one (points to the right page), I read down the page. (moves finger from top line to the bottom line) First I read up here at the top (points to the print at the top), then I read the part in the middle (points to one line of print in the middle of the page), and then I read down here at the bottom. (points to one line of print at the bottom of the page)

Table 6.5.   Identifies directionality of top of the page to the bottom: brief review

Provide an explanation during shared reading by saying, "I start reading up here (tracking the first line of print), and then I go to the next line (tracking left to right beneath the second line) and read each one until I come to the bottom of the page (moving a finger down the page to the bottom line). I read each page from top to bottom."

After several reading sessions during which this explanation has been given, check for the child's comprehension of this concept by asking, "Which way do I read now?" after reading and tracking the first line of print on the page.

Praise the child's correct response (i.e., moving a finger down the page or pointing to the second line of print), and provide assistance if the child seems unsure or responds incorrectly.

Jenny:	Like this? (moves a finger down the page)
Teacher:	Exactly! I read from the top of the page to the bottom. Shall we try it together? You point and I'll read, okay?
Jenny:	Okay. Here. (points to the top line)
Teacher:	"The colt was silly." (tracks print while reading and pauses for Jenny to point)
Jenny:	Here. (points to the middle line)
Teacher:	"The filly was bad." (tracks print while reading and pauses; Jenny points to the bottom line)
Teacher:	"The day the goose got loose." (tracks print while reading) Excellent job! You helped me read!

Identifies the Top and Bottom of a Page   Children may acquire this concept when the previous strategy is implemented (i.e., reading from the top of the page to the bottom) because the explanation includes the terms *top* and *bottom*. If this strategy has not yet been tried, please refer to the previous explanation and example for a description of how to approach this concept. Table 6.6 provides a brief review. When emphasizing this concept, it is important to select a storybook that contains a few pages in which the print appears at both the top and bottom of the page.

Knows that Print Tells a Story   If the first print concept of differentiating print from pictures has been attempted, this explanation has most likely facilitated an understanding that print is what tells the story. Explicitly talking to the child about the print on one or two

Table 6.6.   Identifies the top and bottom of a page: brief review

On one or two occasions during shared reading, provide a brief explanation of how reading proceeds; for example, "I read up at the top of the page first (pointing to the top line of print), and then I read each line down the page until I get to the bottom." (moving a finger down the page until it reaches the bottom) If the book has only one line of print at the top and one at the bottom, then it would be appropriate to say, "I read the print at the top before I read the print at the bottom." (pointing to each)

After providing this kind of explanation for about a week, check to see if the child understands this concept by saying, "Show me the top of the page" or "Can you show me the bottom of this page?"

Praise the child's correct response (i.e., pointing to the top upon request), and provide assistance if the child seems unsure or responds incorrectly.

occasions during shared reading by saying, "These are the words that tell the story," will help acquaint the child with this concept. To determine whether a child understands this concept after repeated explanations, the professional could say, "Show me on this page where the words are that tell the story," or ask, "What do these words do?" Praise the child's correct response. If the child indicates that the pictures tell the story, it may be helpful to explain: "The pictures *do* show some of the story, but they cannot tell the story by themselves. Only the print tells everything in the story." Repeat the strategy if necessary for the child's full understanding of this concept. Table 6.7 provides a brief review of this strategy.

Identifies First Letter in Own Name   To address this concept, the initial letter of the child's first name will be the target. For example, if the child's name is Brad, use the letter *B*. The letter should be presented in the form of a capital because all proper names begin with a capital letter. Select a book that has two or three words that begin with the target letter. For example, if the child's name is Leo, choose three words that begin with a capital *L* (e.g., *Lion, Look, Later*). No words containing the lowercase *l* would be used because that would require the child to associate uppercase and lowercase letters, which is a more advanced skill. One final note: If three different words with the target capital letter are difficult to find in a particular book, then three instances of the same word may be used (e.g., *Lion, Lion, Lion*).

Before shared reading begins, explain to the child that he or she will be looking closely at some words to find a particular letter. Tell the child what the letter is and show a written example. Explain that this is the first letter in his or her name. During shared reading of the chosen book, interrupt the story when the first target word appears and ask, "Can you point to the letter *B* in this word?" If the child does not respond or points to an incorrect letter, use the child's finger to help him or her point correctly. Remind the child that this is the same letter in his or her name by saying, for example, "This letter *B* is the

Table 6.7.   Knows that the print tells the story: brief review

On one or two occasions during shared reading, point to the print and explain to the child, "These are the words that tell this story."

After providing repeated explanations, check for understanding by saying, "Show me which part tells the story," or asking, "What do these words do?"

Praise the child's correct response. Provide assistance or further explanation if the child seems unsure or responds incorrectly.

Table 6.8.   Identifies first letter in own name: brief review

Determine the first letter in the child's name. Select a book that contains several words that begin with this same letter using the uppercase form (e.g., the first letter in *Michael* is *M* and the book contains the words *Mouse, Man, Mile*).

Before shared reading begins, explain to the child that he or she will be looking closely at some words and finding a particular letter. Tell the child what the letter is and show a written example. Explain that this is the first letter in his or her name.

During shared reading, interrupt the story when reaching the target words and ask, "Can you point to the letter *M* in this word?"

Give assistance, and praise all attempts. If the child does not respond or points to an incorrect letter, use the child's finger to help him or her point correctly. Remind the child that this is the same letter in his or her name.

Provide continued practice until the child is able to identify the letter correctly.

---

same letter that begins your name, Brad." If desired, have the child trace the letter with a finger, which may help him or her to remember its shape. Then, proceed with the story. On reaching the second target word starting with the letter *B*, ask, "Where is the *B* in this word?" Provide assistance in finding the letter as needed, and be sure to praise the child's attempt or correct response. Continue this procedure with the third target word in the same way. By making two or three references to the target letter per book for about a week, children will begin to remember this letter and associate it with the one in their name. Table 6.8 provides a brief summary of this strategy.

In the conversational excerpt following a reading of *Spot Sleeps Over* (Hill, 1990), the parent has targeted the letter *W* based on the child's name, *Will*, in the words *What, Where,* and *Watch.*

Parent: And that's the end. (pauses) I like this book. (closes book and hands it to Will)

Will: Me, too. (opens the books and looks under the flap on each page)

Parent: (stops Will on the fourth page) Before you turn the page, can you look at this word up here for me? (points to the word *What* and pauses for Will to look at the word)

Will: This one? (looks at the word *What*)

Parent: Yes, that's the one. Can you point to the letter *W* in this word?

Will: I can't see it.

Parent: (takes Will's finger and places it on the *W*) Here it is. This is a *W* just like the *W* in your name, *Will.* The letter goes down, up, down, and up like this. (uses Will's finger to trace the letter)

Will: Where's my name?

Parent: Well, the story doesn't have your name in it. But we can see your name on the special bookmark Sissy made for you. (places the bookmark containing Will's name beneath the word *What*) Can you find the *W* in your name?

Will: Here (points correctly to the *W* in *Will*) and here. (points to the *W* in *What*)

Parent: Yes, indeed—very good! Let's find another one, okay?

Knows Some Letters of the Alphabet   This concept may be approached in basically the same way as the previous one. It expands on the previous concept and introduces other letters to the child. Begin by choosing a letter and finding a storybook that contains two or three instances of words beginning with that letter. As in the previous strategy, it is suggested that letters be emphasized one at a time until the child shows mastery with that letter. This strategy may be repeated over time to introduce as many letters as the professional wishes—teaching just a few or all 26 letters.

Before shared reading begins, explain to the child that he or she will be looking closely at some words and finding a particular letter. Tell the child what the letter is and show a written example. Interrupt the story on two or three occasions when the target words appear to say to the child, "Show me the letter *J* in this word," or "Can you put your finger on the letter *D* in this word?" Praise all attempts and correct responses. If the child is unable to point to the correct letter, provide assistance. When the child is able to identify the target letter with consistency, a new letter may be selected. See Table 6.9 for a summary of this strategy.

Understands that Words Are Made Up of Letters   If a child has experienced some success with the previous two concepts (i.e., identifying the first letter in his or her own name and some letters of the alphabet), he or she will likely have a basic understanding

Table 6.9.   Knows some letters of the alphabet: brief review

Select a letter that is used at least three times in a storybook.

Before shared reading begins, explain to the child that he or she will be looking closely at some words and finding a particular letter. Tell the child what the letter is, and show a written example.

During shared reading, interrupt the story on two or three occasions when the target words appear and ask, "Can you put your finger on the letter *T* in this word?"

Praise all attempts and correct responses. Provide assistance if the child responds incorrectly.

Continue practicing until the child is able to identify the target letter with consistency.

that words are made up of letters. However, employing a strategy whereby children count the letters may also be used to further strengthen this concept. Begin by selecting two short words in a storybook that contain only two or three letters (e.g., *am, be, cat*). Longer words should be avoided because many young children cannot count to more than the number 3. If possible, select words that contain at least one letter that the child knows. During shared reading, interrupt the story and point to one of the words selected. Ask, "How many letters are in this word *cat*?" and help the child point to the letters as he or she counts. When the child is finished, provide praise—"One-two-three. Good work! There are three letters in this word." At this point, letter identification could be attempted by asking, "Can you name any of these three letters in *cat*?" Provide assistance in naming the letters as needed. Refer to Table 6.10 for a brief summary of this strategy.

Conducting this strategy in just a few reading sessions will help to reinforce a child's understanding that words are composed of letters.

Table 6.10.   Understands that words are composed of letters: brief review

Select two or three words in a storybook that contain two or three letters (e.g., *boy, up, on*). If possible, select words that contain at least one letter that the child already knows.

During shared reading, interrupt the story and point to one of the selected words. Ask, "How many letters are in this word?" and help the child point to the letters as he or she counts. When the child is finished, provide praise such as, "One-two. Good work! There are two letters in this word."

If desired, attempt letter identification by asking, "Can you name either of these two letters?" Provide assistance in naming the letters as needed. Praise correct answers and attempts.

If counting confuses the child, simplify the task by asking the child to name the letters seen in specific two- or three-letter words and omit the counting.

Remember that the intent is for the child to comprehend the concept that words are made up of letters rather than to count correctly or name all of the letters in a word. Therefore, provide counting assistance if needed and do not insist that all letters be named correctly. If counting is especially difficult or confusing for the child, this strategy may be simplified to naming letters in two- or three-letter words.

The following shared-reading excerpt from *Spot Bakes a Cake* (Hill, 1994) shows this strategy being implemented with a pair of preschoolers:

Teacher: "We have to go shopping." Keeva, it's your turn to lift the flap.

Keeva: (lifts the flap) Here's the mouse, and he wants some cheese. I remember him from the last time!

Teacher: Good! Do you recall if cheese is put on the list? (points to the shopping list)

Keeva: Uh-huh—they buy cheese and *loads* of chocolate. It's yummy for the tummy! Yummy for the tummy!

Teacher: Yes, yes, we do like chocolate, don't we? But before we go on to check that shopping list, I have a question about this word right here. (points to the word *go*) Whose turn is it to answer?

Doug: It's *my* turn 'cause she did the last one.

Teacher: Okay, Doug. How many letters are in this word *go*? Count them for us and be sure to use your finger this time, okay?

Doug: Okay. One-two. (points to each letter as he counts) Two letters. (holds up two fingers)

Teacher: You're exactly right! That was perfect this time! Now, Keeva, can you name any letters in the word *go*?

Keeva: Yeah, I know one of 'em. That's an *o*. (points correctly to the letter *o*)

Teacher: Super! That other letter is a little hard, isn't it? (points to the letter *g*) Maybe Doug can help because that is the last letter is his name.

Doug: Okay—D-o-u-g. (whispers and spells by counting on his fingers) It's a *g*.

Teacher: Oh, good job! You're right. We have two letters in *go*—a *g* and an *o*. Nice work, you two!

Identifies the Space Between Two Words   The space that appears between words helps readers distinguish one word from another. Consider how the sentence "My dog loves to chase a ball" would look without any spacing: "Mydoglovestochaseaball." The space between words helps children to see word boundaries—that is, where one word stops and another begins. Technically, this is referred to as *concept of word*. This strategy is intended to assist children in understanding the concept of word. Select a storybook that is familiar to the child and locate a few places where two short words are next to each other (e.g., *is red, will go, the zoo*). During shared reading, interrupt the story briefly and point to the selected two-word phrase. It is recommended that the surrounding words be covered so that the child sees only the two short words being targeted. Ask, "How many words do you see here?" Assist the child in pointing to each word to count up to two. Provide praise and a brief explanation; for example, "One-two. Very good! There are two words here. There is a space between them to keep the words apart. Can you put your finger on the space between the two words?" Direct the child's finger if necessary to point to the space between the words.

If a child requires an explanation of what the word *space* means in this context, it may be helpful to explain that it is an empty place on the page in which nothing is written—no letters, numbers, or signs—and that it remains open or blank so that it is easy to separate one word from another. Some educators explain to students that this is like a parking space between the words. Doing this on two occasions during shared reading over a period of a week will help the child begin to understand this concept. Continue practicing this concept until the child can respond correctly without assistance when asked to put a finger on the space between two words. Table 6.11 provides a brief summary of this strategy.

In the following example, the parent chose not to interrupt the story to employ this strategy. Instead, she and her child enjoy looking back at the story to talk about it after it has been read. During this conversation she chose to discuss the print. The book used in this example is *Where's Spot?* by Eric Hill (1980).

Parent: "Sally finally found Spot! The end." (pauses to allow Michael time to look at the book at his leisure)

Table 6.11.   Identifies the space between two words: brief review

Locate three places in a storybook where there are two short words (one to four letters each) next to each other (e.g., *in here, to the*).

During shared reading, point to the two words selected and cover all of the surrounding words so that only the two are visible. Ask the child, "How many words do you see here?" Assist the child in pointing to each word to count to two. Provide praise.

Say to the child, "There's a little space between these two words to keep them apart. Can you put your finger on that space?" Direct the child's finger, if necessary, to point to the space between the words.

If the child requires an explanation of what the word *space* means in this context, it may be helpful to explain that it is an empty place on the page where nothing is written—no letters, numbers, or signs—and that it remains open or white to keep the words apart (or keep the words from touching).

Continue practicing this concept until the child is able to point to the space between two words independently.

Michael: (turns back through several pages to lift the flaps and look inside) "Nope, he's not under the bed." (turns the page) " 'No,' says the monkey." (turns the page) " 'Not here.' The lion says, 'No.' " (turns the page) "Is he in the piano?" (lifts the flap to look) "Hippo says, 'No.' "

Parent: Do you know that you said the exact words on this page? (points to the words)

Michael: I did?

Parent: Yes, let's look at these words for a minute. It says, "Is he in the piano?" (tracks print as she reads) When I cover these words (covering "in the piano" with her hand), how many words do you see?

Michael: One-two. (says while pointing to "Is he")

Parent: That's right—two words. And there is a space between them. Can you put your finger on the space between the words? (Michael points to area above the words)

Parent: That was a good try, but you pointed to the space up above. Right here is the space in between. (points to the area between the two words)

Michael: Right here? (points correctly)

Parent: That's right. It's not a big space, it's a tiny space—just enough to keep the words from touching. So it goes like this: word, space, word. (points to each in succession)

Michael: Word, space, word. (points to each in succession)

Parent: You've got it!

Points to Words as An Adult Reads   When a child is able to follow along as the professional reads, it shows a good understanding of print in several ways. First, by pointing to words as they are being read, a child must be able to recognize the presence of individual words and understand that the words being spoken are represented on the page. This is referred to as *print-to-speech mapping.* Second, to recognize the presence of a word, a child must see that an individual word is separate from the word ahead of it and the one that follows it. Third, this skill requires a child to know proper directionality (left to right on a line). Consequently, this skill demonstrates the acquisition of several print concepts and moves children one step closer to being prepared to read. However, pointing to words individually as the adult reads does *not* mean that a child is reading. Instead, it means that the child is learning that printed words go with spoken words.

To promote this skill, select a storybook that is somewhat familiar to the child and has at least one page with only one or two lines of print. This is the page to use when asking the child to point to the words. It is important to avoid using pages with too many lines of print, as this may be too difficult and tiresome for the child. During shared reading of this particular page ask the child, "Can you do something for me? Can you point to the words on this page as I read each one?" When reading the print on this page, read at a slightly slower pace than usual, especially at first. Take the child's finger and guide it to begin the activity—pointing to each word as it is read. Try this for the first several words and then release the child's finger so that he or she can perform the task unassisted. When the page is finished, praise the child even if complete assistance was needed. Then resume reading the story without further interruption. See Table 6.12 for a brief summary of this strategy.

As an alternative, consider asking the child to point to the words in the title of the storybook as they are read on the front cover when the book is first presented. That way the strategy may be employed before the story has begun and an interruption will not be needed. Provide the child with as much assistance as necessary to point to the words as they are read to him or her. When the child is able to point to the words in one or two sentences as they are being read, he or she will have mastered this concept.

Table 6.12.   Points to words as the adult reads: brief review

Select a page in a storybook that contains at least one page where there are only one or two lines of print.

Ask the child, "Can you do something for me? Can you point to the words on this page as I read each one?"

Reading at a slower pace, guide the child's finger for the first several words and then let the child continue independently. Provide further assistance if needed.

Upon finishing the one or two lines of print, praise the child's performance even if assistance was necessary for the entire task.

Continue practicing once per shared-reading session for several days until the child is able to point with little or no assistance.

In the following reading excerpt from *The Snowy Day* (Keats, 1962), this strategy is illustrated by a parent who has practiced it previously with his son:

Parent: "He thought it would be fun to join the big boys in their snowball fight, but he knew he wasn't old enough—not yet." Looks like he got whacked with a snowball.

Paul: Daddy, are they playing at nighttime?

Parent: No, they just made this picture dark so you could see the snowballs flying.

Paul: (looks closely at the picture) That looks like fun!

Parent: You and I can make snowballs this winter and give it a try with Uncle Jeff.

Paul: Yeah, we can beat Uncle Jeff for sure! (turns the page)

Parent: Okay, Paul, here is where you do your part. Do you remember what to do?

Paul: You read—I point.

Parent: Right! Here we go: "So . . . he . . . made . . . a . . . smiling . . . snowman . . . and . . . he . . . made . . . angels." (reads words slowly so Paul can point to each one) Well done! You got every word that time.

Paul: I did *two* pages!

Parent: Yeah, you did. You're getting real good at this. We'll do it some more later on.

Phonological Awareness

As described in Chapter 5, phonological awareness is when children are cognizant of the sounds of a language and are able to manipulate these sounds in a purposeful way. It is often seen in young children's sound play and rhyming with words. Tasks involving phonological awareness require children to attend to the sounds of particular words rather than the meaning of these words. This is a challenging concept for young children, but it is very important to their literacy development. The strategies presented in this chapter will require children to understand and use terms such as *sound, word, first, same,* and *different.* Also, keen listening skills will be necessary for children to compare one sound with another. Like written language awareness, these skills may take considerable time to develop. However, this time will be well spent when children acquire an understanding of the sounds of their language because this helps prepare them for the phoneme–grapheme correspondence necessary in reading.

Specific Strategies for Phonological Awareness

The following strategies provide suggestions for brief conversations during shared reading that will assist children in becoming aware of and learning about sounds. Table 6.13 lists the skills associated with phonological awareness to be addressed. The reader will see that they each involve knowledge of sounds only—no reading ability is required. In fact, no reference to print is required at all unless desired. However, children will be required to listen closely to hear the sounds and words. Each strategy is illustrated through a shared-reading excerpt and summarized in a table for quick reference.

Recognizes Word Boundaries

This skill appears to be elementary, but, in fact, it can be difficult for some children to acquire. It requires children to think about language in a more abstract way. Instead of focusing on the meaning of the words, children need to comprehend how many words are spoken. In essence, children need to ignore the meaning and focus instead on the words themselves. For example, in this phonological awareness task, if the adult said, "Throw ball," the child would be expected to tell you that he or she

Table 6.13.   Phonological awareness concepts

An ability to recognize word boundaries (e.g., *blue ball* consists of two words)

An ability to identify the number of syllables in words (e.g., *book* has one syllable, *airport* has two syllables, *lollipop* has three syllables)

An ability to rhyme words by changing the first sound (e.g., *Jill/bill/sill/mill*)

An ability to identify the first sound of words (e.g., *peach* begins with the /p/ phoneme)

hears two words rather than respond to the statement by picking up a ball and throwing it. To accomplish this task, children need to understand the concept of *word* and have some understanding of numbers. Number knowledge only up to 3 or 4 will be needed. This task should not require children to identify more than three or four words because it is too demanding on their short-term memories. Given these requirements, children who are very young may need a great deal of support to participate in this strategy. Professionals may wish to postpone introducing this activity until they believe that children are ready.

To emphasize this skill during storybook reading, select a book that the child has heard several times. This is suggested because repeated readings increase a child's familiarity with the vocabulary used in the storybook. If unfamiliar words are used in this activity, the task will be much more difficult (and frustrating) for the child. Select three areas in the storybook in which word boundaries will be discussed. This should include one instance of a single word, one instance of a two-word phrase, and one instance of a three-word phrase in this order. Order of presentation is important on the first day only because if the child has difficulty understanding the task with the single word, which is the easiest, subsequent tasks will need to be adjusted. Once the child understands the task and can perform it with single words, two-word phrases, and perhaps three-word phrases, the order of presentation should be varied to reduce predictability.

To illustrate word selection, consider the storybook *There's an Alligator Under My Bed* by Mercer Mayer (1987). In this storybook, selections could include the single word *under* (from page 2), a two-word phrase *put cookies* (from page 15), and a three-word phrase *on the stairs* (from page 16). When the concept is introduced for the first time, the activity should be demonstrated using a two-word phrase from the title of the book (e.g., *My Bed*). When deciding on which words to select, preference may be given to those words that the child appears to already know and use. Also, simpler, shorter words (e.g., *cup, hat, sleep*) will be easier for children than those with multiple syllables (e.g., *basketball, firefighter, refrigerator*).

When introducing the storybook, read the title and then explain to the child that he or she is to listen closely for some words from the book that will be repeated. Explain by saying, "What I want you to do is clap your hands to show me how many words I say, like this: *bed*—clap once (adult claps hands once); *my bed*—clap twice. (adult claps twice) Now I want *you* to try it: (pause) *bed* (wait for child to clap once and then pause) *my bed* (wait for child to clap twice)." Provide assistance with clapping if the child is unsure or claps incorrectly. Praise the child's correct responses.

Begin shared reading and interrupt the story briefly when the selected words appear, starting with the single word. Tell the child to listen carefully for a moment to hear how many words are said. Pause briefly, say the word, and then pause for the child to clap once. Provide a reminder if the child gives no response or responds incorrectly. Give praise for all attempts and then resume reading the storybook. By talking about words and giving feedback (e.g., "You clapped one time for one word"), the professional will be helping the child understand the concept of word. Even when a child's performance is inaccurate, the feedback given will help him or her to think about words differently.

If the child has difficulty identifying a single word correctly on the first occasion after the example, it is suggested that only single words be presented during the rest of the reading session because asking about two- and three-word phrases will be beyond the child's ability on that day. Consequently, adjustment of the selected phrases will be needed to reduce them to single words. The two-word phrase *put cookies* could be reduced to *put,* and *on the stairs* could be changed to *on.* It will be appropriate to increase the number of words presented from single words to two-word phrases once the child masters the task with single words. Likewise, once the child shows mastery with two-word phrases, a progression to three-word phrases may be attempted. To make certain that the child is distinguishing the number of words and not merely clapping an expected number of times, it is necessary to vary the number of words presented; for example, a two-word phrase may be followed by a single word, then a three-word phrase is presented last. However, none of the phrases should exceed more than three words at any time.

This strategy is not as conversational as many of the others suggested and consequently the adult and child may find that it interferes with the enjoyment of the story. If this is the case, it is suggested that the strategy be employed immediately after shared reading of a storybook. Simply tell the child before the reading begins that when the story is over, he or she will be asked to do something when the story is finished. Then when the story has been completed, go back to the designated pages and conduct the activity. Table 6.14 summarizes this strategy for quick reference.

Table 6.14.   Recognizes word boundaries: brief review

Select a single word, a two-word phrase, and a three-word phrase from a familiar storybook.

Before shared reading begins, provide a demonstration of what the child is expected to do using a two-word phrase in the title; for example, "When I say the word (pause) *bed*, I am saying one word, so I clap once. (clap once) When I say (pause) *my bed*, that is two words, so I clap two times. (clap twice) Now you try it. Listen to what I say: (pause) *bed*." (child should clap once) Provide assistance if necessary. Praise the child's correct response.

Begin shared reading of the storybook. When the first target appears (the single word selected), say to the child, "Listen closely and tell by clapping how many words you hear. Are you ready? (pause) _____." Here the child should clap once to indicate one word. Provide assistance as needed. Praise the child's correct response.

If the child responds correctly, continue reading until the two-word phrase appears and repeat the procedure. If the child is unable to understand the task with a single word, reduce the two-word- and three-word phrases to single words. Likewise, if the child can do single words but has difficulty with the two-word phrase, reduce the three-word phrase to two words for further practice at that level.

The following shared-reading excerpt from *There's an Alligator Under My Bed* (Mayer, 1987) illustrates this strategy with a three-word phrase:

Teacher: "There used to be an alligator under my bed." (pauses for Tina to look at the pictures)

Tina: Here he is. (points to the boy) Where did the alligator go?

Teacher: I think we'll see the alligator in a minute. He's hiding right now.

Tina: He's under the bed, right?

Teacher: I think so. According to the story, the alligator is "under my bed." (tracks these three words while reading) (pauses) Tina, before we turn the page, let's practice the word game, okay?

Tina: Okay.

Teacher: Remember, you show me how many words I say by clapping your hands. Ready to listen? (pauses) "under my bed"

Tina: "under" (claps) "my bed" (claps)

Teacher: Good try, but you missed something. Let's try it again. I'll say them a little slower this time. Ready to listen? (pauses) "under my bed"

Tina: "under" (claps) "my" (claps) "bed" (claps)

Teacher: Excellent! "Under my bed" is three words, and you gave three claps. That was a hard one, but you got it! Now, let's continue with our story and look for that alligator.

Identifies the Number of Syllables in Words   Recognizing the number of syllables in words is a highly challenging task for some children even after reading instruction has begun. Consequently, this concept has been adapted for young children by having them compare words of different lengths to determine the bigger word. This task may be difficult, especially when children have been focusing on words as phonological units, as in the last activity, and now they are asked to think about syllables. The concept of a syllable is one that may remain elusive for many preschool children. However, young children may gradually become sensitive to how words vary in their syllable structure by comparing words of different lengths. This activity is easier than counting syllables, yet it will give children experience with recognizing another way that words can vary.

This activity will ask children to compare a one-syllable word and a three-syllable word to determine which one has more parts. Select a storybook that the child has heard several times so that the book's vocabulary words are familiar. Choose two pairs of words; a pair consists of a one-syllable word and a three-syllable word. Each pair should appear on the same page in the storybook. As an example, you might select the words *house* and *everyone* from page 1 of *The Napping House* by Audrey Wood (1984) and the words *cat* and *slumbering* from page 12.

Begin shared reading of the storybook and interrupt the story when the first pair of target words appears. Explain the task to the child by saying, "Listen very closely. I will say two words and clap as I say them. I want you to tell me which word has more parts." Say the two words while quietly clapping along and providing a brief pause between the words. When saying the three-syllable word, use a slightly choppy pronunciation so that the syllables are clearly divided (e.g., *eve-ry-one*). Then, ask the child, "Which word has more parts to it, *house* or *everyone*?" Praise the child's correct response and provide assistance if he or she is incorrect or cannot decide. Resume shared reading until the second pair of words appears. Repeat the procedure with the second pair with one difference—present the three-syllable word before the one-syllable word. By changing the position of the longer word, children will be required to answer based on listening rather than guessing based on expected order of presentation.

It may take some children considerable time to master this concept, so several weeks or even months of practice may be required. It may help to provide a visual cue during the activity to bolster the auditory cues when first getting started. If that technique is desired, the professional may point to the individual words in the book immediately before they are spoken and clapped. The visual cue may help children understand how one word is longer or has more parts than another. Once the child is successful in identifying that a three-syllable word is longer than a one-syllable word based on auditory cues alone, a more difficult comparison may be introduced by having the child compare one-syllable words with two-syllable words using the same strategy. Refer to Table 6.15 for a brief summary of this strategy and consider the example of a shared-reading excerpt from *Owen* (Henkes, 1993) that follows:

Parent: "That night Owen's parents told Owen to put Fuzzy under his pillow. In the morning Fuzzy would be gone, but the Blanket Fairy would leave an absolutely wonderful, positively perfect, especially terrific big-boy gift in its place."

Leo: Is that like the tooth fairy?

Parent: It's the same idea. You put something under your pillow and get a surprise in the morning.

Leo: Was the Blanket Fairy going to leave him money?

Parent: Well, I think that would be a good guess. (pauses) Leo, I see a couple of words on this page that I want you to listen to. Can we pause for a minute to do that?

Table 6.15.   Identifies the number of syllables in words: brief review

Choose two pairs of words: a one-syllable word and a three-syllable word. Each word pair should appear on the same page in a storybook with which the child is familiar.

Interrupt shared reading when the first word pair appears. Say to the child, "Listen carefully as I say two words from the story. I want you to tell me which word has more parts. Ready? (pause) *house* (quietly clap once while saying *house*; pause), *eve-ry-one*." (quietly clap three times while saying *everyone*)

Praise the child's correct response (i.e., *everyone*). Provide assistance if necessary (e.g., repeat the word, explain that more claps means more parts to the word).

Resume reading and repeat this procedure when the next word pair appears, except that the three-syllable word should be presented first this time. Praise a correct answer and provide assistance when the child answers incorrectly or not at all.

Leo: Okay.

Parent: Good. I'm going to say two words, and I'll clap along as I say them. Listen carefully and when I finish, tell me which one has more parts to it, okay?

Leo: Yeah, okay.

Parent: *night* (softly claps once as it is spoken; pauses) *won-der-ful* (softly claps three times as each syllable is spoken) Which word has more parts to it: *night* or *wonderful?*

Leo: That's an easy one—*wonderful* does.

Parent: Terrific! I knew you were a good listener! Shall we see what happens with the tooth fairy?

Leo: You mean the *Blanket* Fairy!

Parent: Oh, yeah. How could I ever forget about the *Blanket* Fairy!

Rhymes Words by Changing the Initial Sound   One simple way to rhyme words is to change the first sound in a word to create another word. To facilitate this process, select a storybook that contains a word that sounds like at least two other words except for the initial sound. Some examples might be *bake/take/make, tell/bell/ fell, look/book/took, sand/band/land, light/tight/fight,* and *ring/ sing/ wing.* The objective is to use real words rather than made-up words, which is often what children want to do in this endeavor. During shared reading, interrupt the story when the target word appears to make a comment such as, "This word *tea* sounds like the word *sea.* The words *tea* and *sea* rhyme, which means that they sound the same except for the very first sound. *Tea* starts with a "tuh" sound and *sea* starts with a "sss" sound. Can you change the first sound to make another word that rhymes with *tea* and *sea?*" Be prepared with some examples if the child needs help (e.g., *me, we, key, knee, he, Lee, bee*). Praise all attempts and then resume your reading. Repeat the activity with the same word in future reading sessions until the child shows an understanding of the concept by telling you at least one word that rhymes with *tea.* At that point, a new word for rhyming may be attempted following the same procedure.

    Sometimes it takes children a while to catch on to the rhyming strategy. If the child appears to be having difficulty, two suggestions are offered. First, it may help to use a rhyming book such as *Shoes* (Winthrop, 1986) or *Brown Bear, Brown Bear, What Do You See?*

(Martin, 1983) to introduce the rhyming concept. Commenting on words that rhyme in such a book may be one way to help the child hear the similarity between certain words. Once the child is familiar with the words in the book through repeated readings, he or she may be able to fill in words when requested. It is similar to what happens when children learn simple rhymes through repetition. When the adult begins "One, two, buckle my _____" the child eventually learns to complete the phrase by saying "shoe." A second suggestion might be to extend the activity to a paper-and-pencil task. Begin by showing the child the word in the storybook and then print it on a piece of paper (e.g., the word *back*). Write down a few sounds to consider for making new words that rhyme (e.g., the phonemes /t/, /s/, /p/, and /l/). Show the child how the new sounds, when combined with the last part of the word *back* (i.e., *-ack*), make new words (*t-* and *-ack* form the word *tack*). Then, say the two words in succession so the child can hear them together (e.g., *back/tack*). Adding the written component may help the child understand this process more quickly.

Rhyming is a fun activity for children once they figure out how to accomplish it. However, it may take children some time to master this skill, so introducing this strategy casually over a period of time might be a helpful approach. For example, this strategy could be earmarked for presentation just once or twice a week over a period of months rather than focused on during every shared-reading session. This may reduce the chance of frustrating a child who is unable to master the concept quickly. Table 6.16 provides a brief summary of this strategy for quick reference, and the following shared-reading excerpt involving a storybook created by the teacher about her new puppy titled *Lulu Finds a Home* provides an illustration.

Table 6.16.   Rhymes words by changing the initial sound: brief review

Select a storybook that contains one word that rhymes with at least two other words by changing the initial sound (e.g., *tea/sea/key, tell/bell/fell*).

During shared reading, interrupt the story when the target word appears and make a comment such as, "This word *tea* sounds like the word *sea*. The words *tea* and *sea* rhyme, which means that they sound the same except for the first sound. *Tea* starts with a 'tuh' sound, and *sea* starts with a 'sss' sound. Can you think of another word that rhymes with *tea* and *sea*?"

Praise correct responses. If the child cannot provide any words, consider making the task easier by giving the child a choice of which word rhymes. "Which word sounds like *tea*? Listen: *tea–key* or *tea–book*?" Give further explanation if necessary.

Repeat this activity with the same word in future reading sessions until the child is able to provide at least one rhyming word, and then move to a new word.

Teacher: Look at this picture that shows Lulu taking a walk. "When little Lulu comes back from her walk, she wants to take a nap." (pauses) Jasmine, did you hear the word *nap*?

Jasmine: Uh-huh. (nods her head)

Teacher: Yes, it would be a lot of work for *anybody*. (pause) "When he's done, he'll probably want to take a nap." (pauses) Jasmine, did you hear the word *nap*?

Jasmine: Uh-huh. (nods her head)

Teacher: I just thought of another word that sounds like *nap*. (pauses) *cap*. *Nap* and *cap* rhyme, don't they? *Nap* starts with "nuh" and *cap* starts with "kuh."

Jasmine: *nap* and *cap*.

Teacher: Right! Can you think of another word that rhymes with these two words?

Jasmine: Map!

Teacher: That's a *good* one! *Nap, cap, map.* Suppose we changed the first sound to "tuh"?

Jasmine: Ah, let's see. "tuh"… ah…"tuh."

Teacher: Need some help? (pauses) When the word starts with "tuh" it would be *tap*.

Jasmine: Yeah, *tap*.

Teacher: So we have four words that rhyme. Can you remember what they are?

Jasmine: Uh-huh. *Nap, cap, map,* and *tap*.

Teacher: Very good, Jasmine!

Identifies the First Sound of Words   This task requires children to listen to the sounds in individual words, which may be more difficult than any other concepts presented. In this task, only the first sound of a word is targeted for the children's attention. No other sounds in the word are to be emphasized, as this constitutes a phonemic awareness activity whose introduction is more appropriate during formal reading instruction.

Although there are many sounds in the English language, it is not necessary to focus on every one. Professionals and parents may wish to emphasize just a few or several depending on children's interest and success. However, keep in mind that the more sounds children can recognize before formal reading instruction begins, the better prepared they will be. Consequently, it is suggested that between six and eight consonant sounds be emphasized (one at a time, of course). Be advised that this strategy focuses only on the sound and not on an alphabet letter because many letters represent a variety of sounds, which will only confuse young children at this point.

When selecting a target sound, there are four issues to consider. First, try to select sounds that the child is able to produce correctly. For example, if a child has difficulty pronouncing the phonemes /r/ or /s/, it is suggested that those sounds be avoided. Second, be sure that the target sound appears in different words in the storybook so that opportunities may be offered with various words. Finding a storybook that contains at least three different words with the same first sound is suggested rather than three repetitions of the same word. Third, select simple words that are familiar to the child because more complex and unfamiliar words may make the activity unnecessarily difficult. Fourth, avoid consonant clusters that appear at the beginning of words because this may alter how the sound is produced and may be much more difficult for children to perceive. For example, if /b/ is selected, avoid words like *broom* or *black* and instead choose *back* or *bear,* in which the consonant is immediately followed by a vowel. Some consonant sounds to be considered are /p/, /b/, /t/, /d/, /k/, /g/, /m/, /n/, /l/, /w/, /r/, /s/, and /z/. Be sure to emphasize only one consonant sound at a time so as not to overwhelm or confuse the child. Only when the child is able to recognize the target sound reliably at the beginning of different words (e.g., *book, bee, bike*) should a new target sound be considered.

Once a target sound has been selected following the previous four guidelines, and a storybook has been identified that contains at least three different words with this same first sound, shared reading may begin. Interrupt the story when the first target word appears. In this first instance, provide the child with a brief explanation and an example using the target word, such as, "All words are made up of sounds. When I say a word, I want you to listen to the very first sound and tell me what you hear, okay? So when I say the word *dog,* you will listen for the first sound. Listen (pause) *dog.* The first sound in *dog* is 'duh.'" In all cases, make reference to the sound rather than the letter because the letter and sound often are pronounced differently (i.e., /d/ sounds like "duh" whereas the letter *d* is pronounced as "dee"). Ask the child to repeat the sound "duh" once or twice and then repeat the word *dog*. Then, explain that some other words in this story use this sound, too. Resume reading until the second target word appears. This time, ask the child to listen to a new word and to tell you the first sound (e.g., "Listen [pause] *door*. What is the first sound in *door*?"). If necessary, repeat the word again with emphasis on the "duh" sound to help the child hear the sound. Provide assistance as needed and praise the child's attempts. Repeat this procedure with the third and final target word (e.g., "Listen [pause] *donut*. What is the first sound in *donut*?").

Repeat this strategy with the same words and the same book if desired until the child is able to identify the target sound. However, it also is acceptable to use this sound in different words from another book; just remember to concentrate on the same target sound until the child shows mastery. Once the child is able to identify the first sound in the target words without any assistance, he or she is ready to focus on a new target sound. When the child is acquiring new sounds, old sounds may be reviewed on occasion to help the child remember these and to provide practice in discriminating one sound from another. Table 6.17 provides a brief review of this strategy. An excerpt from a small-group shared-reading session in a preschool

Table 6.17.   Identifies the first sound of words: brief review

Select a target consonant sound that the child is able to say without any difficulty. An example might be the /t/ phoneme. Always refer to this as the *sound* (pronounced as "tuh") and not as the *letter* (pronounced as "tee").

Select a storybook that contains this sound at the beginning of three different words (e.g., *to, take, time*). Avoid all words with consonant clusters (e.g., *try, twine*).

During shared reading, interrupt the story when the first target word appears. Provide a brief explanation and an example using the target word: "All words are made of sounds. When I say a word, I want you to listen to the first sound and tell me what you hear. When I say the word *to*, you hear the 'tuh' sound. Can you hear the 'tuh' in the word *to*?" Then explain that some other words in this story begin with this sound, and resume reading.

When the second target word appears, say to the child, "Listen to this word (pause) *take*. What is the first sound in the word *take*?" Praise a correct answer. If the child is incorrect or fails to answer, repeat the word again with an emphasis on the "tuh" sound to help the child hear the sound.

Repeat the procedure with the third target word when it appears in the story.

When the child shows mastery with this sound, introduce a new target consonant. Review old targets occasionally to keep them fresh in the child's mind.

classroom provides an illustration of the strategy. The storybook is *The Mitten: An Old Ukranian Folktale* (Tresselt, 1989) and the target sound is the /w/ phoneme (e.g., *wool, warm, wiggle*).

Teacher: (completes reading and closes the book) Children, can we talk about some words that we just heard in this story?

Children: Yeah, OK. Uh-huh.

Teacher: Remember how we listen for the first sound in words?

Children: Uh-huh.

Teacher: When I say a word, I want you to listen to the first sound and tell me what sound you hear. I'll say the word two times, so listen each time and then tell me the sound. Listen and watch me closely: (pause) *wool* (pause) *wool*. (The children do not respond.)

Teacher: Well, let me make it a bit easier for you. Which sound do you hear, "s-s-s" or "wuh?" Now, listen to the word again (pause) *wool.*

Children: The "wuh" sound!

Teacher: Excellent work! The first sound of *wool* is "wuh." Can everybody say that sound and the word?

Children: "Wuh." *Wool.*

Teacher: Very good! Now let's try another word.

SUMMARY

The conversational strategies presented in this chapter are intended to promote children's emergent literacy skills during shared reading. These strategies offer suggestions for presenting concepts regarding written language and phonological awareness to young children. They should not be viewed as the only acceptable method of presentation because there are many different ways to explain to children the features of alphabet letters, print conventions, and sounds. Also, the reader is reminded that there may be many natural opportunities throughout the day to discuss these concepts with young children (e.g., when children sign their names to their artwork, examine product labels, look at a classroom calendar, or learn the words to a new song).

In Chapter 7, the reader will find some suggestions for working with young children who resist the shared-reading experience. These ideas are based on the theory of multiple intelligences (Gardner, 1993). Although the suggestions are intended to increase reluctant readers' participation in shared reading, willing participants may find them useful as well.

7

Suggestions and Strategies
for Reluctant Readers

This chapter addresses the problems encountered when children show a dislike for books and are resistant to shared reading with others. Suggestions for identifying possible causes of reading problems with these children are given. Various strategies are presented that may facilitate children's willingness to participate in shared reading.

Some children take to books like ducks take to water, as the saying goes. They are drawn to books and enjoy sharing them with others. Such children are excited when they receive a book as a gift and may look at or play with books on their own initiative. When this interest develops early, storytime is a true pleasure because these children sit with rapt attention and eagerly engage in conversation. As a result, these children are poised to make significant gains in their oral language and emergent literacy development during their preschool years.

Some young children do not find books to be especially interesting, preferring toys, games, physical play, or television viewing instead. In fact, not only do they prefer these other activities, they may actively resist books and storytime. Although it may be common for many children under the age of 3 to prefer more active play, it is important for all children to accept storytime and to explore books so that they can acquire the language and emergent literacy skills necessary for future learning. Research shows that for young children who are not yet reading, those who enjoy being read to and who seek out reading experiences are inclined to develop language and early literacy skills more quickly than those who do not (Frijters, Barron,

& Brunello, 2000). Later, when children are able to read on their own, those who read often and well will develop word recognition and reading comprehension skills more rapidly than children who read infrequently (Stanovich, 2000). Consequently, it is important to stimulate children's interest in books at an early age.

When thinking about interest in shared reading, a child's orientation likely lies somewhere between the extremes of total rapture and intense dislike. Consider the hypothetical continuum of children's interest levels as seen in Figure 7.1. This continuum ranges from no interest at one extreme to high interest at the other. On such a continuum, it is possible for a child's interest to fall anywhere within this range. Keeping in mind that the particular book selected for reading, the time of day, and the availability of a more preferred activity all factor into the equation, after a week or two of reading opportunities, most parents and professionals are usually able to determine a child's general interest level. This chapter focuses on those children who are reluctant readers, meaning those who would score at the lower end of the continuum based on their active resistance to storytime. Some experts suggest that about 10% of children are very reluctant readers (Teale, 1986), although for children who have developmental disabilities that affect their language achievement, this number may be even higher (Kaderavek & Sulzby, 1999).

Although children's interest in books may grow over time as they develop and mature, it is important to help this interest emerge as early as possible so that they do not miss valuable opportunities to acquire language and emergent literacy concepts during their preschool years. If these skills are not developed during this important time period, children will be at a disadvantage when beginning school because they will need to spend considerable time understanding concepts that others have already acquired. Therefore, it is recommended that every attempt be made to entice reluctant readers to explore and accept books at an early age and to come to view books as objects that warrant their attention and interest.

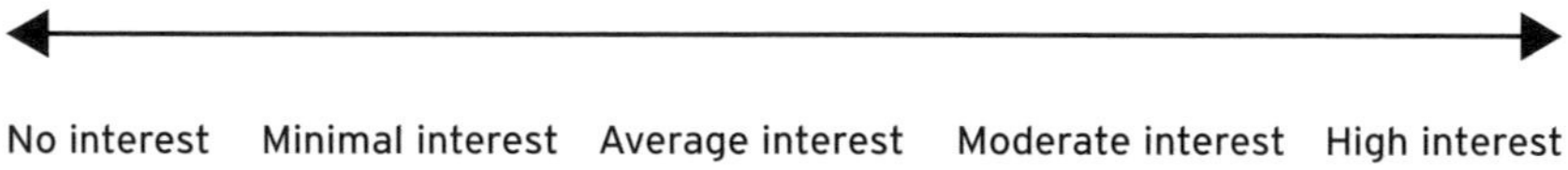

No interest   Minimal interest   Average interest   Moderate interest   High interest

Figure 7.1.   Hypothetical continuum of children's interest in books and storytime.

FACTORS THAT INFLUENCE
CHILDREN'S PARTICIPATION IN SHARED READING

There are several possible reasons why children may not enjoy story-time and eventually become reluctant readers. Four factors that may influence children's participation are 1) interest level, 2) individual temperament, 3) success with the activity, and 4) the adult's reading style.

Interest Level

When children are interested in a book, they exhibit a curiosity or intentness about it. This feeling of curiosity provides a reason for children to attend and listen as the story is being read. This interest or curiosity serves as a positive motivator to participate in storytime and highlights the importance of presenting books that children will find attractive and engaging. This includes not only the topic of the children's book but also how the book may be presented so that it capitalizes on a child's individual strengths. The concept of tailoring the presentation of a book to a child's interests and abilities is discussed in greater detail later in this chapter.

Individual Temperament

A second factor that appears to influence children's motivation to participate in storytime is their individual temperament. Temperament is an aspect of a child's constitution or personality that contributes to his or her approach to solving problems and being able to tolerate frustration, among other things. It may explain why some children are able to persevere in novel or challenging activities whereas others remain sensitive to the difficulties or constraints of such activities (Kagan, 1994). Book reading is an activity that can be highly challenging for some children, especially those with language problems, because the language and literacy demands of the task may be far in excess of their current abilities. Therefore, the demands of the task with respect to a child's language ability and temperament should be examined to see whether adjustments may be needed in the complexity of the reading material or how the child is expected to participate.

Success with the Activity

A third possible factor is a child's feeling of success during shared reading. It is quite possible that many children who are resistant to books and storytime have not found the experience to be rewarding. Children will not be motivated to look at storybooks or will actively resist story-time if they have experienced failure or repeated frustration. The savvy professional knows how to shape shared-reading interactions so that a child is challenged but still can achieve success. Young children are able to achieve success when proper guidance and support is pro-vided. A supportive professional uses language that the child under-stands, presents questions or requests that the child can respond to with some assistance, and provides praise so that the child knows what was done well. This situation will help to establish a positive learning cycle whereby children's success in acquiring new skills will motivate them to participate in future learning opportunities. It is the role of professionals to make certain that shared reading is always a positive experience for young children. For children who already show an interest in books, this is relatively easy because the youngsters are eager to engage in the activity. However, for those children who are reluctant readers, who show no interest in books and resist any form of shared reading, building a series of successful reading experiences will be more difficult but is ever that much more important.

Adult's Reading Style

A fourth factor that could influence children's participation in shared reading may be the adult's chosen reading style. When young children are acquiring language and knowledge about their world, they rely on verbal interactions with adults. It is important for professionals to be aware that some reading styles promote open interaction more than others. For example, consider the comment from the second author's 2-year-old daughter Addie as she "read" a storybook to her mother. While Addie was "reading," her mother periodically interjected ques-tions about the book (e.g., "What was the little boy's name?") and commented on the story (e.g., "This is such a great book!"). Each time she did so, Addie would look at her mother with great serious-ness and say, "Stop talking. Listen to the words!" In this role play, Addie was demonstrating a particular interaction style as the reader, which apparently she had experienced in a previous reading en-counter. This reading style is referred to as a noninterrupting, performance-oriented style (Reese & Cox, 1999) in which the reader shares the story without interruptions. When adults use this reading style, they may not welcome inquisitive children's questions or comments, which could eventually thwart some children's enthusiasm for the shared-reading activity.

As mentioned in Chapter 2, it is common for adults to have their own preferred style toward sharing books with children, and each of these styles has its own benefits. In addition to the noninterrupting, performance-oriented style described previously, two other naturally occurring reading styles have been reported: 1) the describer style and 2) the comprehender style (Haden, Reese, & Fivush, 1996; Reese & Cox, 1999). The describer style involves frequent interruptions during the reading by adults and children, with adult commentary typically focusing on describing pictures, labeling actions and objects, and talking about print and book features (Justice & Ezell, 2002; Reese & Cox, 1999). The comprehender style also involves frequent interruptions, but the adult commentary focuses on inferring, predicting, and reasoning about story events. Based on the findings of Reese and Cox (1999), the describer style appears to provide benefits for developing receptive vocabulary and print skills when compared with the other styles of reading. However, children's level of benefit from the various reading styles appears to be related to their current skills. The describer style was found to be beneficial in developing print skills when children had higher comprehension skills at the beginning of the study. For children with lower initial comprehension skills, the noninterrupting, performance-oriented style was more effective. Dickinson and Smith (1994) found that receptive vocabulary development was supported more when preschool teachers engaged children in quality discussions before and after shared reading than when interrupting styles were used.

Interestingly, the most common naturally occurring reading style preferred by adults who read to preschool children is the performance-oriented style in which conversation occurs before and after the book has been read (Hammett, van Kleeck, & Huberty, 2003). Also, it should be noted that adults tend to be fairly stable in their preferred reading styles over time, maintaining the same approach even as children grow older (Haden et al., 1996).

When addressing the dilemma of reluctant readers, it may be worthwhile for professionals to consider whether their chosen reading style is maximally effective for engaging these children in shared reading. Although the preferred style of many adults seems to be a noninterrupting style in which little discussion is interspersed during the reading, the exclusive use of the noninterrupting reading style may not be the best approach for engaging reluctant readers in shared reading. As noted throughout this book, shared-reading conversations are viewed as a vehicle for adults and children to engage collaboratively in learning tasks to build language and literacy foundations and to develop relationships with each other. One measure of its benefit is the child's response to this activity. If the child responds negatively to a noninterrupting reading style, professionals may wish to consider expanding their repertoire to include the describer and comprehender styles as well.

COMMON RESISTANT BEHAVIORS

It is common for young children to refuse shared reading from time to time when a highly desirable activity competes for their attention. For instance, shared reading may be viewed as a less desirable alternative to playing outside on a sunny afternoon or visiting a neighbor with a new puppy. Also, every child may experience restless behavior on occasion or feel bored by a particular book. All of these are normal experiences and may be expected even from children who are usually interested in storytime. Normal variations in motivation toward reading should be differentiated from a real resistance, which is cause for concern. Three measures are suggested for determining whether a child's behavior constitutes resistance. The first is the average number of times children are willing to participate in shared reading when invited. As a general rule of thumb, resistance may not be a problem if a child willingly participates in shared reading an average of three times for every five opportunities over a period of several days, even if it is only for part of a reading session. For children younger than 3 years old, it may be more realistic to expect participation to average two times for every five opportunities.

The second measure to consider is how often a child seeks out shared-reading experiences, specifically how often a child asks an adult to read to him or her. If the child asks to be read to at least once a week, it is likely that the child has an affinity for the shared-reading experience. If the child rarely or never asks to be read to, shared reading may not be a desirable experience for the child, particularly if he or she often requests other activities. Some research has suggested a correlation between the frequency with which children request being read to and their emergent literacy and language skills (Justice & Pence, 2004).

Table 7.1.   Resistant behaviors toward books and shared reading

Refusing to select a book to borrow or to purchase when invited to do so

Refusing to open and look through a storybook with a familiar adult

Refusing to allow a familiar adult to read any portion of a storybook

Refusing to allow a familiar adult to simply talk about a book as the pages are turned

Exhibiting one or more undesirable behaviors (e.g., screaming, crying, hitting, biting) during storybook reading that result in the reading session being discontinued

Exhibiting destructive behavior (e.g., tearing, cutting, marking, soiling the pages) specifically toward books

Hiding, destroying, giving away, or discarding books

A third measure to consider is the nature of a child's reading resistance along with its frequency, intensity, and duration. This may include refusing to select a book for storytime when the invitation to do so is offered or displaying uncooperative behavior during a reading session. It may also include destructive behavior toward books, such as tearing pages or attempting to destroy the books in some way. A few other examples of resistant behaviors are listed in Table 7.1. Certainly, on one or two occasions a cranky child could display any of these behaviors. The second author's child mentioned earlier in this chapter, who is very motivated toward shared reading, occasionally rips and chews on her books, as she does with other favored items. The difference lies in the frequency and intensity of the behavior and whether it continues or escalates over a period of time. A child who refuses to participate in shared reading for a week or two, but who then resumes his or her usual involvement, would not be considered to be exhibiting an established pattern of resistant behavior, as occasional episodes of periodic resistance are commonly seen during children's normal development. During these temporary phases, resistant behavior often does not escalate into more severe problems but fades away instead. However, if a child is destroying books on a regular basis and his or her hitting behavior during shared reading is becoming more frequent and intense, a resistance to books or shared reading may be emerging.

WHEN CHILDREN'S RESISTANCE
MAY BE A SYMPTOM OF ANOTHER PROBLEM

For children who are clearly resistant to reading, it is important to consider whether this behavior is part of a larger problem. Tearing pages from a book or crying to avoid shared reading may be a child's way of expressing frustration about another issue or a way of seeking attention from an adult. It may not be specific to books and shared reading at all. Although it is sometimes difficult to determine whether a child's behavior is specific to books and shared reading or whether the child would resist whatever an adult presented at that time, there are at least two ways to distinguish the difference. The first is to determine whether the child displays resistant behaviors at other times during the day, not just during shared reading. For example, a professional working in a child care setting may find that one child resists shared reading when first arising from an afternoon nap. However, if books are presented to this child in the morning, little or no resistance is observed. In contrast, a second child may always resist shared reading but may willingly accept all other activities (e.g., physical play, group games, fingerpainting, sing-alongs). A third child may be resistant to everything, no matter when it is presented or by whom. Each of these children shows a different pattern of behavior, but only the second child appears to be resistant solely to the shared-reading activity.

A second way to determine whether resistance is specific to books is to consider a child's manipulation and interaction with other objects. If destructive behavior involves other objects, such as toys, clothing, or the belongings of others as well as storybooks, then this behavior may represent a broader issue. In those cases, addressing the negative behavior toward storybooks will be confronting only part of the child's problem.

In order to determine whether resistance to shared reading is a symptom of a larger problem rather than a sole aversion to books, it is necessary to observe the child in several different situations over a period of time to see what patterns may emerge. In the event that the child acts out during other activities and demonstrates inappropriate behavior toward a variety of objects, then the child's behavior may represent a broader social or emotional problem. If this situation is suspected, it is recommended that the child be referred to a psychologist or behavior specialist for evaluation. These professionals are likely to be helpful in pinpointing the exact cause of the child's frustration or anger, which may explain his or her inappropriate behavior. Unless a cause for the behavior is discovered, intervention will only be attending to its symptoms (e.g., breaking toys, soiling books, refusing to participate) and may not be as effective in the long term as when the underlying reason is fully diagnosed and treated.

GENERAL SUGGESTIONS FOR
ENHANCING THE APPEAL OF SHARED READING

Before specific suggestions are offered for helping reluctant readers to accept shared reading, the reader should be aware of some general procedures that may encourage children's interest. Table 7.2 provides a list of recommendations for making shared reading more appealing to all young children regardless of their interest in books. These include procedures such as reading with enthusiasm, pausing at exciting points, using different voices to represent characters, and interspersing questions to link the story content to the child's life. It is suggested that readers scan the list and determine which of these activities are routinely present and which may be missing from current reading practices. Explore the way different activities or behaviors may influence children's responsiveness to shared reading routines and how they promote reading interactions. Each of these activities should be in place for all children, especially those who are reluctant readers. In a sense, these general suggestions constitute a foundation for the shared-reading experience to which other strategies may be added. Therefore, they represent the beginning point for addressing children's resistance to shared reading.

Table 7.2.   Suggestions for increasing children's interest in storytime

Book selection suggestions:
    Offer books about topics in which the child demonstrates interest.
    Select books about topics of which the child has background knowledge.
    Encourage the child's participation in book selection.
    Select books that are appropriate for the child's developmental level by examining the amount of print, story length, complexity and visual appeal of the illustrations, and inclusion of special features (e.g., lift the flaps).
Reading suggestions:
    Read with enthusiasm by pausing at exciting points, using different voices to represent the characters, and varying volume so that some passages are quiet and others are loud.
    Intersperse occasional questions about the story that invite active participation.
    Invite the child's comments and questions even if they have little relevance to the story.
    Repeat and extend what the child says to demonstrate listening skills and to promote dialogue about the storyline.
    Find ways to relate the story to the child's own personal experiences.
    Allow the child to end the reading session when he or she is bored or tired.
    Praise the child's behavior or demonstrated knowledge during every reading session.
    Promote the child's control of the storybook interaction by allowing him or her to hold the book, turn the pages, and direct the pace of discussion.

ADDRESSING RESISTANCE TO BOOKS AND SHARED READING

Once a child's resistance has been determined to be specific to books and shared reading, the question becomes how the situation may best be addressed. As just mentioned, incorporating all of the activities presented in Table 7.2 into shared reading would be a starting point. For some children, increased control over the situation may result in a positive outcome. Simply allowing the child to select the book, hold it, turn the pages, and control the pace of the discussion may elicit an increase in cooperative behavior. However, a paradigm shift in approaching the shared-reading session may be needed when resistance has been especially intense or has been exhibited over an extended period of time. For those situations, the theoretical framework of multiple intelligences (Gardner, 1993) may offer some ideas.

THEORY OF MULTIPLE INTELLIGENCES

According to Howard Gardner (1993), the theory of multiple intelligences proposes that individuals have seven different methods of processing information and solving problems. These seven intelligences are 1) linguistic, 2) logical–mathematical, 3) spatial, 4) musical, 5) bodily-kinesthetic, 6) intrapersonal, and 7) interpersonal. Recognizing that children may process information in different ways may help explain why some children display less interest in books than in other activities. Simply put, some children may not prefer books and the usual routine of shared reading because this activity is unable to sustain their interest and attention. Professionals and parents often recognize that this is a problem; however, its solution is not always clear because what may work for one child may fail to work for another. This is where the theory of multiple intelligences may be useful. This approach may assist professionals in understanding children's individual differences and preferred learning styles.

As described by Sue Teele (2000), the theory of multiple intelligences offers some promising educational applications for young children. In *Rainbows of Intelligence,* Teele provides suggestions for educational activities that complement each of Gardner's multiple intelligences that would be a helpful resource for both professionals and parents. Following the multiple intelligences theory and its potential educational applications (Gardner, 1993; Teele, 2000), this chapter offers some strategies particular to each of the seven domains of intelligence for addressing children's resistant behavior to shared reading. Of course, knowing which domains of intelligence may be relevant to a particular child will need to be determined either through observing the child during structured activities and free play or through assessment. Teele (1992) has developed the Teele Inventory for Multiple Intelligences (TIMI), which may be used if desired. This inventory, which has been used with preschoolers, involves a simple picture-selection task whereby the child picks one of two choices of activities for 28 items. As children are selecting items that show what they like to do, the answers are neither right nor wrong. This inventory is designed to reveal the dominant intelligences that a child possesses.

Strategies Following the Theory of Multiple Intelligences

When addressing resistant behavior, a few guidelines are offered. First, for each of these suggestions, it is important to tell the child about the activity before shared reading is introduced so that he or she understands how the reading session will be different from prior sessions. Second, it is recommended that individual reading sessions (i.e., one adult to one child) be conducted when addressing children's resistant behavior, as group sessions may hinder or complicate this process. One exception to this rule would be when working with a child who displays interpersonal intelligence. Third, depending on the strategy selected, it may be necessary to scale back how much of the storybook is read to the child in a single session to provide time for the additional activity. For example, if the child will be drawing a picture about the story, reading only a portion of the story is recommended so that the child will have time to complete the drawing. This would be considered a reasonable accommodation for the child, especially when a strategy is first being introduced. Fourth, considering that a child could have several strong intelligence domains, the professional may decide to use suggestions from more than one domain simultaneously rather than a single domain exclusively. For example, if a child displays strong interpersonal and musical intelligences, strategies for each of these domains could be applied in the same reading session in various combinations. Last, it is important to remember that the goal is for the child to experience success and fun during shared reading so that he or she is motivated to participate the next time. Therefore, every effort should be made to engage the child fully and to ensure his or her success.

A few strategies are suggested for each of the seven intelligences proposed by Gardner (1993). Once the professional discovers more about a child's learning style, other activities in the same vein may be attempted. Table 7.3 provides an abbreviated summary of all suggestions offered.

Linguistic   Children with linguistic intelligence will enjoy learning through reading and writing, word games, and listening. In all likelihood, they will not be resistant to shared reading because this activity complements their learning style. These children may be expected to respond positively to the language and emergent literacy strategies presented in Chapter 4 and Chapter 6, respectively. Nevertheless, shared reading may be enhanced in a few other ways not previously mentioned. For example, these children may enjoy retelling stories that they have heard through shared reading. They may enjoy talking about the new words that they hear in stories. Children with good auditory memory skills could be given a part to "read" in the story by providing a short phrase that is used repeatedly through the book on the adult's cue.

Table 7.3.   Strategies for addressing resistant behavior based on the theory of multiple intelligences

---

Linguistic: Have the child retell the story, look up new words, and "read" a part of the story.

Logical-mathematical: Incorporate mathematical problems into the story where appropriate; ask the child to predict events in the story; encourage the child to keep a tally of the books read.

Spatial: Select books with appealing illustrations; invite the child to draw pictures about the story; introduce new stories through a movie version first.

Musical: Provide soft instrumental music during shared reading; introduce rhyming books and encourage the child to compose songs about them; allow the child to snap fingers as a signal to turn the page.

Bodily-kinesthetic: Read to the child in a rocking chair; use books with hands-on features (e.g., lift the flaps); allow the child to act out part of the story through movement or puppetry.

Intrapersonal: Read in a quiet setting; ask for the child's feelings about the story's events; allow solitary time for further book exploration; encourage the child to keep a journal of books read and a personal rating for each.

Interpersonal: Allow the child to invite a friend to shared reading; encourage the child to retell the story with the friend at the end of the session; create a book discussion group for the child to share ideas from stories and book recommendations with peers.

Logical-Mathematical   Children with these intellectual preferences like to sequence, question, and predict events. They enjoy solving mathematical problems, conducting experiments, and making lists, charts, or graphs. To incorporate some of these activities into shared reading, consider selecting storybooks that offer opportunities for mathematical problems. For example, in *The Doorbell Rang* (Hutchins, 1986), the child could be asked to count the number of children who enter each time the doorbell rings and record this on a piece of paper. At the end of the story, the child could count the tally marks or add the numbers to find the total number of children. In other storybooks, the child could be asked to predict what will happen in the story at key junctures. When shared-reading sessions have been completed, the child could be encouraged to create a list of the books that he or she has read and keep a running total to post in the classroom.

Spatial   Children with spatial intelligence are attracted to the visual qualities of objects and materials. Consequently, they will enjoy activities that involve art, graphics, diagrams, maps, and movies, to name a few. These children may be interested in some of the print awareness tasks from Chapter 6. When selecting books for these children, it will be especially important to choose books that have highly appealing illustrations. When children enjoy illustrations from a particular book, they may want to seek other books illustrated by the same artist. These children may like drawing a picture about the story or the main character after the shared-reading session. An art portfolio of these self-made illustrations could be developed or displayed. Also, consider introducing storybooks through movie viewing first. Many stories are accessible through both movies and books. For instance, Disney is one company that is known for producing both movie and book versions of children's stories. After finding a movie that the child enjoys, introduce a book that tells the same story.

Musical   Children with musical intelligence are keenly aware of sounds, enjoy singing and listening to music, and respond to rhythm. To draw these children into shared reading, attempt to play soft music in the background during the reading session. Instrumental rather than vocal music is recommended so that the child does not attend more to the words in the song than the words in the story. Another strategy would be to introduce the child to rhyme books that have a rhythm or cadence to the language such as *This Old Man* (Jones, 2000). The child could be encouraged to compose a song using some of the words in the story as lyrics. Also, the child may be invited to make sound effects, as they would be relevant to the story, or to snap his or her fingers as a signal for turning the page.

Bodily-Kinesthetic   Children who have bodily-kinesthetic intelligence are hands-on learners who enjoy using manipulatives and physical activities that allow them to process information through bodily sensations. Activities that involve movement will likely appeal to these children. Although successfully introducing movement into shared reading may seem difficult, it can be accomplished. For instance, one subtle way to introduce movement is to have the child sit on the adult's lap in a rocking chair to experience a quiet rocking motion during shared reading. Also, books that give the child an opportunity to use his or her hands to lift flaps, pull tabs, or touch objects would introduce a hands-on feature to the reading session. Some books, such as *Ted and Dolly's Magic Carpet Ride* (Fowler, 1994), provide character cutouts that can be pushed through a slot on each page. In the experience of the authors, even the most reluctant readers appear to enjoy this hands-on type of book. Another activity that may be incorporated is having the child act out parts of the story either during or after shared reading. An alternative to this might be allowing the child to use hand puppets to do this.

Intrapersonal   Children who exhibit intrapersonal intelligence may prefer more solitary activities. They may enjoy working independently rather than within a group. They may like talking about or focusing on personal feelings. Some children may initiate their own activities independent of what others are doing. When working with these children the professional may want to ensure that shared reading takes place in individual sessions in a quiet location. During reading or once the story is finished, conversations could focus on the child's feelings about various events in the story. Also, a noninterrupting reading style might be considered if the child wishes to listen to the story without disruption. When the reading session and conversations are completed, the child could be offered some time alone to explore the book independently if desired. The child could be encouraged to keep a journal about the books he or she has read. This could be done by photocopying the front book cover for the child to place in a folder. The child could then "rate" the story with a star system indicating how much he or she liked it.

Interpersonal   Children who exhibit interpersonal intelligence enjoy being with other people and participating in social activities. They may have several friends and may appear to be sensitive to their friends' moods and feelings. They like discussing information with others. For these children, small-group reading sessions could be considered. The professional could ask the child to invite a friend to join the reading session. The child may also enjoy story retelling with this peer once the reading session is completed. This child may be interested in a story discussion group with other children that focuses on sharing book ideas and recommendations. Activities that focus on developing pragmatic language skills during shared reading as described in Chapter 4 may be of interest to these children, too.

SUMMARY

Suggestions for modifying shared-reading sessions to complement one or more of a child's preferred intelligences have been outlined. These may be helpful in making the shared-reading experience more interesting and rewarding for reluctant readers. By using the general reading guidelines, accommodating a child's preferred intelligences, and ensuring positive outcomes, it is anticipated that most reluctant readers will accept books and shared reading to a greater degree. However, it may be unrealistic to expect that a reluctant reader will become an enthusiastic reader in just one or two sessions. Instead, it is more likely that change may be gradual as the professional becomes successful in linking the child's interests and preferred learning style with shared reading. The ultimate goal is to help the child accept and benefit from storybook reading at least to some degree. This is vital not only to the child's future academic success but also for ultimately accepting the role that books play in lifelong learning and reading for pleasure.

8

Shared Reading for Children with Special Needs

This chapter describes the importance of shared reading with children who have special needs. Strategies for establishing two foundation skills considered necessary for shared reading, attending and conversational turn taking, will be presented. A few suggestions for accommodations that may be made for children with particular disabilities are offered.

LANGUAGE AND LITERACY DEVELOPMENT FOR CHILDREN WITH SPECIAL NEEDS

Children with special needs are those who have unique qualities that affect their learning rates and styles. As a result, these children may learn more slowly than other children, and they may learn in different ways. Children with special needs may have diagnosed disabilities, such as mental retardation, autism, or sensory impairments. Or they may be children who have no diagnosed disability, yet seem to have trouble learning. This latter group includes children who, for no apparent reason, appear to develop a little more slowly than other children; for instance, they may be slow to walk, to say their first word, or to be toilet-trained. As preschoolers, these children may have difficulty learning the alphabet, acquiring fine motor skills (e.g., drawing, coloring), or interacting with others.

For all of these children, those with diagnosed disabilities and those with more subtle learning differences, early supports for language and literacy development are essential. As mentioned throughout this book, early book-reading experiences that enhance children's language and emergent literacy skills can provide the foundation for later academic achievements. The same is true for children with special learning needs. In fact, children who have learning difficulties require even more attention to language and literacy development than other children, as they are not as likely to acquire these skills as effortlessly as children without learning disabilities.

As young children, special learners have a variety of needs; for instance, they may need extra assistance in acquiring self-help skills such as feeding, toileting, bathing, and dressing. These needs are immediate and require considerable attention from parents and other caregivers. However, it is important not to overlook other areas of children's development such as language and literacy. Although the majority of research on literacy in young children has focused on children who are developing typically, studies that have looked specifically at children with special needs suggest that these youngsters have fewer literacy experiences than other children. For instance, Craig's (1996) research on literacy opportunities available in the homes of children with visual impairments suggested fewer print resources compared with other homes. Research on children with Down syndrome showed that although print resources in their homes were similar to print resources in the homes of other children, the children with Down syndrome had relatively little opportunity to interact with these resources (Fitzgerald, Roberts, Pierce, & Schuele, 1995). Parents of children with disabilities may have strong beliefs about the importance of supporting their children's language and literacy development, but they nonetheless experience many barriers to translating these beliefs into everyday practices that support their children (Goin, Nordquist, & Twardosz, 2004). When children with disabilities, even those with severe or profound disabilities, are provided ample opportunity to experience print through books and writing, they make considerable gains in language and literacy achievements (Katims, 1994).

Children with disabilities, like their typically developing peers, require high-quality, frequent opportunities to interact with written and oral language to foster their early and later achievements in language and literacy. Just like other children, children with even the most severe learning challenges may experience considerable language and literacy growth across the entire span of early childhood when ongoing supports are provided at home and at school. The opportunity to participate in quality shared-reading interactions with sensitive adults is a critical means to ensuring these gains. Although language and literacy may seem less important during the preschool years, they are vital for future academic and long-term success. Because of the critical period of development, which was discussed in Chapter 3, professionals must realize that with language and emergent literacy acquisition, time is of the essence.

FOUNDATION SKILLS FOR SHARED READING

Many children with disabilities love looking at storybooks, and, like their typically developing counterparts, they require ongoing encouragement to develop this interest. However, not all children with disabilities show an early or continued interest in book reading. Some estimates suggest that as many as 40% of children with disabilities may resist storybook reading interactions (Kaderavek & Sulzby, 1998a). When parents of children with disabilities were interviewed by Goin and colleagues (2004), several noted that their children became less interested in books as they made gains in mobility, and that they "were easily distracted and would not sit for as long as they had prior to achieving independent mobility" (p. 205).

For children whose positive regard for shared reading wanes over time, or for those who have never developed this preference, professionals may need to "set the stage" for effective shared reading. Depending on the severity of a child's problem, it may be necessary to establish a few prerequisite skills so that children are able to fully participate in the shared-reading process. To implement the strategies presented in this book, children will need to bring to the activity at least two foundation skills: 1) an ability to attend to the task and 2) an ability to take conversational turns. Attending, at least for several minutes at a time, is essential for the child to become aware of the activity and to acquire information from it. Conversational turn taking, which is an ability to initiate or respond to a conversational partner, will be needed for discussing ideas and concepts. Children who are able to attend and participate in shared reading through conversational turn taking will be positioned to benefit from this activity to the fullest extent for language and emergent literacy acquisition.

In the authors' opinion, attending and turn taking will need to be established before any other skills are to be emphasized because when a child remains inattentive or unresponsive, his or her skill acquisition will be hindered. Many children with moderate to severe developmental delays may need to begin at this foundation level. If a child is already able to attend and take conversational turns appropriately during the reading of at least one brief storybook, then working to establish these skills will be unnecessary. However, in the event that these skills remain undeveloped, some strategies for assisting children in acquiring them are provided in the following sections.

Attending Strategy

Joint attention or shared attention is one of the most essential prerequisites for children's early learning, and it refers to occasions in which children and adults share a mutual focus of attention on an object such as a toy, a book, a clothing item, or food (Adamson & Chance, 1998). Children who are typically developing engage in brief periods of joint attention by about 5 or 6 months of age, and periods of sustained joint attention increase gradually as they mature. By 18 months of age, children are able to skillfully execute their coordination of attention with adults in frequent, sustained periods of joint attention (Adamson & Chance, 1998). What is important here is that early and sustained joint attention is a critical developmental achievement in which children "master ways of interrelating their own interests with those of their social partners" and that learning in early childhood is more than learning specific skills (Adamson & Chance, 1998, p. 30). Engaging in sustained periods of joint attention focused on books is a crucial achievement for furthering children's language and literacy skills in the shared-reading context.

For children with developmental disabilities, the achievement of joint attention may occur at a much slower pace relative to children without disabilities. Some experts believe that the inability to engage in periods of joint attention is a major impediment to learning for children with disabilities, as joint attention is a critical avenue to language and literacy development during early childhood. Difficulties with joint attention may also likely contribute to the increased prevalence of reading resistance seen in children with disabilities (Kaderavek & Sulzby, 1998a) and to the delays in language and literacy development for these youngsters. Therefore, promoting attending behaviors is an important and necessary goal for children with disabilities as well as for others who have difficulty sustaining joint attention to books. During shared reading, indicators of attending behaviors may include sitting quietly, listening to the story, looking at or pointing to illustrations, and asking questions or making comments about the story. All of these behaviors demonstrate on-task, attending behaviors. Increasing attending is appropriate for children who do not tolerate shared reading well in that they tend to leave the reading session before a book has been completed. If a child attends for the reading of only one or two pages before becoming distracted and leaving the session, then implementing the attending strategy may be appropriate.

It should be noted that at times it may be difficult to determine whether a child's behavior is due to poor attending skills or reflects a resistance to shared reading, as it is possible for resistant behavior to have emerged from an attending problem initially. There are no definitive guidelines for this, but seeing the child's pattern of behavior will usually indicate which behavior is evident. For example, a child's resistant behavior may include a refusal to participate, general whining, or an aggressive outburst, but when attending is a problem, the child may simply walk away from the adult to become involved in another activity. This child may be able to be redirected back to the reading session at a later time, whereas a reluctant reader may show continued resistance.

A long-range goal would be to gradually increase the length of time children remain focused on a book, until eventually they are able to participate during shared reading of an entire book. For example, if a child loses interest after three pages, a first step would be to aim for completion of four pages. The next goal might be five pages, then six pages, and so forth. It is not realistic to expect children, especially those with special needs, to improve their attending skills by several minutes in a single session. Attending for several minutes longer over a period of several weeks might be a more reasonable expectation.

Setting a Goal   It is suggested that a short-term goal be established so that a child's progress may be viewed in sequential steps. The goal could be in length of time (e.g., attending for 5 minutes) or in the number of pages read (e.g., attending through six pages), depending on the professional's preference for method of measurement. The important point is to have a target for which to aim. It is suggested that a written record of the child's daily progress be maintained in order to monitor his or her improvement. Once the child achieves the first goal, a new short-term goal can be established. Continue in this way until the child is able to sit and attend for an entire storybook.

Conducting the Reading Session   Select a storybook with minimal text (e.g., no more than one or two lines of print per page) and colorful, attractive illustrations. Read the story using an enthusiastic manner and appropriate inflection to help maintain the child's attention. Point out interesting features of the pictures and interject occasional questions to keep the child actively involved. Whenever possible, give the child a role in the reading session such as turning the pages. Be sure to pause for the child to look at the pictures and talk about what he or she sees. When the target time has been achieved or the target page has been completed, praise the child by saying, for example, "You did a nice job of helping me read today," "I really liked how you sat so still," or "You did a great job listening to this story!" At this point, it is recommended that the professional end the reading session by saying, "Let's stop here and read some more tomorrow to see what happens." Stopping while the child is still attentive allows the session to finish on a positive note (i.e., with praise) and before the child begins to squirm or walk away. It is desirable for the child to associate positive feelings with shared reading rather than negative ones. If the reading session goes too long, the child is likely to tire, lose interest, and exhibit frustration. Stopping a little too early while the child is still engaged is better than stopping too late when the child is beginning to show signs of frustration.

In the event that the child leaves before the target time or target page has been reached, do not try to force him or her to continue. Insisting that the reading session continue is often counterproductive and may impede future reading attempts. Likewise, little will be gained from scolding the child for leaving the session. Doing so will make storybook reading a negative experience rather than a positive one. Instead, simply ask the child if he or she wants to stop so you can determine if the child intends to return to the session right away or not. If the choice is to stop, consider if any adjustments may be needed for the next reading session (e.g., changing storybooks, selecting a different time of day, reducing potential distractions in the room) so that the child's goal may be achieved next time. A summary of this strategy may be found in Table 8.1.

Turn-Taking Strategy

Turn taking refers to a pragmatic or social custom whereby two (or more) speaking partners contribute to a conversation through a

Table 8.1.   Suggestions for increasing attending skills

Determine current attending behavior by observing how long the child attends in two separate shared-reading sessions.

Establish an attending goal measured in either length of time or number of pages.

Select an attractive book with a limited amount of print on a topic that might interest the child. Read the story with enthusiasm. Give the child a role such as turning the pages or lifting flaps to reveal additional pictures or words.

When the target time or page has been reached, praise the child for paying attention (e.g., "You did a great job listening to the story!") and then end the session. Keep a record of the child's attending time (measured in minutes or number of pages) for each session.

Set new goals and continue with the same strategy until the child is able to attend to the entire reading of one brief storybook.

back-and-forth exchange. A conversational turn may be verbal, vocal, or nonverbal and may consist of asking a question, providing an answer, or making a comment that contributes to the topic.

Conversational turn taking is what makes shared reading an interactive and dialogic event rather than one in which one person does all of the talking. Promoting the dialogue and interaction of shared reading has consistently been shown to accelerate children's early language developments (e.g., length of utterance, receptive vocabulary; Whitehurst et al., 1988). Consequently, turn taking is vital for both the adult and the child to be full and equal partners during shared reading.

This strategy is intended for children who remain passive, unresponsive, and/or verbally reticent during shared reading. These children may remain silent when questions are posed to them, or they may ignore a request to point to a particular picture. When a conversational turn is offered to them, it is rarely, if ever, taken. If a child consistently responds to most of the conversational turns offered, he or she has already developed this foundation skill, and the strategy presented below will be unnecessary.

When considering the child's turn-taking contributions, it is important to ensure that conversational turns are offered by the adult. When children remain passive or verbally reticent, adults may compensate by dominating the session in ways that eventually "squeeze out" the child's turn-taking opportunities. Also, children's responsiveness may vary such that some children enjoy interacting after the story is completed rather than while the story is being read. Therefore, it is suggested that professionals determine the frequency and type of turn-taking opportunities offered to the child, whether offered during the reading session or before and after the session. For children who continue to show passivity or verbal reticence across a variety of adult interaction styles and after numerous turn-taking opportunities are offered, an explicit focus on building the child's engagement in conversational turn taking is recommended.

Types of Turns   Conversational turns may consist of verbal, vocal, or nonverbal responses. Any type of turn is a desirable outcome because it demonstrates a child's response and promotes interaction with the conversational partner. Verbal turns occur when a child poses a question, makes a statement, or answers a question using words. For example, if the professional asks, "What is Spot doing in this picture?" a child's verbal turn might be, "He's decorating the cake." Also, a child may initiate a turn-taking sequence by asking, "What's that?" or by making a comment, "Spot's bowl." Vocal turns occur when a sound is produced rather than a word. For instance, a child could answer the question "What sound does the cow make?" by saying "moo" or by initiating a turn sequence by pointing to a picture of a cow and saying "moo." Sounds need not be limited to animal sounds. For instance, mechanical sounds might include sounds for cars, planes, trains, telephones, or clocks, and human sounds might consist of whistling, snoring, or humming. Children with more severe communicative impairments may use only vocal means to communicate, and thus may communicate or take turns through specific sounds. Nonverbal turns are when a pointing response or some other action is provided. For example, a child would respond to the request "Show me a mouse on this page" by pointing to the mouse in the picture. A child may take a nonverbal turn by responding to other requests such as turning the page, lifting a flap, or touching a picture. Of course, when yes/no questions are presented (e.g., "Is this Spot's daddy?"), children may respond nonverbally using head nods. Generally speaking, nonverbal turns are easiest for children provided they are capable of moving their hands or nodding their heads. Vocal turns are easier than verbal ones because only sound rather than speech is required. Verbal turns are the most demanding because language is required. The reader should be aware of one type of turn that is nonverbal but does involve language, and that is sign language. Some children with limited speech may communicate through sign language or a combination of limited speech and sign language together. For the purposes of this discussion, the reader is asked to consider use of sign language as a verbal turn even though it is not produced through speech.

Setting a Goal   Before shared reading begins, select a goal for the child so that a specific type of target response is determined. To do this, it is important to know the types of turns, if any, that a child already takes. Therefore, it is suggested that a baseline reading session be conducted in which at least five opportunities for turn taking are offered to the child. While reading the story, elicit turns using the following two strategies: 1) ask the child questions about the story and the pictures and 2) make comments about the story and pictures followed by generous pauses. Any response on the part of the child—verbal, vocal, or nonverbal—would be viewed as a turn. It is unimportant whether the child's answer or comment is accurate, as the goal is to document and expand communicative routines. Count how many times out of five opportunities that the child takes a conversational turn. If the child uses three to five opportunities to take a conversational turn, then no further work to establish turn-taking behavior may be needed. If the child responds to fewer than three opportunities, then it may be beneficial to focus on increasing the child's turn-taking behavior. It should be noted that when the child does engage in a turn sequence, the professional should re-spond to the child's turn by acknowledging the turn and repeating or extending the child's utterance. Doing this shows the child that the professional is aware of the child's contribution and recognizes its communicative value.

The child's current mode of response will provide some guidance on which mode of turn taking to target for further development. If the child uses speech for at least one conversational turn (when five are offered), it would be appropriate to increase the frequency of that type of turn. If the child did not produce any conversational turn or did not use any verbal or vocal turns when provided the opportunity, then nonverbal turn taking may be targeted, as this may be easier for the child to achieve in the beginning. Remember to move from easi-est to most difficult (i.e., nonverbal to vocal, to verbal responses) so that the child will achieve success early on. Always keep in mind that the overall goal is to promote shared-reading conversations that are interactive and balanced so that both the professional and the child participate equally.

Conducting the Reading Session   Once a child's turn-taking goal has been determined, it may be helpful to select a book that will promote the type of turn taking being emphasized. For instance, if the child's goal is nonverbal turn taking, a book containing a lift-the-flap feature may provide several natural opportunities for nonverbal responding when the professional asks, "Can you see what's under here?" or "Open the door so we can see what's inside." Of course, any book may be used if no such book is available. Nonverbal turn taking could be requests for the child to turn the pages or point to pictures. If vocal turns are targeted responses, a book that contains bird, animal, or object sounds may be useful. For verbal responses, any book with simple vocabulary words would be appropriate.

During shared reading, intersperse a few opportunities for conversational turn taking, but do not overwhelm the child with multiple requests. As a guide, it may be reasonable to offer five to eight opportunities per session. When a turn is provided, wait at least 10 seconds for the child to respond. If no response is given within 10 seconds, then provide a prompt to assist the child in responding. If the target goal is a nonverbal turn, *gently* guide the child's hand to perform the requested action. Then immediately provide praise to the child for taking this turn. If the target goal is a vocal or verbal turn, model the correct response by making the requested sound or statement. Then ask the child to make the sound or say the words that he or she just heard. When the child makes any attempt at saying the sound or word, give praise. Once the child has taken a conversational turn, resume reading the book. Repeat this procedure for all subsequent turn-taking opportunities. Always provide assistance if the child is unable to provide a conversational turn independently after waiting for 10 seconds. Also, be sure to praise the child whenever a response is given, even if the content of the response is incorrect or assistance is provided. At the end of the reading session, be sure to praise the child again for answering the questions or for following instructions. When the session is completed, it is suggested that the professional record the number of conversational turns the child took and note whether these required assistance. Doing so will help monitor the child's progress and determine when the goal has been achieved.

As the child becomes increasingly responsive through this strategy, less assistance may be required and the adult should gradually relinquish control. What once required gentle physical guidance (e.g., placing the child's finger on the requested picture) may need only a verbal prompt (e.g., "Put your finger on it"). Also, response latency, that is, the time it takes for the child to respond, may gradually shorten (e.g., response time is 5 seconds rather than 10 seconds). All of these changes in a child's response show improved performance and should be considered significant gains in turn-taking behavior. The ultimate goal is for the child to be consistent in conversational turn taking, whether these turns are nonverbal, vocal, or verbal. For the child to become more consistent, the adult must gradually and sensitively withdraw support from the child so that the child may ultimately achieve independence. Once the child is consistent in attending and turn taking, shared reading may shift its focus to developing other skills. See Table 8.2 for a brief summary of turn-taking strategies.

SUGGESTED ACCOMMODATIONS FOR SPECIAL LEARNERS DURING SHARED READING

Once the two foundation skills of attending and conversational turn taking have been established, children will be prepared to be full and active participants in shared reading. Their active participation will open the door to acquiring further knowledge, such as language and emergent literacy, through the strategies described in Chapters 4 and 6. However, the professional may need to make a few accommoda-

Table 8.2.   Suggestions for increasing turn-taking skills

Determine the child's current turn-taking frequency by conducting a shared-reading session and offering five conversational turn-taking opportunities. Note the types of turns, if any, that the child takes (i.e., nonverbal, vocal, or verbal).

Establish a turn-taking goal by specifying the turn type to be targeted (e.g., five vocal turns during one reading session).

During shared reading, offer the child at least five opportunities to take a conversational turn by providing a comment or asking a question and then waiting at least 10 seconds for the child to respond.

If the child fails to respond after 10 seconds, provide assistance. Assistance for a nonverbal prompt would be gentle physical guidance to complete the response (e.g., guiding the child's finger to point to a picture of a train). For vocal or verbal prompts, provide the correct answer (e.g., "choo choo" for a vocal response, "train" for a verbal response) and ask the child to try saying it, too.

Praise the child when he or she responds in any way, as this constitutes a completed conversational turn.

Keep a record of the child's number and types of turns taken during each reading session, and note whether assistance was required. A long-term goal would be consistent and independent responding to all turn-taking opportunities using the form of turn most appropriate for the child (i.e., nonverbal, vocal, or verbal).

tions for some children depending on their particular impairments. A few of these accommodations are described below.

Visual Impairment

When children have a severe visual impairment, they may participate in shared reading in the same way as others except for viewing the book's illustrations. Although they may be able to see little if any of the illustrations, they can listen to the story and participate in conversations. As these children develop, they often become skilled listeners and will appreciate storytime opportunities. Nonetheless, a few reading guidelines are offered. First, because these children rely on their listening skills without visual support, it is important to read in a quiet setting to reduce auditory distractions. Considering that these children will not benefit from the normal visual input, reading should be animated so that it includes variation in pitch and volume to maintain children's interest. Also, providing some description of what appears in the illustrations may be beneficial once the text on a page has been read. Do not avoid using phrases such as "Over here we see . . ." or "This looks . . ." because individuals with visual impairments use these terms, too. Pausing is important; give these children time to process what they hear and to formulate questions if desired. For very young children, presenting objects for exploration when new words are presented in the story may be beneficial. For example, when reading *Spot Bakes a Cake* (Hill, 1994), some items that may be new to the child could be presented when they are mentioned (e.g., a bar of chocolate, eggs, a spoon, a cake pan). This strategy helps the story come alive for these children and improves their comprehension. Professionals may wish to consult a vision specialist for materials and instructional strategies if early braille exposure is desired.

Auditory Impairment

Children with auditory impairment may vary widely in their abilities. Some may speak whereas others may use sign language, and signing skills may range from elementary to advanced. Hearing aids and cochlear implants are commonly seen with young children, although some may use no adaptive device at all. As this illustrates, professionals will need to know how best to communicate with these children before shared reading is conducted. Therefore, consultation with the child's speech-language pathologist, audiologist, or parent is recommended.

If the child is verbal and is able to receive some auditory input, then the professional should be seated on the child's preferred side (i.e., next to the child's best ear). Be sure that surrounding noise is kept to a minimum so that it will not interfere with the child's speech perception. The child may wish to watch the reader's face to capture visual speech cues rather than look at the illustrations during reading. If that is the case, be sure to give the child time to return his or her gaze to the book to examine the pictures once the text has been read. Pausing is also important for these children because children may take time to process what they hear and see before they are ready to move on. Consider allowing these children to turn the pages, which will help them control the pace of the activity.

As another option, professionals might consider use of an amplification system for promoting signal-to-noise quality of shared-reading sessions. One recent study showed the benefit to children's literacy development of conducting shared-reading sessions in a classroom containing a sound field system (Pillow, Justice, & Gray, 2004). In this study, a speech-language pathologist read storybooks with a small group of children with language disabilities over a 3-month period while using a sound field system. Compared with the children who were read to in normal listening conditions, those children whose shared reading featured the sound field system made greater gains in phonological awareness during the 3-month period.

When a child communicates through sign language, the professional may wish to review the story in advance to be certain that signs for all the words are known. A comprehensive sign-language dictionary will be a valuable resource in this regard. During shared reading, the child may be expected to watch the reader rather than look at the book when the text is presented and during conversation. It is recommended that the professional use animated facial expressions to help communicate the feelings that the story conveys. Be sure to pause frequently for the child to process information and to examine the pictures before moving on. Also, be sure to take time to teach the child signs for any new words that appear in the book.

Autism

Professionals may expect to conduct reading sessions in much the same way as they normally would; however, the behavior of children with autism may pose some challenges. Consultation in advance with the child's behavior specialist and speech-language pathologist may help the professional develop an individualized strategy for shared reading with this child. One behavior that is typically seen with these children is an insistence on following a specific routine. This routine could include how the room is arranged, what the child holds in his or her hands, or what book is read. In fact, it may be difficult for these children to accept any book but their favorite one. If the child's routine is disrupted in some way, such as by introducing a new book, he or she may demonstrate inappropriate behaviors such as hitting, biting, or yelling. This is when the wisdom of advance planning and consultation with other professionals becomes evident, for if the child is appeased in one instance, his or her insistence may be even stronger on subsequent occasions. Thus, knowing how to handle this situation in a calm and consistent way will be in the best interest of the child.

Another common behavior seen with these children is echolalia, which is an immediate or delayed repetition of what another person says. Sometimes echolalic behavior can interfere with shared reading because the child repeats whatever he or she hears. When children show echolalic tendencies, it is recommended that their speech-language pathologist be consulted for the best strategy to use when this occurs. Consistency of approach with these children is vitally important.

Language Impairment

Language impairment refers to a situation when children do not develop language in the typical way that others do. For example, their babbling may include primarily vowels rather than both consonants and vowels, they may not reach the usual developmental milestones at the expected time (e.g., speaking first words at age 2 rather than at age 1), or one area of language may be severely delayed whereas the others appear to be on track. It is common for language problems to accompany other problems; however, it is possible for language impairment to be a child's only known problem. It is especially important that children with language impairment receive an abundance of shared-reading opportunities to promote language growth and development. Experts have argued that language impairment is the most well-established risk factor impeding children's timely literacy development, thus increasing the likelihood of exhibiting reading disability during the elementary years (McCardle, Scarborough, & Catts, 2001).

All of the strategies proposed in Chapter 4 that focus on language development would be relevant for children with language impairment. For children who have not yet begun to speak, emphasis could be placed on receptive language development as well as expression of single words. Those who already speak in single words could be encouraged to lengthen their utterances to two-word productions, and children speaking in short sentences could be assisted with adding morphological information such as verb endings and plurals. These examples illustrate how the various language strategies may be used with children at any stage of development.

As for the reading session itself, it is suggested that the professional avoid reading too fast for the child to comprehend, especially using books with more than one line of text per page. Give the child time to process the language through frequent pausing. Be alert for possible misunderstandings and take time to explain concepts if the child appears to be confused. Explain the meaning of words that may be new for the child. Also, consider repeated readings of the same book so that the child has several opportunities to develop a working knowledge of new concepts and words.

Mental Retardation

Mental retardation refers to subaverage intellectual functioning that affects children's learning potential and adaptive behavior. The range of mental retardation is wide and varies from mild to profound. The greater the degree of mental retardation present, the more a child's language development will be affected. Thus, during the preschool years, children with mild mental retardation may be verbal but delayed with respect to typical developmental milestones, whereas those with profound mental retardation may be nonverbal and exhibit low receptive-language abilities.

Professionals reading with children who have mental retardation may follow the same general guidelines as those described for children with language impairment. The various strategies for enhancing language growth described in Chapter 4 may be applied based on the child's level of development. However, for those with severe and profound mental retardation, attending and conversational turn taking may need to be developed first.

One characteristic of children with mental retardation is a problem generalizing newly acquired information to different situations.

This problem may be reflected during shared reading when the professional sees that a child is able to identify the picture for a new vocabulary word only in the book in which the word was first presented but in no others. Consequently, it would be helpful to these children if shared reading could include a variety of books so that generalization of new skills may be enhanced from the very beginning. Avoid doing repeated readings of the same book on a series of consecutive days. Instead, it is suggested that the professional intermix new books with familiar books across reading sessions.

INVOLVING PARENTS OF CHILDREN WITH SPECIAL NEEDS

For all children with special needs, it is critical that professionals invite parents to assume an active role in their children's development. Because many of these children experience brief attention spans, reading sessions may last no more than 5 or 10 minutes at a time. It may be unrealistic to expect preschool children with special needs to attend for longer periods of time, so a natural solution would be to increase the number of reading sessions that occur throughout the day. Engaging parents through home reading programs is one way to accomplish this objective. If parents could conduct brief reading sessions on a regular basis to supplement the shared reading that occurs in the child's preschool or child care setting, then greater strides will be made in the child's acquisition of language and emergent literacy. Professionals are referred to Chapter 9 for suggestions and guidelines in establishing effective home reading programs.

9

Promoting Shared Reading in the Home Environment

Children who grow up in book oriented homes begin to learn to read when they are held in their parents' arms and are read their first nursery rhyme, story, or jingle.

—David B. Doake (1986, p. 3)

Dr. David Doake's quote emphasizes that the earliest beginnings of children's language and literacy acquisition occur at home in the lap of their caregivers. Children with access to books and to quality reading experiences in their homes have more rapid language and literacy development compared with children without such advantages, and they are more able to enter school ready to learn. And although early childhood educational programs can do much to help children develop strong language and literacy skills, there is little substitute for the power of children's rich, positive, and frequent experiences with books within their homes under the sensitive guidance of a parent.

The National Research Council's Committee on the Prevention of Reading Difficulties in Young Children, chaired by Harvard University's Catherine Snow (Snow et al., 1998), was organized to describe ways in which reading difficulties can be prevented among school children. In considering proactive solutions to reading problems, this committee stressed the vital importance of young children's immersion in positive, frequent experiences that directly foster their language and emergent literacy growth in the home environment. One language-rich experience emphasized by the committee is shared storybook reading. Storybook reading experiences are important to children who are developing typically, as well as those who have language, cognitive, or other types of developmental challenges. Indeed, for children with special needs, the committee advised that storybook reading and other language-rich experiences be offered in greater frequency and intensity and be of the highest quality to ensure children's acquisition of essential skills (Snow et al., 1998). The design and implementation of programs that encourage shared reading in the home is a fundamental responsibility of early childhood professionals. Home reading programs are viewed as indispensable for all children, especially those who exhibit developmental challenges or other special circumstances, such as being reared in poverty or acquiring English as a second language.

With so much public attention directed toward improving children's literacy skills in this country, many children in the United States now experience regular storybook reading in their homes. However, professionals who work with young children and their families know that shared reading is not a commonplace event in every household. Data collected from parents through the National Household Education Survey of 1995 (National Center for Education Statistics, 1995) reveal, for instance, that 4 of 10 U.S. children under 6 years of age are read to every day, but 2 of 10 U.S. children under 6 years of age are never read to (Yarosz & Barnett, 2001).

Considering the importance of regular shared reading in the home, it is a grave concern that 20% of U.S. children experience no reading in their home environment and that only 40% of parents report shared reading to be a daily experience. Knowing the potential benefits of regular shared reading at home and the need for more families to adopt this important practice, professionals are encouraged to work with parents to establish and support quality shared-reading experiences in the home.

Designing and implementing a home reading program for parents is one way that professionals can have widespread influence on children's lives. Professionals who work with families and children realize that there is much they cannot control in children's lives. Sometimes, professionals see children for only a few minutes each week. For instance, an SLP who works with a child for 30 minutes each week knows that enlisting the child's parent to provide daily practice could result in more rapid development than the 30-minute session can bring about alone. Some professionals have much more time with children (e.g., a child care provider who cares for a child for 40 hours each week). However, even these professionals recognize the great impact of the home and parents on the child's development. After all, even children enrolled in full-time child care or preschool still spend more time at home.

A successful home reading program informs parents about language and emergent literacy development of children, explains the role of parents in encouraging these skills, provides reading materials or suggestions for selecting appropriate storybooks, instructs parents in effective shared-reading practices, and encourages parents to establish a regular reading habit with their children. When parents understand the importance of shared reading for their children and receive instruction and continued support for establishing this routine at home, the program is likely to succeed and endure.

In this chapter, practical suggestions will equip professionals in designing and supporting home reading programs for the children they serve. Essential elements for creating successful programs are presented and discussed. Some low-cost options are suggested for professionals on a tight budget. Also, answers to some common questions frequently raised by parents about home reading are offered.

STRUCTURE AND OBJECTIVES OF HOME READING PROGRAMS

The general goal of a home reading program is to inform and instruct parents about the importance and benefits of early reading experiences and to establish a habit of regular and effective shared reading with their children. A home reading program is an instructional program designed by a professional specifically for parents to increase the quality and quantity of shared-reading experiences in the home. At a minimum, objectives should include increasing 1) parents' knowledge about their children's language and literacy development, 2) parents' understanding of their role in promoting their children's development, 3) parents' understanding of how shared reading may be designed to enhance development, 4) the quality of parent–child shared reading in the home environment, and 5) the quantity of parent–child shared reading in the home environment. These goals are substantial in both their breadth and depth, and may be a bit daunting on first appearance. However, the parents themselves often will contribute energy and enthusiasm in making reading programs successful. Based on the personal experience of the authors, the appreciation of the parents and the success of the children make any home reading program well worth the effort.

To achieve the first several objectives, professionals will need to provide information to parents. This may be done face to face in individual or group meetings. These meetings will provide an opportunity for parents to learn how children typically acquire language and emergent literacy skills, how children may acquire these skills through shared reading at home, and how parents can promote this development through specific shared-reading techniques. Once parents have received this information and instruction, they will be prepared to begin home reading with their children. At this point, the professional may need to consult with parents to determine the frequency and time of day that shared reading will occur. Regular follow-up conversations about how shared-reading sessions are progressing will be needed to help parents stay motivated and to problem-solve when issues arise.

PLANNING A HOME READING PROGRAM

When offering a home reading program for parents and their children, the professional is encouraged to plan its scope and duration in advance. In the following sections, some suggestions are offered for determining needed resources, length of the program, and content to be covered. The importance of including parents from non–English-speaking homes, with low socioeconomic status, and with children who have disabilities is discussed. Also, particulars about parents' access to children's books, reading schedules, record keeping, and follow-up procedures are described.

Determine Resources Needed

In determining how to deliver quality home reading programs, decisions must be made concerning the cost of the program. When creating a program that may be several weeks in duration, cost is always an important consideration. To the extent possible, programs should be offered at no or minimal cost to parents to ensure the accessibility of home reading programs to those families with the greatest need. However, even low-budget programs will have at least some costs. These may include the professionals' time for developing and implementing the program, instructional materials (e.g., storybooks, instruction manuals, tape recorders for home use), parking and transportation, child care for children when they accompany their parents to meetings, adequate meeting space, and refreshments. If some or all parents are not native English speakers, translation services may be required as well.

Although such costs can add up quickly, several methods can keep costs down so that parents can participate free of charge or for a minimal fee. For instance, professionals (including translators) could donate their time to plan and implement the program; publishers or local bookstores could donate books and other instructional materials; if advertising is needed, it could be created using inexpensive computer software; and if child care is required for children who must accompany their parents to meetings, high school or college students interested in experience with children could be recruited as volunteers. When a large meeting space must be found, local businesses, schools, hospitals, or libraries may be willing to donate meeting rooms. If refreshments are planned for meetings, they could be donated by local bakeries or grocery stores.

As an alternative to seeking donated items and space, it may be possible to find a business, foundation, or agency to underwrite a home reading program. Many organizations are interested in sponsoring such programs as a way of showing their community involvement. When that is the case, funding could be donated by one or more underwriters that will cover all program costs in exchange for being recognized as a program sponsor on all services, materials, gifts, and advertisements. Another possible option is to seek funding through grants available from local, state, or federal sources that provide financial support for projects dedicated to home literacy. In short, because most professionals, organizations, and communities realize the importance of supporting home reading activities, home reading programs can be designed and implemented relatively inexpensively on a shoestring budget so that costs need not be a barrier to delivering a high-quality program.

Determine Program Length

It is suggested that a defined time period for a home reading program be the starting point for planning. A defined time period may solicit more interest and participation from parents than a program that is ongoing for an indefinite time period. For example, a preschool may decide to offer a 4-, 6-, or 8-week program each autumn for all parents. These programs could recruit parents of newly enrolled children or could serve as refresher programs for parents of continuing children. The amount of information, instruction, and discussion to be included will help guide the professional in deciding how many weeks a program should run.

The length of the program to be offered may be determined also by the resources available, not the least of which is the professional's time. When establishing a home reading program for the first time, professionals will need several hours for developing instructional materials, planning agendas for weekly meetings, finding a meeting place, and making arrangements for child care, parking, and refreshments. If funding from a community sponsor is desired, considerable time may be required for finding one or more sponsors to cover costs. However, once this foundation has been established, planning for subsequent programs will be easier and less time consuming because it may be possible to repeat or refine the plans from the initial experience. Professionals may also consider enlisting the assistance of one or more volunteers when organizing a home reading program for the first time.

Determine Participants

Home reading programs may be beneficial to all parents regardless of how often they read to their children. Parents with first-born children may benefit from learning about children's language and emergent literacy development as well as acquiring specific techniques to be used during shared reading. For experienced parents who do not read to their children regularly, getting the reading habit started will be the major objective. For those who do read regularly, participation in a home reading program may help them to improve or refine their reading techniques. Remember, too, that shared-reading procedures may need to be adjusted over time as children grow and develop more language sophistication. This means that eventually all parents may benefit from refresher courses that focus on the changing concerns of their children.

One group for whom participation in a home reading program would be particularly advantageous is maternal caregivers who do not have an education beyond the twelfth grade. In fact, one variable that appears particularly influential on the likelihood of regular shared reading in the home is maternal education (Teale, 1986). Maternal education serves as a marker of socioeconomic status, correlating strongly with household income, and it also correlates well with mothers' own reading behaviors and preferences (Symons, Szuszkiewicz, & Bonnell, 1996). In general, the more educated the maternal caregiver, the more likely children are read to frequently in the home (Yarosz & Barnett, 2001). In 62% of English-speaking U.S. households in which mothers are college educated, mothers report reading to their preschool children every day. The converse is also true: the less educated the maternal caregiver, the less likely children are read to at all in the home. Consider that in English-speaking U.S. households in which the mother has less than a 12th-grade education, 20% of preschoolers are never read to compared with just 10% of preschoolers when the mother has completed high school. In non–English-speaking households in which the mother has less than a 12th-grade education, 50% of preschoolers are never read to; this drops to 25% when the mother has completed high school (Yarosz & Barnett, 2001).

It is worth noting that the relationship between maternal education and home reading practices is not as simple as these data might suggest. In homes that are headed by mothers who are not well educated, chronic maternal depression and parenting stress are observed more frequently compared with homes headed by well-educated mothers (National Institute on Child Health and Human Development [NICHD], Early Child Care Research Network, 1999). Maternal education also tends to be lower for immigrant families, particularly when the parents are not native speakers of English.

Beyond maternal education and socioeconomic status, it is also worth noting that in some homes, book reading may not be viewed as important for children as other activities. This may be true for children who exhibit a disability and whose other needs may seem more pressing, such as learning toileting or basic self-care skills (Marvin & Mirenda, 1993). For example, children with cerebral palsy may miss out on important literacy experiences because of the time devoted to developing motor, speech, and self-care skills. Although parents' efforts in promoting the health and overall development of their children with disabilities should be commended, professionals need to provide special supports so that a focus on language and emergent literacy can be included as well. Early childhood educators and professionals working with young children are cautioned against assuming that home reading is a routine occurrence for the children they serve, even when homes are advantaged and the parents are well educated.

Therefore, it is recommended that professionals who work with young children consider inviting all families to participate in home reading programs.

Determine Meeting Location

If a professional's workplace has insufficient space to accommodate a group of parents, it is necessary to find an alternative setting. Suggestions include public or private schools, hospitals, libraries, community colleges, or local community centers. As an example, a 5-week home reading program offered by the authors was delivered at a speech and hearing clinic at a public university (Ezell, Justice, & Parsons, 2000). When selecting an appropriate space, at least four points should be considered. First, think about the number of participants expected to attend and try to find an appropriately sized room that is accessible to people with disabilities. Having a meeting room that is too large or too small can make participants uncomfortable and ill at ease. Also, accessibility for people with disabilities ensures that everyone can participate. Second, keep in mind the instructional methods planned. For instance, the availability of video equipment will be needed if parents will be viewing videotapes. If small-group discussions will be employed, the room may need to be arranged with moveable chairs and small tables. Third, if child care will be offered to parents while they attend the meetings, one or more rooms that are close by will be needed for this purpose. These rooms should be child friendly with safety devices in electrical outlets and low-pile carpeting on the floor. Fourth, availability of parking and public transportation should be considered. An adequate number of parking spaces for all participants should be conveniently provided. Avoid locations that are off the beaten path and difficult to find. Remember, too, that some parents may need to use public transportation, so be certain that this is close by if needed.

Determine Program Content

In planning a home reading program, professionals may wish to emphasize three primary topics: 1) the sequence of children's typical language and emergent literacy development, 2) the parents' role in promoting children's development through shared reading, and 3) the techniques to be used by parents during shared reading to assist children's development in these areas. Generally speaking, presenting these major topics in the order stated may help parents understand the rationale for shared reading at home, which is of primary importance. Regarding this rationale, a brief explanation of the nature of shared reading will help parents understand their role in children's development. Figure 9.1 may be used to describe the complexities of shared reading. In this model, all of the variables interact with and influence one another. This means that the child's current skills and attitudes toward shared reading are influenced by parental beliefs and shared-reading practices and vice versa. Providing such a rationale for parental involvement might serve as an introductory topic of reading instruction as seen in the sample home reading program outlined in Table 9.1.

Children's Typical Language and Emergent Literacy Development   A high-quality home reading program will provide a foundation of knowledge about children's development in language and literacy. This basic information may include 1) a definition of language and children's major developmental milestones, 2) a definition of emergent literacy and major milestones, and 3) a description of the relationship between early language and literacy and later academic achievements. Much of this background information is provided in Chapters 3 and 5 of this book, although the professional may wish to

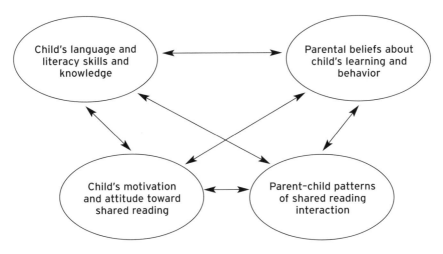

Figure 9.1.   The multidimensional nature of parent-child shared reading. (*Source:* Stone, Bradley, & Kleiner, 2002.)

Table 9.1.   Sample outline of a 6-week home reading program

Session (1 hr)	Topic of meeting	Home activity for parents
Week 1	Introduction Program goals Parents examine their current reading style	Tape record shared reading of three books (provided); listen to the tapes and write down some of your comments and questions and how your child responded.
Week 2	Information provided about children's language and emergent literacy development	Go to the library with your child and look through five different books; explore each book from a language and emergent literacy perspective (e.g., new vocabulary words, use of morphological structures, print features); select two books and write down ideas for shared reading; check out these books to use next week.
Week 3	Information provided about parents' role in children's development through shared reading	Read the two library books selected last week to your child three times and tape record the sessions; listen to the tapes. How does your reading change with repeated readings? Does your child respond differently in the second or third reading?
Week 4	Information provided about reading techniques for developing language and emergent literacy skills	Read three books to your child this week (provided); try three different reading techniques for language and emergent literacy during shared reading; make notes on how your child responds to each one.
Week 5	General techniques for increasing reading effectiveness with your child	Read four books to your child this week (provided); try four of the general techniques during shared reading; make notes on how your child responds to each one.
Week 6	Staying motivated to continue shared reading Home reading program evaluation	

supplement what is provided with additional material. All information should be presented simply and clearly by avoiding overly technical terms and jargon that may be unfamiliar to parents. This background information will be helpful for parents to understand the purpose and benefits of the shared-reading techniques to be presented. Including some discussion among the group in which parents can share specific examples of their children's current skills and milestone achievements may help to bridge the gap between the knowledge bases of the parents and the professional.

Parents' Role in Promoting Children's Development Through Shared Reading

Once parents have discussed children's language and emergent literacy development, professionals may explain how parents influence their children's language and emergent literacy development through their daily interactions. Parents need to understand how the conversations they have with their children promote language acquisition in at least two ways. First, children learn about the content or meaning of what is said, and second, they learn how language itself is structured. Many parents may underestimate the impact that these conversations have on their children's development. The same is true for emergent literacy skills. Daily interactions with parents who point out print and explain its value provide young children with basic knowledge about printed language and how it corresponds with oral language. Once parents begin thinking about the seemingly ordinary interactions they have with their children, such as when reading storybooks, they may be able to provide numerous examples of how their children acquire new sounds, words, and concepts.

Informing parents of the benefits of shared reading will be a first step in motivating them to examine their current reading practices. A list of the possible benefits of shared reading may be created to illustrate how effective reading positively influences children's skills. When discussing possible benefits, make every attempt to keep them brief and to the point. For example, one point might be explaining that when parents direct their children's attention to print while reading, print concepts, alphabet knowledge, and word concepts may be enhanced (Justice & Ezell, 2002). Another example could be explaining that book reading is a language-rich experience that helps increase the amount of verbal interaction taking place in the home and that a lower amount of verbal interaction in the home is related to lower vocabulary scores in children. Increasing verbal interaction is an important foundation skill for future reading (Hart & Risley, 1995). Thus, increasing the amount of reading in the home may further children's vocabulary growth. These are just a few of the benefits that may be explained; others may be added, as shown in Table 9.2.

Appendix A provides a list of possible questions that parents may have about shared reading in the home. Professionals may find this material useful for large- or small-group discussion, for handouts that parents take home, or for occasional newsletter installments.

Reading Techniques to Assist Children's Development

Effective home reading programs work with parents to instruct them in effective reading techniques. Initially, parents should be given an opportunity to explore their current reading behaviors and to consider ways to modify their reading behaviors to bolster the developmental value of shared reading. For instance, are parents having brief conversations that depart from the book's text? If so, do these conversations focus on learning new vocabulary words, developing sentence structures, or recognizing print? Likewise, are children permitted to select which book to read, hold the book, and turn the pages? Do children seem to enjoy reading books with their parents, including the conversations taking place during this activity?

Table 9.2.   Possible benefits of shared reading

Parental reading behavior	Possible benefit to the child
Parent reads books often with child	Child-parent social relationship is strengthened
Parent follows the child's focus of attention in the storybook	Child may initiate conversation more often
Parent praises child's active participation in shared reading	Child develops a positive regard for storybook reading as a leisure activity
Parent points to letters and words in the storybook	Child develops alphabet knowledge, print concepts, and an interest in print
Parent defines and discusses new words that occur in the storybook	Child's vocabulary skills are strengthened
Parent reads storybooks of many different genres	Child's knowledge of different texts and genres is strengthened
Parent reads rhyming and verse books	Child's awareness of the sound structure of language is strengthened
Parent repeats and extends what the child says during reading	Child's syntactic and morphological skills are enhanced

Professionals may teach parents any number of strategies to improve reading effectiveness. Strategies that focus on language and emergent literacy development that are described in Chapters 4 and 6, respectively, may be presented to parents for use during shared reading at home. Professionals could present only one or two of these to introduce parents gradually over several home reading programs or could present an overview that covers them all and have parents select one or more to try. For example, professionals might suggest that parents select one language strategy and one emergent literacy strategy to try initially.

In addition to specific strategies for promoting language and emergent literacy growth, some general reading strategies are recommended for parents. Appendix B provides a list of these general strategies that collectively provide an excellent assortment to introduce to and practice with parents in a home reading program.

These techniques may seem simple and commonsense, but researchers have shown that parents tend not to use these sorts of strategies when reading with young children. Some studies have shown, for instance, that parents do not often depart from the text when reading with their children—instead, reading by parents tends to leave little room for conversation (Ezell & Justice, 1998). However, it is the conversation that extends beyond the text that is so important to children's language and literacy growth. When conversations do occur beyond the text, parents tend to control the topic and the pace, using a preponderance of questions rather than comments that follow on the child's topic and interest (Justice & Kaderavek, 2003). Consequently, parents may need extensive practice learning these different strategies to understand the rationale for using the techniques and to learn their application in order to become comfortable with them.

Determine Instructional Methods

A variety of methods may be needed to present instructional material to parents to make the meetings interesting and to address the goals discussed in the prior section. Techniques may include general lecture, large- and small-group discussion, observation and modeling of specific techniques, role play, and written handouts. This variety of instructional techniques will help meet the concerns of diverse learners and will address topics in different ways. Lectures and discussions are useful for providing some information, including details on children's early language and literacy achievements. For instance, the professional might deliver a 15-minute lecture on children's early print concepts, followed by an open discussion in which parents identify ways in which their children have shown knowledge of specific print concepts. Observation and modeling may be useful in teaching parents specific strategies to use during shared reading. For example, parents could watch videotapes of other parents reading storybooks with children to identify different strategies that were used. Also, parents could observe a professional modeling the use of a specific strategy while reading with a child. Role play could accompany observation and modeling to allow parents to practice specific strategies with one another. As for providing written handouts to parents, this technique should not be overlooked. Many parents want to take home written material to look over at their leisure. Handouts or an instructional manual may serve as an important reference and reminder of what to do at home when a professional is not available to answer questions.

Determine How Parents Will Have Access to Storybooks

A major objective of any home reading program will be to ensure that families have a variety of children's books available for reading and exploration. Some families may already have books for their children and will be interested in exploring new books for shared reading. However, some children may not have any books in their homes, so providing books for these families will be essential. In either case, parents will need to have ready access to books not only during the home reading program but in the months that follow.

In an ideal home reading program, parents are provided with children's books each week of the program to practice specific techniques and to find out more about their children's reading preferences and their own reading behaviors. Funds for these books may be donated from agencies who wish to underwrite the home reading program. Also, some publishers are willing to donate books for this purpose or sell them at a reduced cost if prior arrangements are made. Looking beyond the home reading program itself, it is advised that additional supports be considered so that families can continue their shared reading practices with additional books. Several suggestions are presented here for building access to books over the long term.

Use the Local Library   Parents should be encouraged to join their local libraries. Instruct and assist parents in signing up for a library card and accessing services such as story hours. Suggesting specific tasks to do involving the library (see Table 9.1) may help parents and their children become acquainted with the local library and its personnel. Professionals might consider establishing an incentive program for frequent library patronage (e.g., providing a gift book whenever a child visits the library three times in a month).

Establish a Lending Library   With sufficient funding, professionals may be able to establish their own lending library for the children they serve. This library could be stocked with donated books and those purchased by sponsors. Parents and their children could be allowed to select books to borrow using a procedure similar to a local library's. As an alternative, a "backpack" program could be offered that allows children to take a backpack home each week that contains a book with a special learning activity.

Provide Gift Books on Special Occasions   Professionals may consider providing gift books to the children they serve at specific times. Examples could include when children are first enrolled for service, on children's birthdays, and for other holidays or special events.

Offer Catalog Purchases   Some publishers such as Scholastic provide a low-cost option for families to purchase children books. Scholastic publishes a variety of catalogs each month, which schools and other learning institutions send home to children. Catalogs contain a listing of books sold at a low cost with a few books available for less than one dollar. Teachers receive bonus points from the orders for their classrooms and can purchase additional books for classroom use or as gifts for children. Professionals delivering home reading programs can join Scholastic as "teachers" and have the same privileges, including access to low-cost books and bonus points for receiving free books.

Determine a Reading Schedule

In implementing home reading programs, parents may need some guidance on how often and how long to read. Although it is desirable that parents conduct shared reading on a daily basis, this may not be possible for all families. Consequently, a range of five to six sessions per week may be offered to parents as a way to ease the daily pressure. Also, professionals could provide alternatives for parents to consider when a particularly hectic week occurs. For instance, another reader, such as a grandparent, an older sibling, or a babysitter, could be solicited for the child.

Professionals may need to help parents set a specific time for shared reading in the home (e.g., by asking which time is more likely to be available for regular shared reading—early in the morning, before a nap, after dinner, or at bedtime). Also, professionals might ask parents to consider their children's temperament and when they may be most amenable to storytime. If the typical naptime routine involves a cranky child, this may not be the best opportunity in the day for shared reading. Once a few suggestions are offered, parents can explore the timing that best suits their own children.

Although reading on a regular basis is probably more important than the length of any individual reading session, parents may ask for guidance on how long to read. As for the recommended length of shared-reading sessions, it would be appropriate for parents to aim for sessions that are at least 10 minutes in length. When parents use conversational strategies that have a language or emergent literacy focus, shared-reading sessions are likely to grow longer—perhaps to 15 minutes or more. However, parents should be advised against watching the clock to shorten or lengthen a session to meet a certain time limit. Rather, they should consider shared reading as a time to explore important language and literacy concepts with their children in a relaxed and leisurely manner.

Determine Use of Record Keeping

When establishing new habits and practices, a daily log is often useful for documenting progress toward a goal and achievement of objectives. Examples of these in everyday life are recording one's daily weight or food intake when following a weight-loss program or recording the length of daily walks when following an exercise program. In working with parents to establish home reading habits, a reading log may be a helpful tool. An example of a reading log is provided in Figure 9.2. Reading logs may be designed by the professional to be unique for each parent if desired. They may be simple or complex depending on the program's goals. Provide parents with a reading log

Home Reading Log			
Parent: _____	Child: _____		Week of: _____
	Books we read today	Approximate time we spent reading	Things we talked about while reading
Sun			
Mon			
Tues			
Wed			
Thurs			
Fri			
Sat			
Notes (e.g., things we liked or didn't like, techniques I used to help my child):			

Figure 9.2.   A reading log for a home reading program.

to record their shared reading and to bring to the home reading program meetings each week for discussion. Reading logs are useful for discussing specific books, for length of shared-reading sessions, and for monitoring different reading techniques. Once parents and children both derive enjoyment from reading and some other positive outcomes, reading often becomes rewarding in itself and will require little encouragement or monitoring to continue.

When parents begin to use the specific strategies suggested in this book, children's language and literacy skills are likely to grow by leaps and bounds. For instance, when parents begin to talk about print during shared reading, children may become more aware of print in other situations. Likewise, when parents define and discuss new words, children may begin to understand and use these words in their speech. Helping parents to document their children's language and lit-

Month: _____		
Date:	During book reading today, my child said:	During book reading today, my child did:
Date:	During book reading today, my child said:	During book reading today, my child did:
Date:	During book reading today, my child said:	During book reading today, my child did:
Date:	During book reading today, my child said:	During book reading today, my child did:
Date:	During book reading today, my child said:	During book reading today, my child did:

Figure 9.3. A language and literacy development record for parents.

eracy growth can be motivating for parents as they establish the home reading habit. It is like writing down when children speak their first words or take their first steps, or measuring their height as they grow taller. Parents can be encouraged to consider these early skills as their children's "baby steps" in acquiring literacy. Professionals can provide parents with a development record similar to the one in Figure 9.3 to encourage parent documentation of children's language and literacy gains observed during shared reading at home.

Determine Follow-Up Procedures

An important consideration in delivering quality home reading programs is to follow up with parents on a regular basis. Establishing high-quality, frequent shared reading in the home for families new to this practice takes great effort for busy mothers, fathers, and other caregivers. Thus, frequent and sensitive follow-up is critical for parents' continued success. This practice demonstrates a professional's commitment to working with families to ensure children's future academic success.

Monitoring parents' shared reading may be handled in several ways (e.g., telephone contact, exchanging notes, occasional group meetings with parents, listening to shared-reading sessions recorded on audiotape by parents, even e-mail when this option is available). When parents understand that the professional wants to lend support and assistance, they will welcome such discussions. Topics to cover include how the child is progressing with his or her language development, whether the child is beginning to show increased awareness of print and sounds, which books the child is particularly enjoying, how often library visits occur, how frequently shared reading occurs, and whether any problems have arisen for which the parents need assistance.

10

Resources and Tips
for Selecting Storybooks

This chapter discusses the particular features to consider when selecting books to read. The chapter also suggests ways to help children participate in choosing books themselves and makes recommendations regarding the use of electronic books. Suggestions for books and web sites are also provided to assist with selecting storybooks.

BOOK FEATURES

Throughout this book the interactive nature of shared reading has been emphasized, with a particular focus on developing language and emergent literacy skills through conversation. However, one of the most important elements in shared reading is the actual book itself, for if the book is lacking or deficient in some way, the quality of the reading session is diminished. As all adults know through personal experience, when a book is interesting, reading is a pleasure; but when the material lacks interest, reading becomes a dreaded chore. Young children will find the same to be true. Thus, it is important to consider the various features of children's books in order to select ones that will be of interest to the child and maximize the potential of each and every reading session. Children's interest may be influenced by various book features.

Three features should be considered when selecting books: 1) narrative content, 2) print, and 3) physical characteristics. Each of these has the potential to facilitate various objectives discussed in this book (e.g., building children's vocabulary knowledge or print awareness), as well as to contribute to the general interest of a book. Thus, it is suggested that professionals consider these features in some measure, depending on the specific objective of a reading interaction. For example, if the professional intends to focus on print, then the primary feature to consider is the size, amount, and placement of the print in a book. If vocabulary enrichment is desired, then the language within a book's narrative should be a primary consideration. When reading to children who lack an interest in books, the story itself may be the most important feature to consider.

Narrative Content

It is recommended that the theme or story of the book be considered first and foremost for two primary reasons. First, it is desirable to consider the theme so that young children are presented with wholesome and age-appropriate material. Selecting a book that is too advanced for a child is counterproductive because the material will not be understood. When that occurs, children lose interest and may terminate the reading session prematurely. Second, it is important to find books that are suitable based on children's interests. As noted earlier, if the topic of a book is of no interest to the child, the reading session will be less pleasurable for both participants, and repeated readings of this same book will likely be out of the question.

Generally speaking, there are a few topics that appeal to most children. These include stories describing an adventure or fantasy event, stories about pets or animals, and stories that describe a familiar experience to which children can relate (e.g., learning to share with playmates or siblings). Concept books are also popular with young children. These are books that emphasize alphabet letters, counting or numbers, colors, shapes, and opposites (e.g., hot/cold, up/down, open/closed). Informational texts are increasingly being developed for young children to expose them early to the nonfiction expository genre, which is important for learning new information. For young children, informational texts on such topics as dinosaurs, puppies, weather, and transportation might be enjoyable. The only drawback to concept books and informational texts is their sole focus on the concept or information and lack of a story. Rhyming books, which are written in verse and can be on any topic, are an additional source of reading material for young children. These sometimes appeal to young children for their repetitive and melodic qualities and may be considered if a focus on sound awareness or word play is desired.

After considering the general topic of a book, determine whether its length is appropriate by considering the amount of text on each page. Although many children's books are approximately 32 pages in length (for publishing purposes), they vary tremendously in the quantity and complexity of the text. Quantity of text refers to the sheer number of words and sentences. Complexity of text refers to the grammatical quality of the text; for example, whether it features primarily simple sentences or whether there is a great deal of clausal embedding and compound sentences. Books may have a high quantity of text but may be fairly simple grammatically, or the reverse may be true, whereby a book has relatively little text but is very grammatically complex. Both quantity and complexity of text should be considered. Longer text will require a longer reading session, which may not be suitable for young children's short attention spans. Text that is complex may be more difficult for children to understand and thus may not be suitable for children whose language skills are underdeveloped or delayed. Naturally, as children mature, they will be able to attend for longer periods of time and be able to handle more complex text, but for those below 4 years of age, attention may be brief, particularly if the text is demanding. If the book is an exceptional one and fits in every other way except its length or complexity, then it may be possible to consider reading the book across multiple sessions rather than in a single session. An individual child's attention span should be the guide here.

Third, consider a book's vocabulary level, which will be closely associated with the topic. Children are likely to gain from reading experiences in which they understand at least 90% of the text; too many words in the text that they do not understand can detract from both comprehension and enjoyment. For very young preschool children, the overall level of vocabulary should not be too advanced or contain too many novel or abstract words. For example, if the story involves baking a cake, vocabulary may include basic words such as *cake mix, bowl, spoon, eggs, stir,* or *pour.* If some of these concepts are new to children, they can be defined or discussed prior to, during, or after the reading session.

For children in the later preschool and kindergarten years, many of the books used during reading sessions are likely to contain at least several challenging vocabulary words that are novel to children. The book *Otis* (Bynum, 2000), for instance, contains such potentially challenging words as *hauled, ripe, sidelines, silky,* and *spotless.* Likewise, *Swimmy* (Lionni, 1963) contains the words *gulp, marvel, midday, invisible, swaying,* and *swift.* These are words that Isabel Beck and her colleagues call *Tier 2 words*—words that are neither basic nor rare but are common in mature conversations and not specific to a certain context (Beck et al., 2002). Because of this, Tier 2 words (e.g., *power, temporary, supply, tend, fortunate*) are likely to be found in storybooks read with preschoolers and kindergarteners.

How can these higher level Tier 2 vocabulary words be identified? Generally, word length and specificity are associated with higher level vocabulary. For instance, words often increase in difficulty and become more descriptive when they contain more syllables (e.g., *happy/jubilant, picture/illustration*). Of greater importance, however, is specificity, or the level of detail words provided. Compare a general word such as *tool* to specific words such as *screwdriver* or *socket wrench.* Children typically develop the basic word (e.g., *tool*) first and then develop more specific words to discuss this broader concept. A Tier 2 word is appropriate for discussion between the professional and the child when the child understands the basic concept underlying the more specific Tier 2 word (Beck et al., 2002). For instance, the Tier 2 word *silky,* which occurs in the book *Otis* (Bynum, 2000), can be readily discussed with a child who has a concept of how different materials feel and who may use other words to describe textures (e.g., *scratchy, smooth, soft*). The word *silky* adds more precision to the child's vocabulary, and the storybook provides an excellent anchor for helping the child understand this new word.

When considering the vocabulary contained in a book, an additional consideration is to determine which words, particularly those that may be novel or challenging, are depicted in the illustrations or simply presented in print. Many nouns, verbs, and adjectives may be featured in illustrations; however, this is not always the case, so it is important to check. For example, in the book *Dear Zoo* by Rod Campbell (1982), animals are illustrated on each page, and animal characteristics are described. Some of these characteristics (e.g., *tall, heavy*) are apparent in the illustrations but others (e.g., *grumpy, scary*) are not. Consequently, the book may be ideal for helping children see some adjectives described but not others. Although this would not exclude the book from being selected, the adult should be prepared with other means of explanation if no illustrations are provided to help decipher challenging words (e.g., using a synonym that the child knows, acting out the meaning).

Print Features

When selecting a book to help children develop print awareness and knowledge of the alphabet, consider the size, amount, and location of print in the book. Larger print is preferable to smaller print because it is easier for young children to see various features that might be pointed out by the adult. For instance, differences in the number and shape of letters within words are easier to discern when print is larger. Some books for young children use bold print to make it even more prominent, which can be helpful.

As for the amount of print needed, it is suggested that one word per page would be considered the minimum amount needed for print awareness. The book *Red Bear* by Bodel Rikys (1991), for instance, has just one word on each of its pages, specifically a color word (e.g., *red, yellow, brown*) to go with the illustrations, which show a bear getting dressed. Although the adult and child can explore the color concepts depicted in the pictures of this book, the large, bold color words presented on the pages also provide an excellent opportunity for talking about different letters and the sounds that go with the letters. Almost all books contain at least this much print per page, although wordless books (those that contain pictures without any print) would not meet this minimum. More print than one word per page is useful for other print activities such as helping children learn to count words, to point to words as the adult reads, and to recognize the space between words. One excellent example of a book that contains relatively few words per page is *Freight Train* by Donald Crews (1978). This richly illustrated book averages fewer than four words per page, with words presented in large print that varies in color. If print directionality is emphasized, print should appear on both the left and right pages with more than one line of print on a page. Consider, too, that the amount of print is often associated with print size; books containing an abundance of text often use a smaller print or font size. This can be seen by comparing the large, bold print in *Where's Spot?* (Hill, 1980) with the smaller print used in *The Very Hungry Caterpillar* (Carle, 1987).

The print's use within illustrations or elsewhere on the page also must be considered. Many storybooks feature print beyond the narrative by incorporating it into the illustrations (e.g., *The Wing on the Flea,* by Ed Emberley [2001]). This colorful and educational storybook, which talks about different shapes, features print in a variety of ways as a rich complement to the illustrations. For instance, characters on one page are shown yelling "WHEE!" and on another page a pirate and his parrot are examining a map containing much print (e.g., *dig here, big log, 4 giant steps north*). On yet another page a mat labeled "WELCOME" sits in front of a door, and a calendar with numbers sits on a shelf. When print appears within the illustrations, it provides additional opportunities for adults and children to identify and talk about these occurrences. As explained elsewhere in this book, these conversations provide an important means for developing children's knowledge of print concepts.

Some book illustrators make print salient by changing fonts, by varying print color, and by altering the arrangement of letters. For instance, a page of a storybook that discusses a mountain might use print as a complement to the text by using brown type and arranging the print to move diagonally up the page. Some book illustrators also use print to label items in illustrations, as in Lois Ehlert's *Feathers for Lunch* (1990) in which different flowers are labeled for the reader (e.g., tulip, geranium). Other illustrators incorporate speech bubbles to depict what characters are saying, as in Eric Hill's *Where's Spot?* (1980). In this book, speech bubbles are used by an assortment of animals to answer questions about where Spot might be found (e.g., "Is he behind the door? 'No!' says the bear."). These various approaches to making print a salient feature—by manipulating print, color, and arrangements—are important considerations when selecting books to facilitate children's interactions with print.

Physical Characteristics

At least three primary physical characteristics may enhance children's enjoyment of a book. These include a book's composition and shape, its illustrations, and its packaging. Regarding composition, books may be made from heavy cardboard, vinyl, or paper. Heavy cardboard books are referred to as board books and are ideal for infants and toddlers who lack sufficient fine motor control to avoid crinkling and tearing paper pages. Board books are very durable and thus are an ideal part of children's personal libraries and the libraries of classrooms and child care centers. Vinyl books, which are also known as bath books, will withstand water and soiling. Children who are very fond of books may want to take books into the bathtub or into the pool. Vinyl books are useful for serving this function, and a variety of reasonably priced titles are available in this format. Also, in preschool classrooms, vinyl books may be incorporated into water-table activities and may withstand regular cleaning. Paper books come with either soft covers, which are light and travel easily, or hard covers, which are more durable. Books with soft covers tend to be less expensive than hardcover books, and thus make up much of children's own libraries and the libraries in early childhood educational environments. Some book publishers, such as Scholastic, make paper books accessible to children and classrooms by offering a variety of books at very low costs.

Books vary in size from mini books to big books that are created for reading to groups of children in a library or classroom. Some books use their shape to appeal to young children (e.g., those shaped like trains, cars, animals, houses, or purses). Others may have "windows" on the front cover that let the reader see into or through the book. Although a book's composition or size may have a particular purpose for the reader, its special shape is meant to enhance the book's appeal to young children or to suggest a book's theme.

The illustrations of a book are central to sustaining children's interest in the story and to enhancing children's comprehension of the story events. Illustrations and narrative text work in tandem to create a story that is comprehensible and interesting to young children. Thus, it is suggested that books with attractive and colorful illustrations be used whenever possible. Illustrations that are abstract and difficult to interpret should be avoided with young children; otherwise, children's comprehension of the story may be compromised. Some books have illustrations that invite children's active participation and promote turn taking. Such features may include flaps to lift for revealing words or pictures, tabs to pull for activating movement in the illustration, buttons to push for producing sounds or lights, and various textures to touch or feel that represent concepts in the book. Some books even provide a means for inserting a child's own photograph into the book so that the child becomes a character in the story. Consider these special features for all young children but especially for those who may be less enthusiastic about books and book-reading activities. Allowing children to lift flaps, pull tabs, push buttons, and touch and feel various parts of a book are important ways to entice children who may be reticent or reluctant to participate. These devices invite children to take an active role during shared reading that requires minimal ability and is virtually risk free.

The third physical characteristic concerns how books are packaged. Some books come packaged with a toy or object that is relevant to the story. This may include a doll or action figure, a piece of jewelry, or some other object. These accompanying toys create additional interest for children in two important ways. First, adults may use the toy to open a discussion about the book and to invite the child to guess how the toy relates to the story. Second, once the story is read, the child may use the toy during play to recreate the story or as a reminder of the story, which might promote repeated readings of the book. In other words, accompanying toys such as these help the story to "come alive" for young children. The use of props by preschool teachers to help children act out stories and to describe new vocabulary or concepts contained in a story can promote children's language and literacy gains from shared-reading activities (Wasik & Bond, 2001).

CHILDREN SELECTING THEIR OWN BOOKS

Having children select their own books provides an opportunity for preschoolers to exert some control over their reading experiences. It also provides an occasion for children to learn more about books in general. Initially, most young children may select a book based on the cover illustration suggestive of a particular topic, or they may select a book with which they are familiar, having read it previously. This selection strategy may work exceedingly well in most cases. However, there will be times when this strategy is unsatisfactory, as children may select books that are not likely to be appealing to them or ones that are beyond their skills conceptually. Children may need to learn additional ways for choosing books, and this can be modeled for them by adults, older peers, or siblings. Additional methods include examining illustrations throughout the book, investigating story length, looking for special features (e.g., flaps for lifting), and attending to the author's name.

The professional may begin the process of examining storybooks by asking children what they liked or disliked about a particular book. If a child is able to explain his or her feelings about a book, then the professional may help direct the child to focus on that particular element. If children enjoy the lift-the-flap features, they can be directed to leaf through a book to see what is inside and whether this feature appears. When a book is disliked because it is too lengthy, children can learn to pay attention to story length, deciding when a book is too long, too short, or just right. When children like the main character in a story, professionals can direct attention to the book's author and help them find other books about this character that were written by the same author. So even though young children may not be able to read yet, they may learn several ways to select books that might interest them when borrowing, buying, or choosing from a given assortment. Such conversations with children about book features help them to become aware of different genres and stylistic features of books, a knowledge base that becomes increasingly important to children as they enter the primary grades.

ELECTRONIC STORYBOOKS

In the current technological age, it is no surprise that children are increasingly using electronic storybooks (e.g., Leap Pad, CD-ROM). There are a number of electronic picture storybooks available for children of preschool age. Unlike their paper counterparts, electronic storybooks provide children with opportunities to explore sounds, animations, words, and games corresponding to the story.

There is every reason to believe that electronic storybooks can be helpful to language and literacy development in young children, and that many of the same principles and strategies discussed in this book can be used with electronic storybooks. One way in which electronic storybooks might actually be superior to paper storybooks is in helping children attend to written language. In paper storybooks, illustrations are often the most salient aspect of the book. However, in electronic storybooks, the printed text may be highlighted and made particularly prominent with colors and icons, sometimes with links to follow for more information about letters and words. There is some evidence from recent research that children may learn more about letters and words when reading electronic storybooks (de Jong & Bus, 2002).

However, leaving a young child alone with an electronic story-book cannot substitute for shared reading that includes adults and children together. The discussion and social interaction that takes place between the adult and child in a reading session provides opportunities for sharing ideas and experiences that reading in isolation cannot possibly achieve. Aside from the social interaction benefits, paper storybook reading by adults and children vary in other ways from electronic storybook reading by children alone. When adults and children read storybooks together, they typically read the whole book from beginning to end. This is usually not the case with electronic storybooks. When reading electronic storybooks, children follow links to explore text or illustrations, or leave the storyline to play linked games. Consequently, children reading electronic storybooks often do not read all of the pages of a book. In fact, one study by researchers de Jong and Bus (2002) in the Netherlands showed that kindergarten children reading electronic storybooks spent only about half of the time actually reading the storybook, with the other half of the time spent playing games. In contrast, when given paper storybooks, children spent the whole time reading the storybook. This is important because exposure to storybooks in their entirety allows children to experience the natural flow of a story. This sequence or flow is important to children's development of story grammar (e.g., understanding that stories have a beginning, a middle, and an end). Also, valuable language concepts and vocabulary are missed when children fail to read all of the pages in a story.

There is a place for electronic storybooks in the lives of young children, as familiarity with such texts is important for developing computer mastery. They may be viewed as providing additional opportunities for children to engage with books either on their own or in the accompaniment of peers, siblings, parents, or teachers. In addition, electronic storybooks may be very appealing to children, even those who do not enjoy reading paper storybooks, and their use may be an effective strategy for enticing unmotivated or reluctant readers. However, it is suggested that electronic storybooks be used to complement or build on the shared reading of paper storybooks by adults and children rather than to replace them.

RESOURCES FOR SELECTING BOOKS

Many reference books are devoted to the topic of book selection for young children. Several excellent references are included here to provide further suggestions for the reader. Some of these include textbooks such as *Literacy Difficulties* by Cathy Collins Block (1997) that primarily provide instructional information about reading but also intersperse book suggestions throughout the text. Others provide lists of books that are arranged by children's age groups, reading levels, and so forth. Librarians will be familiar with these and may be able to recommend other sources as well.

The Internet is another source for book suggestions. Organizations that promote emergent literacy such as Beginning with Books Center for Early Literacy now have web sites that include book suggestions along with information about their programs. Children's authors sometimes have personal web sites that list their published books, which is an excellent source for finding other books by the same author when children love a particular book. Consider making a list of all of these resources available to parents when establishing and/or updating home reading programs.

Books

Bauer, C.F. (1983). *This way to books.* Bronx, NY: Wilson.

Block, C.C. (1997). *Literacy difficulties.* New York: Harcourt Brace College.

Butler, D. (1998). *Babies need books.* Portsmouth, NH: Heinemann.

Cullinan, B.E. (1992). *Read to me: Raising kids who love to read.* New York: Scholastic.

Friedes, H. (1993). *The preschool resource guide.* New York: Plenum.

Gebers, J.L. (1990). *Books are for talking too!* Tucson, AZ: Communication Skill Builders.

Immroth, B.F., & Ash-Geisler, V. (1995). *Achieving school readiness: Public libraries and national education goal No. 1.* Chicago: American Library Association.

Kimmel, M.M., & Segel, E. (1988). *For reading out loud!* New York: Delacorte Press.

Lipson, E.R. (2000). *The New York Times parent's guide to the best books for children.* New York: Three Rivers.

Little John, C. (1999). *Talk that book: Booktalks to promote reading.* Worthington, OH: Linworth.

Odean, K. (1997). *Great books for girls.* New York: Ballantine.

Odean, K. (1998). *Great books for boys.* New York: Ballantine.

Pilla, M.L. (1990). *The best high/low books for reluctant readers.* Englewood, CO: Libraries Unlimited.

Trelease, J. (1989). *The new read-aloud handbook.* New York: Penguin.

Vukelich, C., Christie, J., & Enz, B. (2002). *Helping young children learn language and literacy.* Boston: Allyn & Bacon.

Web Sites

Beginning with Books Center for Early Literacy

http://www. beginningwithbooks.org
Beginning with Books Center for Early Literacy is an outreach program based in Pittsburgh, PA, that promotes reading to young children in the home. Along with a description of the program, reading tips and book suggestions are provided.

Born to Read

http://www.borntoread.org
Born to Read is a project originally created by the Vermont Business Roundtable but is now directed by the Vermont Chapter of the American Academy of Pediatrics. It is a book-distribution program that provides books for all newborns in the state of Vermont. Book suggestions are categorized by children's ages.

International Children's Digital Library

http://www.icdlbooks.org
The International Children's Digital Library stated mission is "to select, collect, digitize, and organize children's materials in their original languages and to create appropriate technologies for access and use by children 3–13 years old." At this web site, actual books can be seen for online reading.

International Reading Association

http://www.ira.org/choices
The International Reading Association has a "Choices Booklists" section that provides three separate lists: children's choices, teachers' choices, and young adults' choices.

The New York Times

http://www.nytimes.com
The New York Times is known for its bestseller lists of books. At the newspaper's web site, under Books, Best-Seller Lists, popular children's books are listed in the section All Children's Books Lists.

References

Adams, M.J. (1990). *Beginning to read: Thinking and learning about print.* Cambridge, MA: The MIT Press.

Adamson, L.B., & Chance, S.E. (1998). Coordinating attention to people, objects, and language. In A.M. Wetherby, S.F. Warren, & J. Reichle (Eds.), *Transitions in prelinguistic communication* (pp. 15–38). Baltimore: Paul H. Brookes Publishing Co.

Akhtar, N., Jipson, J., & Callanan, M.A. (2001). Learning words through overhearing. *Child Development, 72,* 416–430.

Arnold, D.H., Lonigan, C., Whitehurst, G.J., & Epstein, J.N. (1994). Accelerating language development through picture book reading: Replication and extension to a videotape training format. *Journal of Educational Psychology, 86,* 235–243.

Badian, N.A. (2001). Phonological and orthographic processing: Their roles in reading prediction. *Annals of Dyslexia, 51,* 179–202.

Beck, I.L., McKeown, M.G., & Kucan, L. (2002). *Bringing words to life.* New York: Guilford Press.

Bennett, K.K., Weigel, D.J., & Martin, S.S. (2002). Children's acquisition of early literacy skills: Examining family contributions. *Early Childhood Research Quarterly, 17,* 295–317.

Bergin, C. (2001). The parent–child relationship during beginning reading. *Journal of Literacy Research, 33*(4), 681–706.

Block, C.C. (1997). *Literacy difficulties.* New York: Harcourt Brace College.

Bus, A.G., van IJzendoorn, M.H., & Pellegrini, A.D. (1995). Joint book reading makes for success in learning to read: A meta-analysis on intergenerational transmission of literacy. *Review of Educational Research, 65,* 5–142.

Bynum, J. (2000). *Otis.* New York: Harcourt.

Campbell, R. (1982). *Dear zoo.* New York: Little Simon.

Carle, E. (1987). *The very hungry caterpillar.* New York: Philomel Books.

Chaney, C. (1994). Language development, metalinguistic awareness, and emergent literacy skills of 3-year-old children in relation to social class. *Applied Psycholinguistics, 15,* 371–394.

Christelow, E., (1989). *Five little monkeys jumping on the bed.* New York: Clarion Books.

Clay, M.M. (1979). *The early detection of reading difficulties* (3rd ed.). Portsmouth, NH: Heinemann.

Craig, C.J. (1996, May–June). Family support of the emergent literacy of children with visual impairments. *Journal of Visual Impairment and Blindness,* 194–200.

Crews, D. (1978). *Freight train.* New York: Greenwillow Books.

Curenton, S., & Justice, L.M. (2004). Low-income preschoolers' use of decontextualized discourse: Literate language features in spoken narratives. *Language, Speech, and Hearing Services in Schools, 35,* 241–255.

de Jong, M., & Bus, A.G. (2002). Quality of book reading matters for emergent readers: An experiment with the same book in a regular or electronic format. *Journal of Educational Psychology, 94,* 145–155.

Dickinson, D.K., de Temple, J.M., Hirschler, J.M., & Smith, J.A. (1992). Book reading with preschoolers: Co-construction of text at home and at school. *Early Childhood Research Quarterly, 7*(3), 323–346.

Dickinson, D., & Keebler, R. (1989). Variations in preschool teachers' storybook reading styles. *Discourse Processes, 12,* 353–376.

Dickinson, D., & Smith, M. (1994). Long-term effects of preschool teachers' book readings on low-income children's vocabulary and story comprehension. *Reading Research Quarterly, 29,* 105–122.

Doake, D.B. (1986). Learning to read: It starts in the home. In D.R. Tovey & J.E. Kerber (Eds.), *Roles in literacy learning* (pp. 2–9). Newark, DE: International Reading Association.

Ehlert, L. (1990). *Feathers for lunch.* Orlando, FL: Harcourt Brace.

Ehlert, L. (1993). *Nuts to you!* San Diego: Harcourt Brace Jovanovich.

Ehri, L.C. (1995). Phases of development in learning to read words by sight. *Journal of Research in Reading, 18,* 116–125.

Emberley, E. (2001). *The wing on the flea.* New York: Scholastic.

Ezell, H.K. (2005). *The Legend of the tooth fairy.* Unpublished manuscript.

Ezell, H.K., & Justice, L.M. (1998). A pilot investigation of parents' questions about print and pictures to preschoolers with language delay. *Child Language Teaching and Therapy, 14*(3), 273–278.

Ezell, H.K., & Justice, L.M. (2000). Increasing the print focus of adult–child shared book reading through observational learning. *American Journal of Speech-Language Pathology, 9,* 36–47.

Ezell, H.K., Justice, L.M., & Parsons, D. (2000). Enhancing the emergent literacy skills of preschoolers with communication disorders: A pilot investigation. *Child Language Teaching and Therapy, 16,* 121–140.

Ferreiro, E., & Teberosky, A. (1982). *Literacy before schooling.* Exeter, NH: Heinemann.

Fitzgerald, J., Roberts, J., Pierce, P., & Schuele, C.M. (1995). Evaluation of the home literacy environment: An illustration with preschool children with Down syndrome. *Reading and Writing Quarterly: Overcoming Learning Difficulties, 11,* 311–334.

Fowler, R. (1994). *Ted and Dolly's magic carpet ride.* Tulsa, OK: Educational Development Corporation.

Frijters, J.C., Barron, R.W., & Brunello, M. (2000). Direct and mediated influences of home literacy and literacy interest on prereaders' oral vocabulary and early written language skill. *Journal of Educational Psychology, 92,* 466–477.

Gardner, H. (1993). *Multiple intelligences.* New York: HarperCollins.

Gebers, J.L. (1990). *Books are for talking too!* Tucson, AZ: Communication Skill Builders.

Gillam, R.B., & Johnston, J.R. (1985). Development of print awareness in language-disordered preschoolers. *Journal of Speech and Hearing Research, 28,* 521–526.

Girolametto, L., & Weitzman, E. (2002). Responsiveness of child care providers in interactions with toddlers and preschoolers. *Language, Speech, and Hearing Services in Schools, 33,* 268–281.

Gleason, J.B. (2000). *The development of language* (5th ed.). New York: Macmillan.

Goin, R.P., Nordquist, V.M., & Twardosz, S. (2004). Parental accounts of home-based literacy processes: Contexts for infants and toddlers with developmental delays. *Early Education and Development, 15,* 187–214.

Goodman, Y.M. (1986). Children coming to know literacy. In W. Teale & E. Sulzby (Eds.), *Emergent literacy* (pp. 1–14). Norwood, NJ: Ablex.

Greenhalgh, K.S., & Strong, C.J. (2001). Literate language features in spoken narratives of children with typical language and children with language impairments. *Language, Speech, and Hearing Services in Schools, 32,* 114–125.

Haden, C.A., Reese, E., & Fivush, R. (1996). Mothers' extratextual comments during storybook reading: Stylistic differences over time and across texts. *Discourse Processes, 21,* 135–169.

Hammett, L.A., van Kleeck, A., & Huberty, C.J. (2003). Patterns of parents' extratextual interactions during book sharing with preschool children: A cluster analysis study. *Reading Research Quarterly, 38,* 442–468.

Hart, B., & Risley, T.R. (1995). *Meaningful differences in the everyday experience of young American children.* Baltimore: Paul H. Brookes Publishing Co.

Henkes, K. (1993). *Owen.* New York: Greenwillow Books.

Hill, E. (1980). *Where's Spot?* New York: Puffin Books.

Hill, E. (1981). *Spot's first walk.* New York: Puffin Books.

Hill, E. (1985). *Spot goes to the beach.* New York: Putnam.

Hill, E. (1990). *Spot sleeps over.* New York: Putnam.

Hill, E. (1992). *Spot goes to a party.* New York: Putnam.

Hill, E. (1994). *Spot bakes a cake.* New York: Putnam.

Hoff, E. (2000). *Language development* (2nd ed.). Pacific Grove, CA: Brooks/Cole.

Hutchins, P. (1986). *The doorbell rang.* New York: Greenwillow Books.

Inkpen, M. (1990). *The blue balloon.* Boston: Little, Brown.

International Reading Association (IRA) and the National Association for the Education of Young Children (NAEYC). (1998). Learning to read and write: Developmentally appropriate practices for young children. *Young Children, 53*(4), 30–46.

Jones, C. (2000). *This old man.* Wiltshire, England: Child's Play International Ltd.

Justice, L.M., & Ezell, H.K. (2000). Enhancing children's print and word awareness through home-based parent intervention. *American Journal of Speech-Language Pathology, 9*(3), 257–269.

Justice, L.M., & Ezell, H.K. (2001). Written language awareness in preschool children from low-income households: A descriptive analysis. *Communication Disorders Quarterly, 22*(3), 123–134.

Justice, L.M., & Ezell, H.K. (2002). Use of storybook reading to increase print awareness in at-risk children. *American Journal of Speech-Language Pathology, 11,* 17–29.

Justice, L.M., & Ezell, H.K. (2004). Print referencing: An emergent literacy enhancement technique and its clinical applications. *Language, Speech, and Hearing Services in Schools, 35,* 185–193.

Justice, L.M., & Kaderavek, J. (2003). Topic control during shared storybook reading: Mothers and their children with mild to moderate language impairment. *Topics in Early Childhood Special Education, 23,* 137–150.

Justice, L.M., & Pence, K. (2004). *Children's reading interest and literacy development.* Unpublished raw data.

Kaderavek, J., & Sulzby, E. (1998a). Emergent literacy issues for children with language impairment. In L.R. Watson, T.L. Layton, & E.R. Crais (Eds.), *Handbook of early language impairments in children. Volume II: Assessment and treatment.* New York: Delmar.

Kaderavek, J., & Sulzby, E. (1998b). Parent–child joint book reading: An observational protocol for young children. *American Journal of Speech-Language Pathology, 7,* 33–47.

Kaderavek, J., & Sulzby, E. (1999). *Issues in emergent literacy for children with language impairment* (Center for the Improvement of Reading and Achievement Rep. No. 2-002). Ann Arbor, MI: Center for the Improvement of Reading and Achievement.

Kaderavek, J.N., & Sulzby, E. (2000). Narrative production by children with and without specific language impairment: Oral narratives and emergent readings. *Journal of Speech, Language, and Hearing Research, 43,* 34–49.

Kagan, J. (1994). *Galen's prophecy: Temperament in human nature.* New York: Basic Books.

Katims, D.S. (1994). Emergence of literacy in preschool children with disabilities. *Learning Disability Quarterly, 17,* 58–69.

Keats, E.J. (1962). *The snowy day.* New York: Puffin Books.

Leseman, P., & de Jong, P.F. (1998). Home literacy: Opportunity, instruction, cooperation and social-emotional quality predicting early reading achievement. *Reading Research Quarterly, 33,* 294–318.

Lindbergh, R. (1990). *The day the goose got loose.* New York: Puffin Pied Piper Books.

Lionni, L. (1963). *Swimmy.* New York: Alfred A. Knopf.

Lonigan, C. (1994). Reading to preschoolers exposed: Is the emperor really naked? *Developmental Review, 14,* 303–323.

Lonigan, C.J., Burgess, S.R., Anthony, J.L., & Barker, T.A. (1998). Development of phonological sensitivity in 2- to 5-year old children. *Journal of Educational Psychology, 90,* 294–311.

Lonigan, C.J., & Whitehurst, G.J. (1998). Relative efficacy of parent and teacher involvement in a shared-reading intervention for preschool children from low-income backgrounds. *Early Childhood Research Quarterly, 13,* 263–290.

Martin, B. (1983). *Brown bear, brown bear, what do you see?* New York: Holt, Rinehart and Winston.

Marvin, C.A., & Mirenda, P. (1993). Home literacy experiences of preschoolers enrolled in Head Start and special education programs. *Journal of Early Intervention, 17,* 351–367.

Mayer, M. (1987). *There's an alligator under my bed.* New York: Dial Books for Young Readers.

McCardle, P., Scarborough, H.S., & Catts, H.W. (2001). Predicting, explaining, and preventing reading difficulties. *Learning Disabilities Research and Practice, 16,* 230–239.

Munsch, R. (1980). *The paper bag princess.* Toronto: Annick Press.

Namm, D. (1990). *Little bear.* Chicago: Children's Press.

National Center for Education Statistics. (1995). *National household education survey.* Washington, DC: Author. Available at http://nces.ed.gov/nhes

National Institute on Child Health and Human Development (NICHD) Early Child Care Research Network. (1999). Chronicity of maternal depressive symptoms, maternal sensitivity, and child functioning at 36 months. *Developmental Psychology, 35,* 1297–1310.

Numeroff, L.J. (1985). *If you give a mouse a cookie.* New York: HarperCollins.

Numeroff, L.J. (1991). *If you give a moose a muffin.* New York: HarperCollins.

Owens, R.E. (2000). *Language development: An introduction* (5th ed.). Boston: Allyn & Bacon.

Penno, J.F., Wilkinson, I.A., & Moore, D.W. (2002). Vocabulary acquisition from teacher explanation and repeated listening to stories: Do they overcome the Matthew Effect? *Journal of Educational Psychology, 94,* 23–33.

Piaget, J. (2001). *Language and thought of the child* (2nd ed.). New York: Routledge Classics.

Pianta, R.C. (2000). *Enhancing relationships between children and teachers.* Washington DC: American Psychological Association.

Pillow, G., Justice, L., & Gray, L. (2004, Winter). Audiologists and speech-language pathologists collaborating to support early literacy. *Educational Audiology Review, 21*(1), 21–23.

Purcell-Gates, V. (1996). Stories, coupons, and the TV Guide: Relationships between home literacy experiences and emergent literacy knowledge. *Reading Research Quarterly, 31,* 406–428.

Rathmann, P. (1994). *Good night, gorilla.* New York: Putnam.

Reese, E., & Cox, A. (1999). Quality of adult book reading affects children's emergent literacy. *Developmental Psychology, 35,* 20–28.

Rikys, B. (1991). *Red bear.* New York: Dial Books for Young Readers.

Scarborough, H., & Dobrich, W. (1994). On the efficacy of reading to preschoolers. *Developmental Review, 14,* 245–302.

Schuele, C.M. (2004, September). *Phonological awareness instruction: Teaching strategies and considerations.* Paper presented at the Rite Care conference of the Vanderbilt Bill Wilkinson Research Institute, Nashville.

Senechal, M., LeFebre, J., Thomas, E.M., & Daley, K.E. (1998). Differential effects of home literacy experiences on the development of oral and written language. *Reading Research Quarterly, 33,* 96–116.

Seuss, Dr. (1963). *Hop on pop.* New York: Beginner Books.

Skinner, B.F. (1965). *Science and human behavior.* New York: The Free Press.

Snow, C.E., Burns, M.S., & Griffin, P. (Eds.). (1998). *Preventing reading difficulties in young children.* Washington, DC: National Academy Press.

Stanovich, K.E. (2000). *Progress in understanding reading: Scientific foundations and new frontiers.* New York: Guilford Press.

Stockham, J. (2002). *Down by the station.* Auburn, ME: Child's Play International.

Stone, C.A., Bradley, K., & Kleiner, J. (2002). Parental understanding of children with language/learning disabilities and its role in the creation of scaffolding opportunities. In B. Wong & M. Donahue (Eds.), *The social dimensions of learning disabilities: Essays in honor of Tanis Bryan* (pp. 133–160). Mahwah, NJ: Lawrence Erlbaum Associates.

Symons, S., Szuszkiewicz, T., & Bonnell, C. (1996). Parental print exposure and young children's language and literacy skills. *The Alberta Journal of Education Research, 27,* 49–58.

Teale, W.H. (1986). Home background and young children's literacy development. In W.H. Teale & E. Sulzby (Eds.), *Emergent literacy: Writing and reading* (pp. 173–206). Norwood, NJ: Ablex.

Teele, S. (1992). *Teele Inventory for Multiple Intelligences.* Redlands, CA: Citrograph Printing.

Teele, S. (2000). *Rainbows of intelligence.* Thousand Oaks, CA: Corwin Press.

Torgesen, J.K., Wagner, R.K., & Rashotte, C.A. (1994). Longitudinal studies of phonological processing and reading. *Journal of Learning Disabilities, 27,* 276–286.

Treiman, R. (1985). Onsets and rimes as units of spoken syllables: Evidence from children. *Journal of Experimental Child Psychology, 39,* 161–181.

Tresselt, A. (1989). *The mitten: An old Ukranian folktale.* New York: Mulberry Books.

Valdez-Menchaca, M.C., & Whitehurst, G.J. (1992). Accelerating language development through picture book reading: A systematic extension to Mexican day care. *Developmental Psychology, 28,* 1106–1114.

van Kleeck, A., Gillam, R., Hamilton, L., & McGrath, C. (1997). The relationship between middle-class parents' book-sharing discussion and their preschoolers' abstract language development. *Journal of Speech, Language, and Hearing Research, 40,* 1261–1271.

Vukelich, C., Christie, J., & Enz, B. (2002). *Helping young children learn language and literacy.* Boston: Allyn & Bacon.

Vygotsky, L.S. (1978). *Mind in society: The development of higher psychological processes.* Cambridge, MA: Harvard University Press.

Wasik, B.A., & Bond, M.A. (2001). Beyond the pages of a book: Interactive book reading and language development in preschool classrooms. *Journal of Educational Psychology, 93,* 243–250.

Wells, G. (1985). *Language development in the preschool years.* New York: Cambridge University Press.

Welsch, J.G., Sullivan, A.K., & Justice, L.M. (2003). That's my name!: What preschoolers' name writing can tell us about emergent literacy knowledge. *Journal of Literacy Research, 35,* 757–776.

Westby, C.E. (1991). Learning to talk, talking to learn: Oral-literate language differences. In C.S. Simon (Ed.), *Communication skills and classroom success* (pp. 334–357). Eau Claire, WI: Thinking Publications.

Whitehurst, G.J., Arnold, D.S., Epstein, J.N., Angell, A.L., Smith, M., & Fischel, J.E. (1994). A picture book reading intervention in day care and home for children from low-income families. *Developmental Psychology, 30,* 679–689.

Whitehurst, G.J., Epstein, J.N., Angell, A.L., Payne, A.C., Crone, D.A., & Fischel, J.E. (1994). Outcomes of an emergent literacy intervention in Head Start. *Journal of Educational Psychology, 86,* 542–555.

Whitehurst, G.J., Falco, F., Lonigan, C.J., Fischel, J.E., DeBaryshe, B.D., Valdez-Menchaca, M.C., & Caulfield, M. (1988). Accelerating language development through picture-book reading. *Developmental Psychology, 24,* 552–559.

Whitehurst, G.J., & Lonigan, C.J. (1998). Child development and emergent literacy. *Child Development, 69,* 848–872.

Whitehurst, G.J., Zevenbergen, A.A., Crone, D.A., Schultz, M.D., Velting, O.N., & Fischel, J.E. (1999). Outcomes of an emergent literacy intervention from Head Start through second grade. *Journal of Educational Psychology, 91,* 261–272.

Whybrow, I. (2000). *Where's Tim's Ted?* New York: Barron's Educational Series.

Winthrop, E. (1986). *Shoes.* New York: HarperCollins.

Wood, A. (1984). *The napping house.* New York: Harcourt Brace & Company.

Yarosz, D.J., & Barnett, W.S. (2001). Who reads to young children?: Identifying predictors of family reading activities. *Reading Psychology, 22,* 67–81.

Appendix A

Frequently Asked Questions About Shared Reading

Several common questions asked by parents during home reading programs are presented here, as well as possible answers to these questions. The professional may anticipate such questions by providing this information in advance during parent instruction or consider presenting portions of this material as a handout for parents during a meeting or in a newsletter. Some of these questions also may be effective icebreakers for stimulating discussion among participants. In short, there are many potential uses for this information when working with parents.

Question: When should I start reading to my child?

Answer: You can begin reading when your child is an infant. Of course, infants will not carefully inspect the pictures, follow the print, or answer questions. However, your infant will hear your voice and enjoy the attention. Reading aloud will provide important language stimulation, and as time goes on your infant will begin to understand your words. Read whatever books please you at this point, because any book will do. When infants begin to grab items and put them into their mouths, use cloth, plastic, or board books so that those with paper pages will not be destroyed.

Question: How often should I read to my child?

Answer: Read to your child every day, if possible. Daily reading will provide the frequent exposure to language and emergent literacy concepts your child needs to prepare for school. In addition, it will help your child develop a reading habit that can last a lifetime. Take books along to doctor and dentist appointments, in the car, when visiting relatives, and on vacation. Whenever your child is left with a baby sitter, provide several storybooks and give instructions that reading is to be conducted. When your child goes to a friend's house to play or to spend the night, pack a book along with the toothbrush and pajamas. In other words, make children's books accessible to your child throughout the day and in a variety of situations.

It can be difficult to squeeze storybook reading into a hectic schedule, and some days it just may not be possible. On such days, consider if someone else in the household could conduct your child's reading session. If another reader is not available, have some talking books on hand so that your child can still listen to a story and look at a book when you are unavailable.

Question: When is the best time to read?

Answer: Although books may be read at any time of the day, many parents like to read at bedtime. Reading is a preferred bedtime activity because it often calms and relaxes children and prepares them for sleep. However, if you wish your child to be an active participant in the reading activity, you may be at cross-purposes if you expect your child to listen quietly while at the same time be an active participant. Two suggestions are offered to resolve such a conflict. First, you may wish to select a different time of day for reading that requires your child to be actively involved and keep bedtime stories for listening quietly. Second, you could read two stories at bedtime. The first would require active involvement and the second could invite quiet listening. It is suggested that you experiment with reading at different times of the day to determine what best suits you and your child.

Question: How long should storybook reading sessions last? What if my child becomes bored or restless and wants to stop?

Answer: Reading sessions do not have to be lengthy to be effective. Generally speaking, children's picture books can be read and discussed within a 10-minute period. Keeping it brief should keep most children from becoming bored or restless. Aim for holding brief reading sessions on a daily basis rather than long reading sessions once or twice a week.

Your second question is likely linked with the first. If sessions are too long, children may become bored. For some children, a 15-minute session is not too long, especially if the book is engaging. However, other children cannot attend or sit still that long. Consequently, it is recommended that you work within your child's attention span. When a child becomes bored or disinterested, there is little benefit from continuing, so simply suggest to your child that the book be continued tomorrow if he or she is ready to stop. Of course, it will always be better to end a session before your child becomes restless. To determine this, be alert to your child's verbal responsiveness, attention to the story and pictures, and posture. Boredom and restlessness may be apparent through these behaviors before a child will tell you that he or she has had enough for the day.

Question: I thought my child's preschool program included storybook reading. Why do I need to do this too?

Answer: Preschools vary in the amount of reading conducted with young children. Some preschools may have books available to children at various times of the day but have few staff to provide one-to-one reading. Others may provide a storytime activity that involves the entire group of children, offering limited opportunities for your child to talk and interact.

Consequently, the amount and quality of reading your child receives may change from day to day. It is suggested that you consider this preschool reading time as a supplement to your home reading sessions rather than vice versa. As the parent, you can provide the consistent, individual attention that your child needs for gaining language and emergent literacy skills. For instance, at home your child will have the chance to examine books at a comfortable pace, ask questions, make an unlimited number of comments, and receive immediate assistance or feedback. This level of quality personal attention is difficult to provide on a daily basis for every child in a typical preschool classroom.

Question: How many books should my child have?

Answer: There is no magic number to answer this question. Clearly, not having any children's books in your home will disadvantage your child because language and emergent literacy skills grow from frequent exposure to books. However, acquiring hundreds of children's books may be overdoing it and not reasonable from a cost standpoint. Aim for what is reasonable for your budget, keeping in mind that a dozen books should be the minimum number your child owns.

Before purchasing books for your child, you may wish to check out books from the library to see which ones your child especially enjoys. When a favorite book is found, consider purchasing it for your child's personal library. These do not have to be purchased in expensive bookstores if you can take advantage of bargains at yard sales, used book sales sponsored by the local library, or thrift shops. Consider giving books to your child as birthday or holiday gifts. If your child receives gifts from relatives such as grandparents, aunts, or uncles, make it clear that books or gift certificates to bookstores are desired presents. Over time, your child can develop a personal collection that will be valued for years to come.

Question: My child wants to read the same book over and over. Is this normal? How do I interest her in new books?

Answer: Yes, asking for repeated readings of a favorite book is normal behavior for young children. Sometimes children will want to read the same book for weeks or maybe even months. They may like this book for its subject, its storyline, its illustrations, or some other feature. Nonetheless, such a situation can become very tiresome for the adult. It is suggested that you try a couple of strategies for broadening your child's interest. First, ask your child why this book is a favorite. If your child can express a reason, it may help you to locate other books that he or she might enjoy on the same topic or by the same author. Your local librarian may assist in this regard. Second, if you typically read only one book per sitting, try reading two books. Explain to your child that you want to read a new book followed by the favorite book. Third, consider making an audio recording of your child's favorite book. This will permit your child to listen and look through the book whenever he or she wishes to do so. That way, shared-reading time may be used exclusively for exploring new books.

Question: My child seems to like e-books. Is this a good thing?

Answer: E-books (electronic books) are popular with children primarily because of the animation that brings a story alive. Some e-books provide children with additional activities or allow them to select alternative endings to a story. It's difficult to find fault with any engaging activity that can promote language, emergent literacy skills, and computer skills all at the same time; so on the whole, e-books have a lot to offer. However, e-books cannot take the place of an adult reader who can answer a child's questions or correct a misunderstanding. They also cannot relate a child's life experiences to events found in stories. Among other things, e-books cannot provide practice with pragmatic skills such as establishing eye contact or continuing a conversational topic. Consequently, e-books are not satisfactory substitutes for one-to-one shared reading with an adult. Rather, they may be viewed as a form of entertainment that contains some positive educational elements.

Question: I hear from some people that putting labels on everything (e.g., bed, dresser, TV) helps children learn to read. Should I be doing this at home?

Answer: Certainly it is important for children to see print in the environment to increase their awareness. However, few children will learn to read simply by looking at labels on objects. If that were the case, educators probably would have figured out a way to have all children reading before they begin school.

What will be helpful to your preschooler will be to learn that print has a purpose. To do this, the print must have a reason for being there. For example, if your child keeps toys in a bookcase, you could label where each toy is to be placed when put away. If you do this, it is suggested that you place the word next to a picture of the toy so that your child can rely on matching toy with a picture at first. If you draw your child's attention to these labels and read them, eventually your child may begin to associate the printed word with the picture or the toy. Keep words short (e.g., *doll, ball, books, games*). Shorten longer words such as *truck* for *dump truck*, and label just a few rather than all. Use large-size print that is easy for your child to see.

Another example might be to put your child's name on a hook where he or she is to hang a coat or hat. Also, your child's name could be placed on personal items such as a backpack or toothbrush. These labels indicate ownership and help children learn to identify their names. Remember that your preschooler is little, so keeping print at his or her eye level will be necessary. It will not help your child if the word is too high to be seen clearly and easily.

Question: What suggestions do you have about limiting television time?

Answer: With television and movies so readily available today for entertainment, it is sometimes difficult to get children interested in books. The auditory and visual stimulation that these forms of entertainment provide make them highly appealing to children. When movies and television are available, books are often viewed as a less interesting alternative. Educators are concerned that television and videos are replacing books in children's lives, which may have lasting effects on their academic achievement.

There is no clear and easy solution to this problem except the obvious—limit television and movie viewing and pick up books more often. Clearly, it is much easier to do this when your children are young. As with most behaviors, it falls to you, the parent, to establish good habits in your children, and interest in books is no different. Take advantage of the fact that young children like to do what adults do. Have one or two evenings a week when no television is allowed for anyone and make these "book nights." If an entire evening is not possible, a "book hour" before any television viewing is permitted would be a good alternative. To do this, you must be prepared with a variety of children's books as well as adult magazines and books. Begin reading some books with your child, and then allow him or her to explore other books alone while you read or look through magazines. If an hour or an entire evening is too long for your child, begin with just 20 or 30 minutes and gradually lengthen the reading time. If you are persistent in presenting books to your children and in making reading interesting and fun, they will enjoy their storytime and learn to value the pleasure books can bring.

Appendix B

General Reading Strategies

These strategies have been shown by researchers to be useful for accelerating children's early language and literacy achievements. Some or all of these reminders could be incorporated into instructional material for a home reading program or in periodic newsletters to parents.

Have fun during shared reading.

Make shared reading an enjoyable experience for children. Adults should be warm, responsive, and sensitive to their children during the reading experience. Resist the temptation to be overly directive throughout the activity.

Follow the child's lead.

When reading with children, focus on the child's object of attention. Parents are reminded to resist the temptation to continually follow their own interests rather than their child's. Children are more likely to attend longer and engage in conversation when the topic is of interest to them.

Repeat children's utterances.

When reading with young children, repeat what they say. This confirms children's verbal participation in the reading interaction and provides an adult model of their own verbalizations. By repeating what children say, parents follow the child's lead and focus on his or her object of attention.

Extend children's utterances.

In extending children's utterances, the parent provides a language model that is slightly advanced of the child's own production. In an extension, the parent repeats what the child says and adds just a little more grammatical or semantic information. When a child says "Fish," the parent can extend this by saying, "It's a big fish," "Yes, this is blue fish," or "That fish looks hungry!" Any information may be added; these examples are simply suggestions.

Balance questions and comments.

Providing both questions and comments keeps shared reading more balanced for children. Often parents reading with children ask too many questions, resulting in an imbalance in the amount and type of participation by the child. Parents can ask questions, but they can also make general observations and comments to share their own thoughts and feelings about the story.

Pause to let the child respond.

It is common for parents to expect young children to respond immediately when taking a conversational turn. Often parents fail to pause long enough for their children to make a comment or provide an answer. Pausing after making comments, asking questions, or reading the text on a page gives children time to process the story, make connections between book events and their own lives, and, if desired, share their own feelings and questions about the content. As a general guideline, pause at least 5 seconds for your child to take a conversational turn; pause even longer if your child has limited language abilities.

Share the book.

During shared reading, allow children to claim ownership of the activity by permitting them to choose the books and to turn the pages during reading. Allowing children to set the pace, turn the pages, and predict what might happen makes them active participants in shared reading.

Talk about print.

When reading with children, talk about the print in the storybook. Point to the print, track the print, ask questions about the print, comment about the print, and show children that print is an interesting part of the storybook—even as interesting as the pictures.

Elaborate on new words.

Stop and talk about words that are new or unfamiliar to the child. Ask the child to repeat the word and explain what it means. Also, link the word's meaning to the story. Use the word four or five times during the conversation to increase the child's familiarity with how the word sounds so it may be recognized when it is heard again.

Choose interesting books.

Choose storybooks that are interesting and motivating to the child. Also, give children opportunities to select their own books for shared-reading sessions. Try to read a variety of books. Have conversations about how the stories relate to experiences in children's lives.

Read the same books over and over.

Children enjoy reading the same books over and over—sometimes in a single reading session and sometimes over a period of weeks, months, or years. To learn new words and concepts, children will benefit from repeated exposure. Repeated reading of storybooks provides children with this exposure in a predictable, familiar, and entertaining context.

Glossary

blend *See* consonant cluster.

bound morpheme The smallest unit of meaning (morpheme) that cannot stand alone and must be attached to another morpheme. For example, when the bound morpheme *-s,* which means more than one entity, is attached to the free morpheme *chair,* it becomes *chairs.* Adding this bound morpheme changes the meaning of the word from one chair to two or more chairs. Some bound morphemes are added to the beginning of words (known as prefixes), and some are added to the end (known as suffixes).

consonant A phoneme that is produced by stopping and releasing or restricting the airstream in some fashion. The English language has 24 consonants. These are listed in Table G.1 along with examples of their use.

consonant cluster *Also called* blend. Two or more consonants appearing adjacent to one another in a word. The English language has several consonant clusters. A few of these may be seen in the following examples: *play, blind, clean, flee, glad, Klondike, sleep, skate, pride, bread, crate, free, green, tree, sweep, screen, splice,* and *street.* Consonant clusters may appear in any position in a word. They may appear at the beginning as in *dream,* in the middle as in *basket,* or at the end as in *weeps.*

critical period The period of time that is believed to be the most productive for children to acquire language. Many consider the critical period to be the first 5 or 6 years of life. After that time, language may still be acquired; however, it appears to develop more slowly and with greater effort.

decoding Synonymous with reading, the ability to decipher a word—particularly an unknown word—by analyzing its letters, arriving at their corresponding sounds, and synthesizing the letter-sounds into the word represented.

directionality The direction in which reading is accomplished in the English language. Convention dictates that a reader follow three directions when reading a book: 1) read the left page before the right page, 2) read left to right on a line, and 3) read multiple lines of print from top to bottom.

Table G.1.   English consonants

/p/ as in pie	/v/ as in vine
/b/ as in bay	/s/ as in say
/t/ as in tea	/z/ as in zip
/d/ as in day	/ʃ/ as in ship
/k/ as in key	/ʒ/ as in treasure
/g/ as in go	/θ/ as in thin
/m/ as in me	/ð/ as in there
/n/ as in no	/ʧ/ as in chin
/ŋ/ as in ring	/ʤ/ as in jam
/l/ as in lime	/h/ as in he
/r/ as in ribbon	/w/ as in we
/f/ as in feet	/y/ as in yes

emergent literacy   The period of time that an individual amasses knowledge about books, letters, numbers, and print prior to being able to read through decoding. The terms *early literacy* and *preliteracy* have also been used to refer to this stage of development, which is viewed as transcending the preschool years. Emergent literacy is generally thought of as occurring before formal reading instruction begins.

environmental print   Print that appears within one's environment at home, at school, and in the community (e.g., on calendars, cereal boxes, toy boxes, restroom doors, billboards, vending machines, restaurant signs, and clothing labels).

expressive language   Language for the purpose of communicating with others. It is different from receptive language, which refers to an ability to comprehend or understand language. Expression may take the form of speaking (the oral mode), writing (the written mode), or signing using some form of sign language (the gestural mode).

free morpheme   The smallest unit of speech that can stand alone and have meaning. The following words are examples of free morphemes: *cup, bird, shoe, swing, pond, go, sit, run,* and *write.*

grammar   *See* syntax.

grapheme   An alphabet letter.

incidental learning   One's ability to acquire knowledge, skills, or new behaviors without the need for direct instruction.

joint attention   *See* joint reference.

joint reference   *Also called* joint attention. A common focus on a particular action or object (e.g., an article of food, a toy, a clothing item, a book) shared by two individuals. When joint reference is shared by a young child and an adult, the situation is ideal for the child to practice emerging communication skills (e.g., new words, gestures) and for the adult to provide language input regarding the referent.

language   The expression of thoughts and feelings through sounds, symbols/print, or gestures/manual signs. Language is a rule-governed system that is acquired by children in the critical period transcending birth through puberty. When language is produced orally, it is through speech. When it is produced in symbols or print, it is through writing. When gestures or manual signs are used, language is being conveyed through sign language. *See also* phonology, morphology, syntax, semantics, pragmatics.

lexicon *See* vocabulary.

metalinguistic awareness A skill describing one's ability to think about and talk about language. This awareness demonstrates a consciousness about words and an ability to view language as a topic of interest.

morphology The formation of words based on the smallest units of meaning, called *morphemes*. Morphemes can be added to words to change their meaning (*un* + *happy* = *unhappy*), and sometimes to change the word class (*trust* + *ful* = *trustful*; changing a noun into an adjective). This system also provides information about number (*cat* + *-s* = *cats*; singular to plural) and about time (*barking* versus *barked*; present progressive versus past tense). Through these changes, morphology provides additional information about word meanings and relationships.

observational learning The action of acquiring knowledge or learning new behaviors by watching (or observing) others.

particulate principle The notion that a very small set of elements can be used to create an infinite number of possibilities. An example of this is how children can produce an infinite number of sentences by using only a few syntactic rules.

phoneme A single sound. Phonemes are the sounds that make up a language. The English language has a total of about 43 phonemes (24 consonants, 14 vowels, and 5 diphthongs). Phonemes are written in phonetic symbols and appear in slashes (e.g., /ʃ/), rather than in alphabet letters (e.g., *sh*).

phoneme–grapheme correspondence The matching of sounds (phonemes) to the corresponding letters (graphemes) when an individual reads. Phoneme–grapheme correspondence is a skill required of beginning readers when they are first learning to decode print. Once reading becomes automatic, decoding is accomplished quickly until an individual comes across unknown or difficult words to pronounce. Also, the importance of this skill reemerges when an individual begins learning a new language.

There are only 26 letters in the alphabet; however, simply learning the letters of the alphabet will not provide all of the sounds of the language. Consider the letter *c*, for example. It represents the /k/ phoneme in *cat*, the /s/ phoneme in *receive*, and is silent in *kick*. Also consider the letter *x*. It represents the /z/ phoneme in *xylophone* and the /ks/ blend in *box*. In a nutshell, this is the dilemma that beginning readers face—knowing which sound a letter represents in any given word.

phonemic awareness A skill describing one's analysis of all of the sounds (phonemes) in a particular word. For example, the word *shoe* consists of two phonemes: the /ʃ/ sound and the "ooo" sound (the first is a consonant and the second is a vowel), whereas the word *fright* consists of four phonemes: the /f/ and /r/ phonemes followed by the "i" sound (as in *hi*), and finally the /t/ phoneme. As can be seen, identifying the number of sounds in a word is not the same as counting the letters in a word. Phonemic awareness is absolutely critical for learning to read. Phonemic awareness is usually acquired during formal reading instruction; however, precursory skills may be observed in some pre-school children.

phonics   The systematic teaching of sound–symbol correspondence. A considerable number of recent studies have shown systematic instruction in phonics to be a critical aspect of a balanced literacy curriculum.

phonological awareness   An emergent literacy skill describing one's awareness of sounds in a language and the ability to manipulate sounds in a purposeful way. The ability to produce rhymes is one example of a phonological awareness skill. Although children learn to speak a language at an early age, they acquire this knowledge without an ability to talk about the experience in an abstract way. Only later do children become aware of the concept of sounds, words, and sentences and can discuss these abstract ideas. Thus, a 1-year-old may be able to say the word *doggie,* but a 4-year-old may be able to tell you that the word *doggie* starts with the /d/ phoneme. This ability is representative of metalinguistic awareness.

phonology   The sound system used to formulate words. Phonological knowledge is important from both a listening and speaking perspective. Distinguishing sounds allows a listener to hear the difference between *pick* and *pack* or between *pie* and *tie.* Likewise, a speaker needs to be able to produce the sounds of a language so that words are articulated clearly and correctly.

phonotactics   The rules of acceptable sound sequences with a given language. For example, in English, the phonemes /b/ and /r/ can appear together forming a consonant cluster /br/ as in the words *broom* or *braid.* However, the phonemes /b/ and /k/ cannot appear together because English does not use /bk/ as a sound sequence. Instead, a vowel must appear between these consonants (e.g., *bike, bake, book*).

pragmatics   The social aspect of communicating with others. Pragmatics requires the appropriate social use of language based on the culture of the participants and the context of the situation. Pragmatics involves appropriate greetings, turn taking during conversation, distance between the speaker and listener, word choice, use of politeness markers (e.g., *please, thank you, excuse me*), and topic maintenance (i.e., staying on the topic of conversation), to name a few.

print awareness   A skill describing one's knowledge that language may be produced in written form as well as in oral form (e.g., speech). Print awareness is an emergent literacy skill that involves an understanding that print carries meaning and that it may be used for myriad purposes. An individual who shows an awareness of print but remains unable to read or decode the print would be considered to be in an emergent literacy stage of development.

receptive language   The understanding or comprehension of language. Receptive language is assessed when a speaker asks a listener to carry out an instruction in a nonverbal way. For example, an adult may ask a child to "point to," "show me," or "touch" an object or picture as in, "Show me the alligator's tail on this page." To demonstrate comprehension, a child may simply use a finger to touch the appropriate part of the illustration; no words are required to answer.

semantics   An aspect of language that refers to word meaning. Understanding word meaning encompasses all levels, from simple to complex. At a simple level, it may be seen when a child understands the meaning of a concrete noun such as *butterfly,* or an abstract noun such as *forgiveness.* However, when a word has multiple meanings, such as *cross,* a child must distinguish which meaning is inferred based on the context in which it is used (e.g., as an adjective to describe an angry person, as a verb to describe an action, as a noun to describe a symbol). At an even more complex level, understanding the meaning of figurative language forms such as similes, metaphors, idioms, proverbs, and irony requires greater semantic knowledge because these words, phrases, and expressions cannot be taken literally.

shared reading   The active involvement and shared interaction of both the adult reader and the child or group of children during book reading that focuses on the words, pictures, and story. Other terms that have the same meaning include *interactive reading, book sharing, reading aloud, storybook reading, adult–child storybook reading,* and *book-reading interaction.*

social register   The knowledge of rules in the area of pragmatics that govern how language is used in social situations. Social register refers to how individuals adjust and regulate their language so that it is appropriate for the situation and the listener. Under this concept, individuals might speak casually to a friend (e.g., inserting slang or jokes) in a relaxed situation and with greater reverence or respect (e.g., addressing men as "sir") to an individual of authority in a formal situation.

storybook   A book written and illustrated for children that contains a written narrative and tells a story. It may also be referred to as a picture book. Books that contain no narrative (called wordless books) or provide pictures and print but do not tell a story (alphabet, concept, or number books) are not considered storybooks.

syntax   *Also called* grammar. The orderly arrangement of words into sentences. Syntax refers to the sentence structure. The most basic sentence structure (which all sentences must ascribe to) is sentence = subject + predicate, as in "Dogs bark." Syntax allows listeners or readers to understand the relationship between the words (e.g., subject, verb, adjective, adverb, phrase, and clause), which promotes comprehension of the thought being expressed.

tracking   The smooth, left-to-right motion of a reader running a finger beneath the words as they are read. Tracking is a nonverbal cue provided to young children during storybook reading that helps draw their attention to print.

universal premise   The notion that regardless of culture or language, children all across the world acquire language in essentially the same sequence and along the same timeline. This concept also includes the observation that children enter the world ready to learn *any* language, meaning that children will learn whatever language they are exposed to at birth.

vocabulary   *Also called* lexicon. The number of words understood and used by an individual. One's vocabulary comprises the receptive vocabulary, or the words that are understood, and the expressive vocabulary, or the words that are used. One's receptive vocabulary is nearly always larger than one's expressive vocabulary. In other words, people tend to know/understand more words than they can produce.

vowel   Speech sounds that, as a class, are produced differently from consonants. The English language has 14 vowels and 5 diphthongs. A diphthong is a phoneme that is produced when one vowel moves to another within the same syllable. These 19 sounds are represented by only a few letters of the alphabet (*a, e, i, o, u*, and sometimes *y*), either alone or in combination with other vowels.

zone of proximal development (ZPD)   Coined by the Russian psychologist Lev Vygotsky, a point in task completion at which learning is achieved most readily. The task is neither easy nor excessively difficult, yet to complete a task within the ZPD, assistance is required. In other words, the zone represents tasks introduced to an individual that are slightly more difficult than can be accomplished independently. As an individual achieves independence on this task, the learning zone then shifts to a higher level. For example, a child may require assistance to distinguish the /p/ phoneme from the /z/ phoneme. The adult who assists may point out how one's mouth looks different when producing these sounds. When the child masters this task, there is no further need to work on these particular sounds because the child can distinguish them independently. At that point, the adult would move learning to a higher level by introducing phonemes that are more difficult to distinguish such as /z/ and /s/. Again, the child would require assistance to discriminate these two sounds at first, but once assistance is provided, mastery occurs. Assistance may be required for a single instance or for many instances depending on the learning potential and the current ability of the child.

Credits

CHAPTER 2

Page 20: From SPOT BAKES A CAKE by Eric Hill, copyright © 1994 by Eric Hill. Used by permission of G.P. Putnam's Sons, A Division of Penguin Young Readers Group, A Member of Penguin Group (USA) Inc., 345 Hudson Street, New York, NY 10014. All rights reserved.

Page 31: Excerpt from THERE'S AN ALLIGATOR UNDER MY BED by Mercer Mayer, copyright © 1987 by Mercer Mayer. Used by permission of Dial Books for Young Readers, A Division of Penguin Young Readers Group, A Member of Penguin Group (USA) Inc., 345 Hudson Street, New York, NY 10014. All rights reserved.

Page 32: From OWEN by Kevin Henkes. Copyright © 1993 by Kevin Henkes. Used by permission of HarperCollins Publishers.

Pages 32–33: From THE DOORBELL RANG by Pat Hutchins. Copyright © 1986 by Pat Hutchins. Used by permission of HarperCollinsPublishers.

CHAPTER 4

Pages 61–62: Reprinted from OWEN by Kevin Henkes. Copyright © 1993 by Kevin Henkes. Used by permission of HarperCollins Publishers.

CHAPTER 6

Pages 92–95: From THE DAY THE GOOSE GOT LOOSE by Reeve Lindbergh, copyright © 1990 by Reeve Lindbergh. Used by permission of Dial Books for Young Readers, A Division of Penguin Young Readers Group, A Member of Penguin Group (USA) Inc., 345 Hudson Street, New York, NY 10014. All rights reserved.

Pages 100–101: From SPOT BAKES A CAKE by Eric Hill, copyright © 1994 by Eric Hill. Used by permission of G.P. Putnam's Sons, A Division of Penguin Young Readers Group, A Member of Penguin Group (USA) Inc., 345 Hudson Street, New York, NY 10014. All rights reserved.

CHAPTER 10

Index

Page numbers followed by *f* indicate figures; those followed by *t* indicate tables.